INTIFADA HITS THE HEADLINES

Indiana Series in Middle East Studies
Mark Tessler, general editor

INTIFADA HITS THE HEADLINES

How the Israeli Press
Misreported the Outbreak
of the
Second Palestinian Uprising

Daniel Dor

INDIANA
University Press
Bloomington & Indianapolis

This book is a publication of

Indiana University Press
601 North Morton Street
Bloomington, Indiana 47404-3797 USA

http://iupress.indiana.edu

Telephone orders   800-842-6796
Fax orders   812-855-7931
Orders by e-mail   iuporder@indiana.edu

Library of Congress Cataloging-in-Publication Data

Dor, Danny, date
  Intifada hits the headlines : how the Israeli press misreported the
outbreak of the second Palestinian uprising / Daniel Dor.
    p. cm. — (Indiana series in Middle East studies)
  Includes bibliographical references and index.
  ISBN 0-253-34333-X (cloth : alk. paper)— ISBN 0-253-21637-0
(pbk. : alk. paper)
  1. Mass media—Political aspects—Israel. 2. Arab-Israel conflict—
1993—Mass media and the conflict. 3. Arab-Israel conflict—1993—
Press coverage—Israel. 4. Press and politics—Israel. 5. Jews—
Israel—Attitudes. I. Title. II. Series.
  P95.82.I75D67 2004
  302.23'095694—dc21
                                    2003011798

1 2 3 4 5 09 08 07 06 05 04

CONTENTS

Preface

Three years after the outbreak of the second Palestinian Intifada, public opinion polls consistently tell a paradoxical story: On the one hand, they show that substantial majorities on both sides, Israelis and Palestinians, understand and accept the basic parameters of the final settlement. On the other hand, the polls also show that each side is deeply convinced that it does not have a partner for such an agreement. The last-minute failure of the Camp David negotiations, in July 2000, and the quick development of the cycle of violence, since October 2000, which eventually led to the reoccupation of the territories controlled by the Palestinian Authority, are taken by both sides to be the ultimate proof that the other side is simply not interested in a peaceful, pragmatic solution. This situation results in a deep and paralyzing sense of despair. In this tragic process, the media on both sides have played a highly destructive role.

This book concentrates on the Israeli side. It attempts to provide a careful, critical analysis of the crucial contribution made by the Israeli press, in the first month of the Intifada, to the development and crystallization of the consensual perception which took over the Israeli collective consciousness: the notion that Israel, under Prime Minister Ehud Barak, did everything possible to achieve a final status agreement with the Palestinians, only to be repaid with an outburst of violence initiated and planned by Yasser Arafat—an outburst of violence that proved, and has kept proving on a daily basis ever since, that the Palestinians are "unripe for peace."

As we shall see, the Israeli press provided its readers with a highly distorted, biased, and anxiety-ridden representation of reality during the entire period at hand. More than anything, this was the result of editorial policy: Working under a complex set of influences, the papers' editors suppressed certain components of reality and highlighted others, even when the materials they received from their own reporters consistently countered the consensual perception of reality. The dramatic gap between the accumulated perspective of the reporters' materials and the final output produced by the editors—the headlines, the allocation of materials to different sections of the papers, the graphic design and choice of visuals—exposes a facet of the relationships between the media, the establishment, and the public that the literature usually neglects: Concentrating on the relationships between reporters and sources, the literature fails to highlight the way editorial policies transform the establishment's propaganda into consensual ideology, a process in which the reporters' work usually plays a rather minor role. As we shall see in chapter 8, no conspiratorial theorizing is needed to explain this very special role played by editorial work.

The core part of this research (chapters 2 through 7) was originally published in Hebrew in September 2001, a year after the outbreak of the Intifada, by Babel Publications, under the title *Newspapers under the Influence*. Unfortunately, the sense of urgency that accompanied the publication of the Hebrew original has not diminished in the least. In fact, the events which have unfolded since then, both on the local and the global level— including the sea change in global ideology since the September 11 attack on New York and Washington—invest it with additional relevance. More than ever before, it seems that democratic societies in crisis find their perceptual horizons dramatically reduced by opportunistic media coverage. This is a highly dangerous situation: In societies conditioned by the liberal-democratic rhetoric of free information flow, these reduced horizons allow governments a troubling latitude in manipulating public opinion.

Acknowledgments

I would like to thank Miran Epstein, Avi Weinberg, Jacky Hugi, Yehiel Limor, Rafi Mann, Moshe Negbi, and Haim Rechnitzer for their help with the original Hebrew version of the book, and Jérôme Bourdon, Dafna Lemish, Gabi Lanyi, and especially Chuck Salmon for their help with the English version. Special thanks to the people at Babel Publications, Amit Rotbard, Jasmine Halevi, Gila Kaplan, and Haim Pessach, for taking such great care of the book, and to my seminar students and the participants in various conferences where parts of this research were presented, for their valuable criticism. I would like to thank my editor at Indiana University Press, Marilyn Grobschmidt, for believing in the book and for her help all along the way; my copy editor, Candace McNulty, for her thoughtful work; and the two anonymous referees for their critically encouraging reviews. Most importantly, special thanks to Lia Nirgad, my very own Lia'le, my best friend, my best reader, my translator, for simply being who she is.

INTIFADA HITS THE HEADLINES

1

Introduction

During the past days, Yasser Arafat has decided to sacrifice Ismael. To further his political aims, he is offering up defense-less Palestinian children on the altar of television images. The purpose of all this is to gain control of the Temple Mount, where, according to Jewish tradition, Abraham, father of our nation, sacrificed his son Isaac. But in the biblical story an internal, divine voice told Abraham: "Lay not thine hand upon the lad." Arafat has refused to heed such voices of grace.

—Dan Margalit, *Ha'aretz,* October 10

On Friday the 13th, October 2000—two weeks after the outbreak of the Palestinian uprising that later came to be known as the "El-Aqsa Intifada"—the local Tel Aviv supplement of Israel's most popular daily, *Yediot Ahronot,* published a survey conducted by the Geocartographia Institute among Arab and Jewish residents of Jaffa. The investigators were trying to find out how the past days had affected the residents of a city that normally, if only superficially, represents the option of true coexistence between Jews and Arabs, a city that during the previous two weeks had seen its streets and alleys flooded with all the violent, pent-up feelings of anger, suspicion, despair, and racism.

Geocartographia's researchers asked the residents ten different questions. The answers, as usual, were presented in the news story in statistical form. Some of the questions elicited interesting, disturbing answers. Thirty-four percent of the Jews, for example, said that since recent events they experienced more negative feelings toward the Arabs—hate or fear or disappointment. About 30 percent of the Jews said that if violence were to continue much longer, they might support drastic measures: closure on Arab residents, annulment of their citizenship, or expulsion to the Palestinian Authority. Forty percent of the Jews thought that in case of war between Israel and the Arab nations, Jaffa's Arab residents would attack the city's Jews. More than 60 percent of Jaffa's Arabs and about 55 percent of the Jews told the researchers that since the outbreak of the Intifada they feared for their lives. But 83 percent of the Arab residents of Jaffa and 55 percent of the Jewish residents also said they believed "coexistence will resume its course."

The editors of *Tel Aviv* chose to publish this survey on their front page. They picked one piece of data for their headline, which they spread in huge white letters above a grim picture in harsh red and black. The picture shows dozens of people standing on one of the city's streets, in front of two private cars, which an angry crowd has bashed and overturned. A fire department vehicle is standing next to these cars, with its lights on. The headline reads:

IN CASE OF WAR—JAFFA'S ARABS WILL ATTACK TEL AVIV

Incredible as it may seem, this was indeed the headline—and it reports a simple, unequivocal "fact": In case of war, Jaffa's Arab residents would attack Tel Aviv. It is quite impossible to imagine a more catastrophic forecast. And how is this apocalyptic headline related to the survey mentioned above? The overline, in much smaller letters, "explains":

ACCORDING TO GEOCARTOGRAPHIAS' POLL, 40% OF JAFFA'S JEWS BELIEVE:

This, then, is the link between the headline and the survey: The headline does not report a factual situation, as its wording, its location, and the lack of quotation marks seem to imply, but rather reflects a belief expressed by the people questioned; it does not reflect the position of all respondents, but only of Jewish ones; it does not reflect the position of all Jews surveyed, but only of a minority; and finally, it does not even report what those Jews actually told the surveyors—this segment said they believed that in case of war, the Arab residents of Jaffa would attack them, the Jewish residents of Jaffa. The headline speaks of an organized attack of Jaffa's Arab residents on the neighboring city of Tel Aviv, and one may confidently assume that even that 40 percent would completely discount this possibility. Moreover, as an angry letter sent to the paper a week later revealed, even the picture spread on the front page was highly misleading: The rioting crowds in the picture happened to be *Jews*, not Arabs. And so this innocent poll, which set out to describe the beliefs and feelings of Jaffa's residents—both Arabs and Jews—was actually molded by the editors of the paper into a piece of incitement against Jaffa's Arabs, defining them, once and for all, as the enemy within the heart of Tel Aviv.

It is possible that some of *Tel Aviv's* readers thoroughly analyzed the survey's results that weekend and figured out the manipulation of its results on the supplement's cover. The vast majority of readers, however, probably did no such research. We may assume that most of them did not even read the story to the end—the list of statistical results is long and tiresome. They probably scanned the paper, read the front page headline and looked at the pictures, and frowned in amazement and dismay: If Jaffa's Arabs truly intend to attack Tel Aviv, then it is probably true—there really is no chance for peace.

Now, there is no real reason to suspect that the paper's editors made a conscious decision to use the Geocartographia survey in order to manufacture this piece of incitement. For all we know, they merely intended to make maximal use of the material at their disposal, and to produce what they hoped would be a strong, moving, dramatic front page. But in the course of their work—in their search for the best piece of data for the headline, in their formulation of the headline itself, in the dropping of the quotation marks, in the process of graphic design—a crucial set of assumptions, feelings, and beliefs, which the editors shared with most Israelis during those difficult days, found its way to the front page: an acute sense of fear, confusion, and ignorance, a whole range of unconscious racial beliefs, and an acutely biased perception of the unfolding events. And all of these created a page that further strengthened these very assumptions and feelings for the readers, taking them yet one little step further on the road of mistrust and nationalistic self-righteousness.

If this front page were an isolated case, an accidental slip-up within a context of independent and restrained journalistic work, it would be possible to simply ignore it. Unfortunately, this front page is all too representative of the way the October 2000 events were portrayed in the Israeli press.

The El-Aqsa Intifada
and the New Consensual Narrative

October 2000, the first month of the El-Aqsa Intifada, is one of the most dramatic and important moments in the history of contemporary Israeli society. After seven long years of fierce political clashes between the supporters of the Oslo peace agreement and its opponents—clashes that reached their tragic climax in the murder of Prime Minister Itzhak Rabin—the first month of the Intifada saw the Israeli collective consciousness withdrawing once again into the defensive, enraged consensus of a society that saw its dream of peace vanish in a cloud of smoke. It only took a few weeks of violence, following what seemed to be the final failure of the diplomatic negotiations, for the public discourse in Israel to re-invent itself in a new form—basing itself on a *new consensual narrative*, which was instantaneously subscribed to not only by the political right but also by the great majority of the voters of the traditional left. In schematic form, this is what the new narrative stated:

(1) Ehud Barak's government did everything it possibly could in order to achieve a permanent status agreement with the Palestinian Authority. At the Camp David summit, which convened in July 2000, it presented the Palestinians with extremely generous offers for withdrawal from Palestinian territories. In fact, polls show that by July 2000 the majority of Jewish Israelis already perceived Barak's positions at Camp David as *too* conciliatory.[1]

(2) The chairman of the Palestinian Authority, Yasser Arafat, refused the generous Israeli offers of Camp David. Barak's "overly conciliatory" position was thus useful in a deep way: It finally uncovered Arafat's "real" intentions, proving that his regime was not interested in peace.[2]

(3) Arafat then initiated a massive Palestinian uprising, the Intifada, which quickly developed into an organized terror attack on Israel, with the purpose of creating international and internal pressure that would eventually lead to further Israeli concessions.[3]

(4) Faced with the severe violence of the Palestinian Intifada, Israel responded with restraint, doing everything in its power to protect its civilians while refraining from the use of military resources to quell the uprising. This sharp contrast between Palestinian and Israeli conduct provided additional proof of the "inherent" differences between the two national cultures.[4]

(5) All the acts of violence committed by Palestinians since the beginning of the Intifada were directed by Arafat, who has maintained full control of the field. Israel was thus patiently awaiting his decision to stop the violence and remains willing to return to the negotiating table the moment violence comes to an end.[5]

The most important feature of this narrative is that it seems, on the face of it, to be absolutely non-ideological—a non-controversial, factual story that naturally allows for a simple and commonsensical interpretation. The traditional ideological debate within Israeli society had centered on whether or not Israel should withdraw from the territories in exchange for peace. Now it turned out that the logical foundation of the debate was flawed: Barak's government offered to withdraw, and the Palestinians rejected the offer. This seemed to imply that peace did not depend on anything Israel could do; the Palestinians simply were not interested in peaceful solutions. This type of commonsensical twist in public perception is one of the most fundamental characteristics of successful hegemonic campaigns (Hallin 1986; Phillips 1996; Gramsci 1971; Stevenson 1995;

Williams 1977). It highlights the absolute importance of those "factual" elements that seem to bestow on the new narrative its non-ideological character. Moreover, it underlines the question of *perception of fact:* How did the majority of Jewish Israelis come to the conclusion that at Camp David, Barak actually presented Arafat with generous offers? How did they become convinced that Arafat rejected these offers and initiated the Intifada? What did they learn about the conduct of the Israeli Defense Forces (IDF) and the Palestinians in the first stages of the Intifada? In short: What made the great majority of Israelis, regardless of their original ideological inclination, accept the new narrative as a factual description of the events they were witnessing? This is, first and foremost, a question about the *news*.

This book attempts to trace the development and crystallization of the new consensual narrative in the news reports published by the Israeli press during the critical month of October 2000. As we shall see, throughout this period the papers provided their readers with a one-sided, partial, censored, and biased picture of reality—a picture that seemingly supported the new narrative and obviously sustained and exacerbated the readers' sense of distress and anxiety, but hardly corresponded with events as they unfolded in reality. Much more significantly, there was a stark contrast between this picture and *the factual reports sent in by the newspapers' own reporters*, the patterns of deviation being first and foremost the result of *editorial policy*. The newspapers systematically suppressed certain elements of reality and emphasized and accentuated others, in a way that provided the "factual" platform for the new narrative and has become ingrained in the Israeli collective consciousness ever since.

The discourse-oriented analysis highlights the complex set of converging influences exerted on the Israeli press at the time: the surge of fear and anger, the undercurrents of racist stances, the deep-seated ignorance concerning the realities of occupation, and most importantly the massive propaganda campaign led by the government and the military establishment. It thus provides vital support to the fundamental contention that the media "construct" the news rather than simply "report" it—and that the modes of construction are intimately related to the media's relationships with the establishment, their perception of their own role in times of crisis, and the culture's general view of reality. Different versions of this view inform the critical analyses of Hallin (1986), Herman and Chomsky (1988), Cohen and Wolfsfeld (1993), Cottle (1997), Liebes (1997), Schudson (1978, 1997), Schlesinger (1989), Shinar and Stoiciu (1992), Wolfsfeld (1997), and many others.

From Reports to Headlines:
Newspapers, Analysis, and Methodology

Three major national Hebrew-language dailies are published in Israel: *Yediot Ahronot*, *Ma'ariv*, and *Ha'aretz*. *Yediot Ahronot* is by far the most popular newspaper in Israel. According to recent estimates, it reaches "three-quarters of all Israel's households" (Caspi and Limor 1999).[6] Published in tabloid form, its daily editions comprise sixty to one hundred pages in several sections: news, a daily supplement containing additional news, feature articles, and culture and entertainment columns, a financial supplement, a sports supplement, and two major weekend supplements. Despite its superficial resemblance to classic tabloids, *Yediot Ahronot* is a "rare cross-breed" between what might be termed a "popular" and a "quality" paper (Caspi and Limor 1999; Limor and Mann 1997). Like classic tabloids, it does include extensive crime reports and "soft news," but these usually appear toward the end of the news section. The first half of the news section is dedicated to political and national issues, and the paper employs some of the most distinguished political and military reporters and analysts. It is owned by the Moses family, which also owns seventeen local newspapers, five periodicals, and a publishing house and is a senior partner in a television franchise holder, a cable television operator, and a recording company.

Ma'ariv is the second most popular paper in Israel.[7] It has been competing fiercely with *Yediot Ahronot* for five decades and in the last decade or so has adopted a strategy of similarity. In terms of format, graphic design, colors, and photographs, and also in terms of the "cross-breed" content composition, the two papers are by now almost indistinguishable. *Ma'ariv* is owned by the Nimrodi family, which also owns local newspapers, three periodicals, a publishing house, and a recording company and is a senior partner in a television franchise holder and a cable television operator.

The third paper, *Ha'aretz*, is probably the best known outside Israel, not just because of its English edition, but also because of its prestige. Owned by yet a third powerful business family, the Shokens, "its status resembles that of elite publications such as the *New York Times*" (Caspi and Limor 1999). The paper enjoys "relatively broad distribution among senior officials, intellectual circles, and the business community," which accords it "influence that greatly exceeds the scope of its circulation" (Caspi and Limor 1999). The Shoken family also owns fourteen local newspapers and a publishing house.

In October 2000, the three newspapers published more than 1,800 Intifada-related news items. All were examined and analyzed according to a long list of discursive, linguistic, and communicative parameters. An additional set of about 800 news items, published from the beginning of November 2000 to the end of March 2001, were analyzed. Most of the analytic parameters employed in the project have been variously used in the past, especially within the paradigm of *critical discourse analysis* (cf. de Cillia et al. 1999; Erjavec 2001; Fang 2001; Fairclough 1989, 1995; Ilie 1998; Teo 2000; and, most prominently, van Dijk 1983, 1985, 1988a,b, 1995); in the literature on *news framing* (cf. Gamson 1992; Iyengar 1991; Pan and Kosicki 1993); in the literature dealing with *second-order agenda-setting* (cf. McCombs et al. 1997; Valkenburg et al. 1999); in the literature on *headline production and comprehension* (cf. Bell 1984, 1991; Dor 2003a; Lindemann 1989, 1990; Nir 1993; Perfetti et al. 1987); and the literature dealing with *headline rhetoric, metaphors, and agency* (cf. de-Knop 1985; Henley et al. 1995; Jenkins 1990; Leon 1997; Phillips 1996; and Semino and Masci 1996). As far as I can tell, however, the integrative usage of the entire set of parameters, within the specific framework developed in this book, is a methodological innovation. These are the parameters:

1. Positioning: Where is each of the news items located in the paper? Is it located on the front page, the first few news pages, the back news pages, the culture and entertainment section, the daily or weekly supplement? Generalizing over the entire set of news items, the following fundamental question was asked: Do news items of the same type, in terms of their factual relationship with the new consensual narrative, consistently get located in the same parts of the paper? More specifically, where are news items that supposedly support the new narrative located? Where do we find news items that potentially threaten the new narrative?

2. Graphic saliency: Where is each news item located on its page? How much space does it occupy in comparison to the other items on the page? How salient is its headline? Does it also have a sub-headline? Is it accompanied by a photograph? In general, do news items of the same type consistently receive similar graphic treatment? Where are they usually located on the page? How much space do they occupy? How salient are their headlines? Do they have a sub-headline? Are they accompanied by a photograph?

3. Front page reference: Is the news item mentioned on the front page? What types of news items consistently get mentioned on the front page? What types are never mentioned?

4. Headline selection: Which pieces of data are consistently picked out from the texts and promoted to the headlines? Which are picked out for the

sub-headline? What types of data are never picked out? Can we find a consistent relationship between these patterns of selection and the new narrative?

5. Headline-text factual correspondence: To what extent do the factual components in the headline accurately copy the information in the body of the text? In what types of circumstances do we find that the factual components in the headlines do not accurately reproduce the information in the body of the text? Can we find a consistent relationship between the patterns of deviation and the new narrative?

6. Rhetorical contribution of headlines: To what extent do the headlines make a rhetorical contribution (hyperbole, emotional overstatement, melodramatization) that goes beyond the rhetoric of the texts? In what circumstances do we find such rhetorical contributions? Can we find a consistent relationship between the rhetorical patterns and the new narrative?

7. Lexical selection of headlines: What semantically constitutive key words, metaphors, names, and verbal constructions are selected for the headlines? Do they also appear in the text? How are the patterns of selection related to the new narrative?

8. Formulation of agency: How does the syntactic formulation of the headlines (especially in terms of the distinction between active and passive voice, and the syntactic positioning of the participants in an event) contribute to the assignment of agency, responsibility, and guilt in the event? What consistent patterns of syntactically based assignment of responsibility do we find in the headlines? How are they related to the new narrative?

9. Epistemic framing: How does the formulation of the headline determine the epistemic status of the information in the text? In other words, does it assign it the status of a fact, a claim, a prediction, an assumption, a lie? How is this assignment related to the source of the information? What consistent patterns of epistemic framing can we find? What types of data are consistently framed as facts, claims, predictions, assumptions, lies, and so on? How are the patterns related to the new narrative?

10. Visual semiotics: How do the visuals surrounding the news items— the photographs, the headline's colors, and so on—contribute to the framing of the news items? What semiotic patterns do we find in the contribution of the photographs to the framing of news items? How are these patterns related to the new narrative?

This integrated analysis allows for a clear distinction between the materials sent in by the reporters on the one hand and the newspapers' editorial policy on the other: In the three newspapers, the reporter's work is done when the text itself, without headlines, is sent in to the news desk. Everything else is determined by the editors: positioning, saliency, headline formulation, photograph selection, and so on.

As we shall see throughout the book, the careful examination of this distinction reveals a clear and fascinating state of affairs: A thorough reconstruction of all the news items—*without their headlines, and regardless of their positioning*—results in a complex, varied, informative, and often contradictory factual picture, which in no way conforms with the new consensual narrative. Obviously, not *every* factual facet of the incredibly complex events is indeed covered by the reporters—this issue shall also be dealt with here—but many of the reports nevertheless cover considerable parts of the complexity. However, this picture goes through a first transformation as it makes its way to the headlines of inner pages, where it already shows patterns of resemblance to the new narrative, and by the time it reaches the headlines of the front pages, it has lost almost all of its complexity: Virtually all the informative elements that do not tally with the new narrative disappear, and we are left with broad, one-sided generalizations—exactly those generalizations that were cemented in the Israeli collective consciousness throughout the month.

This book thus concentrates on the relationships between the reporters' accounts of reality and the newspapers' presentation of these accounts, leaving the debate regarding "objective reality" out of the picture. The reporters' daily reports are taken to be the best first approximations of reality that the newspapers managed to obtain, and the evaluations of bias, in their turn, are based on these first approximations. This methodology thus resolves another difficulty, that of distinguishing issues of bias and issues of accessibility to information: In principle, newspapers may provide their readers with a distorted presentation of reality simply because they had no access to relevant information. Concentrating on those pieces of information the papers actually received, and those to which they had clear access, helps us concentrate on editorial policy, and on patterns of bias.

From Headlines to Hegemony: Interpretation and Suppression

As far as the newspapers' readers are concerned, the above process dramatically constrains the way the news is read and interpreted—for three complementary reasons:

First, the positioning of a news item in a specific section of the paper not only sends a clear message about its significance (the closer the story is to the front page, the more significant it is claimed to be), it also marks the news item as a piece of "hard" or "soft" news (Tuchman 1973). The hard news section is where readers look for "factual presentations of events deemed noteworthy"; it is where "important news" appears (Tuchman 1973, 113–14). In the soft news section, on the other hand, readers look for "features," or "human interest stories"—"interesting" items which, by their very definition, do *not* serve as providers of "factual presentations" of "important news." As Tuchman shows, this classificatory distinction is far from being transparent, and "the same event may be treated as either hard news or a soft news story" (114). Thus, the editorial decision concerning the positioning of a news item in a specific section of the paper may play a crucial role in the readers' perception of its status as "hard" or "soft"—and by implication, in the readers' perception of the "importance" of its "factual representation." As we shall see throughout the book, the majority of crucial factual reports that cast a shadow on the new narrative, and that *did* appear in the papers, were framed as features or human interest stories and were positioned in the "soft news" sections of the papers.

Second, modern newspaper readers are "headline consumers" (cf. Dor 2003a; Nir 1993; Roeh and Nir 1993). As Nir (1993) claims, "for the modern newspaper reader, reading the headline of a news item replaces the reading of the whole story." Modern readers thus "often scan headlines and subheads and only occasionally read entire news stories" (Roeh and Nir 1993, 178). As Dor (2003a) shows, this is an entirely rational mode of behavior, because newspaper headlines come with the "guarantee" of optimal relevance: They offer their readers the optimal ratio between cognitive *effect* (the amount of new and relevant information they provide) and cognitive *cost* (the effort it takes to read and interpret them).[8] News stories contain a lot of information, but they also take a lot of effort to read and interpret. Headlines are much more cost-effective, because (a) they are very short and easy to read, and (b) they are supposed to provide an "initial summary" of the story (van Dijk 1988a). This cognitive calculation, of course, presupposes an unbiased, ideologically neutral summary. When headlines do *not* provide such a true summary of the text, the possibilities for biased representation of the facts are dramatic. Facts that are systematically presented in the back paragraphs of the text and are never highlighted in the headlines or the sub-headlines have a very good chance of not being noticed at all by most readers. And, in fact, the present research confirms this probability.

Third, headlines constrain the set of possible interpretations of their stories, even for those few readers who do read every printed word. Headlines *frame* the context for the interpretation of their stories, and in doing so dramatically reduce the range of possible interpretations (Bleske 1995; Dor 2003a; Gamson and Modigliani 1989; Geer and Kahn 1993; Iyengar 1991; Rhee 1997; Valkenburg et al. 1999; van Dijk 1988a).

We have already looked at one isolated example of all this—the *Tel Aviv* catastrophic headline pronouncing the future attack on Tel Aviv by Jaffa's Arabs—but the following, more elaborate example may be useful at this point in the discussion. In the third week of the Intifada, an emergency summit convened in Sharm el-Sheikh in Egypt. Among the participants were Prime Minister Barak, Chairman Arafat, and U.S. president Bill Clinton. The summit ended on October 17, with an agreement between Barak and Arafat to stop violence. Each side, irritated and weary after a long history of mutual disappointments, set out to check the willingness of the other side to respect the agreement. This was a challenging moment: The atmosphere in the occupied territories was explosive, and any act of violence, on either side, was liable to put an end to the agreement and restart the chain of violence of the past two and a half weeks. On the American presidential airplane, flying back from Sharm el-Sheikh to Washington, a "senior American official" told reporters that "the area is still extremely volatile and dangerous. One person, shooting a gun or throwing a stone, will suffice." As it turned out, the agreement did indeed collapse only a few hours after it was signed.

What happened during those volatile hours? The newspapers' field reporters sent in the following set of facts:

1. At the Erez roadblock, on the border between Israel and the Palestinian area of the Gaza Strip, IDF soldiers killed a Palestinian officer and wounded about fifteen people. Throughout the day, in different locations, various clashes were reported between IDF soldiers and Palestinian demonstrators. According to certain versions (e.g., the one reported in *Ma'ariv*), another Palestinian was killed by soldiers in these encounters. Several people, on both sides, were slightly wounded.

2. In the Nablus area, next to the settlement Itamar, two settlers murdered a Palestinian, Fareed Nassasra, a resident of Beit-Fourik, and wounded three others.

3. Palestinians from the town of Bet-Jalla shot at Gilo—officially a Jerusalem neighborhood, actually a settlement—critically wounding border policeman Shimon Ohana.

4. In the Gaza Strip, Palestinians shot at two trucks and threw a hand-grenade, which did not explode, at the police station in the settlement area of Gush Katif. No one was injured.

5. In the Kissufim area, a shooting exchange took place between IDF soldiers and a Palestinian group that tried to break through the security fence in order to place a bomb on the Israeli side. The Palestinians escaped.

6. In Zikhron Ya'akov, a Jewish town located deep inside the Green Line, hooligans set fire to a greengrocer's store owned by Ahmed Zhalka, age sixty-one, from the Arab village Kara.

How are these facts represented in the October 18 editions of the three newspapers? Let us take them one at a time. *Yediot Ahronot's* main headline on the 18th makes a simple and unequivocal statement:

ARAFAT PUT TO THE TEST

The message sent by this headline is crystal clear: The Sharm el-Sheikh agreement has not put both sides to the test, but only the Palestinians, which means that the future of the cease-fire depends on Arafat, and on him alone. Should the agreement collapse—and on the morning of the 18th this already seemed to be happening—only Arafat is to be held responsible. The sub-headline reads:

TENSE ANTICIPATION IN ISRAEL: IS ARAFAT WILLING AND ABLE TO CEASE FIRE?

Once again, Israel passively awaits Arafat's decision: Should he decide to cease fire, and if indeed he is able to do so, fire will indeed cease. Nothing that Israel, or Israelis, would do may have any causal effect on the situation in the field.

The overline, on the upper right side of the page, reads:

CEASE-FIRE IN SHARM, GUNFIRE ON GILO IN JERUSALEM

The very positioning of these two phrases in the same overline plays a crucial rhetorical function: It highlights the contradistinction between Arafat's declarative agreement to cease-fire and his "real intentions"—revealed in the shots fired by his own people in Jerusalem. The title of the main commentary article on the front page, written by Israel's most distinguished journalist, Nachum Barnea, frames the day's events around the same opposition—**FROM SHARM TO GILO**. Barnea writes: "A one-hour flight separates the Mövenpick conference center in Sharm el-Sheikh, at the tip of the Sinai peninsula, and the Gilo neighborhood of Jerusalem. One hour—and eternity." The "eternal" distance between the conference center and the settlement Itamar, where settlers murdered a Palestinian the day before, is never mentioned.

The banner above the main picture of the page says: **JERUSALEM— CIVILIANS UNDER FIRE**. The picture shows two youngsters in sports outfits, lying on the ground next to each other, taking cover and speaking on their cellular phones. Next to this picture appears a smaller one, that of the wounded border policeman Shimon Ohana, whose heart, according to the caption, was "pierced" by the bullet. The caption then reveals that Ohana is "an only son to his parents, born after five daughters."

Let us move on, then, to the other headlines in the news pages: ARAFAT HAS 48 HOURS TO CALM DOWN THE FIELD (pages 2–3); PALES-TINIAN CABINET: WE WILL CEASE FIRE ONLY AFTER ISRAEL DOES ITS SHARE (page 2); ARAFAT TAKES HIS TIME (page 3); WAR IN THE LIVING ROOM (pages 4–5, dealing with the shooting at Gilo); BULLET PIERCES POLICEMAN'S HEART (page 6); A NIGHT OF SHOOTINGS ON HEBRON, PSAGOT, AND IDF OUTPOSTS (page 6); WE HAVE AN AGREEMENT, BUT THERE'S NO TRUST (page 7). Pages 8–9 present the details of the security codicil of the Sharm el-Sheikh agreement; page 11 deals with the attempts to bring about an emergency coalition between Barak and the right-wing opposition party Likud, headed by Ariel Sharon; and pages 12–13 are dedicated to a huge group photograph of the summit participants. Then, on page 14—the first page of the second part of the paper—appears a report on the murder near Itamar. Nothing in the report indicates that there might be a link between the event and the larger-scale developments of the day. The word *murder*, moreover, never appears in the text, and the headline says: PALESTINIAN KILLED BY SETTLER'S FIRE. Contrast the usage of the verb in the *passive voice* with the *active voice* formulation of the headline on page 6— BULLET PIERCES POLICEMAN'S HEART. The second Palestinian casualty (and there may have been a third) simply do not make it into the paper.

Ma'ariv offers its readers a slightly fuller, more balanced picture. The main headline says:

CEASE-FIRE PUT TO THE TEST

This headline, as opposed to the one offered by Yediot Ahronot, does not explicitly hold the Palestinians uniquely responsible for the cease-fire agreement; it recognizes, implicitly at least, that Israel is also on trial. The front page mentions the shooting at Gilo, as well as the three dead Palestinians, "one of them by settlers' fire." The picture's banner, however, expresses the very same contradistinction highlighted by Yediot Ahronot's front page:

DECLARATION IN SHARM—FIGHTING IN GILO

And another headline, below the picture, says:

BARAK ORDERED CEASE-FIRE YESTERDAY; ARAFAT STALLED

The relative positions of the different elements on this page, as well as the size of the letters, are crucial here: The Palestinian shooting on Gilo is mentioned in four different places on the page—always in very large letters—above the main headline and below it, and in the picture's banner. The three dead Palestinians, on the other hand, appear only once, in small letters, in the lower part of the page. This part is not at all visible when the paper lies folded in the newsstands. Another small headline, in the lower part of the page, refers to the Arab summit, which convened at that time and was about to reach a joint decision with only a "mild" denunciation of Israel, according to *Ma'ariv*. As we shall see, the positioning of statements made by Arab leaders in the papers, throughout the month, is perfectly predictable: Extreme, threatening statements are prominently located, at the head of the page; moderate statements appear, if at all, at the bottom. In its entirety, then, this page is slightly more balanced than *Yediot Ahronot*'s front page, but the message spelled in large letters, at the head of the page, is the very same.

What about *Ha'aretz*? The message conveyed by the paper on the morning of the 18th is essentially the same as that of the other two papers. The shooting at Gilo and the injured border policeman appear in the second headline, and the evacuation of the soldier to the hospital is the subject of the main picture. As in *Ma'ariv*, the murder of the Palestinian near Itamar appears in small letters in the box titled **THE MAIN FACTS**. The other Palestinian who was killed, reported in an item on page 5, is not mentioned at all on the front page. The newspaper's main headline is:

**BARAK STEPPING UP PREPARATIONS FOR
UNILATERAL SEPARATION FROM PALESTINIANS**

As we shall see in chapter 6, Barak's "unilateral separation plan" never passed the stage of a propaganda stunt. It never actually existed as a real plan for action, not only because no one worked it out in detail, but also because such a plan was, and still is, unfeasible. Barak declared that he was "stepping up preparations" for the implementation of this virtual plan in order to try to improve his public standing and to step up pressure on Arafat. According to the news story that appeared under this headline, Barak believed that this plan would be acceptable to Ariel Sharon, then head of the Likud opposition party. The "plan" did not include the evacuation of any settlement and was not conditional on Palestinian approval. In other words, on the very day Barak signed a cease-fire agreement with Arafat—

an agreement including the commitment "to find a way to return to negotiations"—he decided to send a message through the media, announcing
that he was "stepping up preparations" for a "plan" that would effectively
bury any chances of understanding on the permanent status agreement, and
use this plan as a "platform" for a national emergency government with
Ariel Sharon. As we shall see, this analysis of the plan constituted the pre-
vailing view among analysts and commentators, but *Ha'aretz* chose—not
for the first time—to swallow the prime minister's bait, and devote its main
headline to the idea of "unilateral separation."

Thus, on the morning of October 18, each of the three newspapers in
its own way supplied its readers with a partial, censored description of the
complicated state of affairs of the previous day. The belief that continued
violence, in defiance of the Sharm el-Sheikh agreement, resulted from a
choice made by the Palestinians, and by them alone, did not become part
of the readers' view as a result of the facts presented by the papers. Quite
the contrary: This belief already suffused the reports with an unequivocally
commentarial tone, leaving no room for doubt. It dramatically stressed, in
vivid colors, certain elements of reality, and suppressed others, thus effectively preventing readers from exercising their right to form their own interpretation of the events, based on an impartial, full presentation of the
facts at hand. To be sure, many readers would probably have interpreted the
events in the same way, even if they had received a fair presentation of all
the facts. Leftist wishful thinking notwithstanding, full exposure to the
facts does not necessarily turn people into doves. But it may also be reasonably assumed that impartial reporting would have made it possible for
many other readers to form a different opinion. In other words: It is indeed
possible to interpret the facts of October 17 either way, but it is almost impossible to interpret the facts *as they were presented in the three newspapers'
front pages* in any other way than according to the constitutive frame that
determined their presentation in the first place. The right to an independent interpretation is the true meaning of the call for unbiased journalism—and in this sense, none of the three papers rose up to the occasion on
October 18. As we shall see throughout the book, this example accurately
represents the conduct of the press throughout the month.

The Narrative:
From Deconstruction to Reconstruction

The remainder of the book is structured on a narrative grid. It follows the
events of October 2000 on a day-to-day basis, *deconstructing* the narrative

as reported by the newspapers, and *reconstructing* a more balanced narrative based on the full reports sent in by the reporters. As we shall see, this dynamic methodology—reminiscent of historical descriptions and analyses—will help us capture some crucial generalizations, which would disappear in a more static form.

The second chapter deals with the first two days of Intifada coverage, concentrating on the two seemingly factual contentions that came to dominate the Israeli perception of the events: the assertion that Arafat initiated the Intifada, and the claim that the outbreak of violence had nothing to do with Ariel Sharon's controversial visit to the Temple Mount the day before the riots broke out.

The third chapter deals with the key events of the second half of the first week of the Intifada—the Paris summit, the "fight" over the Temple Mount, the withdrawal from Joseph's Tomb, and the kidnapping of soldiers on the northern border—and follows the papers' anxious expression of their own "disillusion" with the peace process.

The fourth chapter starts in the beginning of the second week of the Intifada, when Barak presented Arafat with a forty-eight-hour ultimatum to stop the violence, and continues with an overall examination of the two key concepts the newspapers adopted in their coverage of the IDF's military operations in the occupied territories: the concepts of "restraint" and "response." As we shall see, these two concepts took what was in reality a two-sided war of attrition conducted within the continuous context of occupation and framed it as a one-sided story of inexplicable, rampant violence initiated by the Palestinians—violence to which Israel responded with restraint.

The fifth chapter deals with the tragic events within the Green Line—events in which thirteen Arab Israelis were killed—and analyzes the way in which the newspapers presented the police's patently one-sided version as a "factual" report of "Intifada within."

The sixth chapter surveys the coverage of the events of the second week of the Intifada, from the escalation in the IDF's response until the "Lynch" in Ramallah, and shows how the press joined the campaign of delegitimization of the Palestinian people as a partner for peace, a campaign that lay at the heart of Prime Minister Barak's political strategy.

The seventh chapter deals with the diplomatic developments of the third week of the Intifada—the Sharm el-Sheikh summit and the "political time-out" announced by Barak—and focuses on the completely uncritical reporting of Barak's political moves, the way he conducted negotiations with the Palestinians, and his "generous proposals" for a permanent status agreement.

The concluding chapter deals with a set of theoretical questions having to do with the combined influences exerted on the newspapers, the professional and ideological relationships between editors and reporters, and the relationship between the media, the state, and the public.

2

"Under Arafat's Baton"

> And now all our old wounds are bleeding again across the land. The rattle of firearms, so familiar from battlefields, ambuscades, and raids, has returned to the cities and towns, to the roads that unite near and far. Something old and forgotten, something we thought had become history, has returned and is now in the living heart of the Land of Israel and of Israel.[1] And there is no more then and now, no more here and there; the Green Line is gone.
>
> —Chaim Guri, *Ma'ariv,* October 3

The first newspaper reports of the "El-Aqsa Intifada" reached the newsstands on Monday, October 2, after a weekend extended by the Jewish New Year (*Rosh Hashana*). In the preceding three days, the Jewish residents of the country had watched in fear and anger the harsh, incomprehensible television images: thousands of Arabs hurling rocks, burning tires, and blocking highways; an injured border policeman prevented from reaching the hospital by a crowd of Palestinians; and one small Palestinian child, Mohammed al-Durra, seeking refuge in his father's arms, then shot to death in front of the cameras, on live television. And all this—as far as the Israeli public was concerned—for no conceivable reason, just before the conflict was to end, in the midst of permanent status talks, about a week after Ehud Barak, vaunted as being more accommodating toward the Palestinians than any prime minister before him, played host to Yasser Arafat in his home at Kochav Yair. Worse, this happened not only in the territories, not only on the Temple Mount, that "Islamic volcano," but also in major Arab cities and villages within Israel itself—Nazareth, Um El-Fahem, Faradies—as well as on Yeffet Street in Jaffa, just five minutes away from downtown Tel Aviv. "Something old and forgotten," in Poet Chaim Guri's pathos-ridden words, arose from those images, something that the Israeli collective memory retained despite fifty years of sovereignty, five victorious wars, military might unmatched in the Near East, and more than thirty years of occupation and rule over another people. It was the awesome fear and bottomless anger, the bitter sense of betrayal felt by a Jewish community that perceives itself as being in a constant search for peace and finds itself again, for the umpteenth time, ringed on the outside and besieged from the inside by enemies bent upon its destruction.

Between Ariel Sharon's visit to the Temple Mount on the previous Thursday and the appearance of the Monday morning papers, the Israeli collective consciousness had time to dig its heels deep into the siege mentality of 1948. The Monday papers, together with the Tuesday editions, reflect the War of Independence siege cast of mind on every page, in every headline, with every picture—even in articles written by special guest writers. *Ma'ariv* enlisted poet Chaim Guri, quoted above, probably the most genuinely representative voice of the 1948 generation. On its front page, *Yediot Ahronot* asked another famous veteran of the War of Independence, the former chief of staff and ultra-right-wing ex-member of the Knesset (MK) Raphael Eitan: "What should be done?" The general who led the IDF into Lebanon in the 1980s replied: "If it were up to me, no Arab would be allowed to travel on our roads these days. I would cancel their social security and turn off their water and electricity—before shooting at them."

More than a hundred pictures appear in the three newspapers in these two days, and most of them construct a dramatic contrast between Palestinian *violence*—"the fire kindled by the Arabs" within the Green Line and beyond it, and the Israelis who were victimized by it—and Israeli *restraint*. The pictures show the Palestinians in delirious motion: running, hiding, rolling on the ground, throwing stones. In many pictures they are engulfed in smoke, rushing from one fire to the next. On page 3 of the Monday edition of *Yediot Ahronot,* under the headline WAR OF INDEPENDENCE? there is a large picture in shades of gray and brown. In the foreground a line of soldiers, wearing helmets and vests, stands with backs to the camera and heads turned to a horizon filled with thick blue and gray smoke. In this haze of smoke run two Palestinians. One of them holds a bucket, perhaps running to put out a flame. None of the soldiers is aiming his weapon at the Palestinians. One of them waves a hand at them. His body language is relaxed, almost friendly, expressing restraint. The caption reads: "Battle crosses all lines." On the facing page there is a graphic illustration under the heading FOCAL POINTS OF THE CONFLAGRATION. A small fire marks the location of each incident: Tamra, Kefar Kanna, Nazareth, Kalkilya, Ramallah, Hebron. The entire country is aflame. The Green Line is marked by a faint, barely visible dashed line. *Ma'ariv* favors group pictures of IDF soldiers, sitting on armored vehicles at the entrance to Nablus, or standing on the road to the Temple Mount. The soldiers are never engaged in any particular activity. They are "in a holding pattern," at an "observation post," or "taking up positions." Compare this with the picture that appears on page 3 of Ma'ariv, on October 2, showing three Palestinian policemen holding Kalashnikov rifles, hiding behind a wall, bent low, panting, in the thick of battle. The caption quotes "senior sources in the defense establishment" as saying that "the Palestinians have not yet exhausted their potential for confrontation and intend to continue violent clashes in the coming days." On pages 2 and 3 of Ha'aretz there are three pictures: Palestinian policemen lying on a sandy plain at Netzarim junction, shooting at IDF soldiers; a fire blazing on a central street in Nazareth; and a firebomb exploding on a street in Jaffa.

A few pictures accompany other news items of visual interest: PM Barak and IDF Chief of Staff Shaul Mofaz at the headquarters of the Judea and Samaria army command; mayor Amram Mitznah trying to pacify demonstrators in an Arab-Jewish neighborhood in Haifa; a Palestinian position hit by an IDF missile (no casualties); a Palestinian car set ablaze by settlers, with the caption "Returning fire." Finally, a handful of pictures are dedicated to the victims on the Palestinian side: Yediot Ahronot publishes three very small pictures of injured Palestinians being evacuated; one small picture showing the funeral of a two-year-old killed by IDF fire; and three huge pictures depicting the frame-by-frame death of Mohammed al-Durra—the significance of which is a complex matter: This tragic incident infuriated the Israeli public more than anything else during that week. As far as common perception was concerned, the Palestinians pushed the child to his death in order to score points in the battle waged on television screens worldwide. We shall return to this subject in chapter 4.

The headlines printed by the papers project the same message. Of 41 headlines in the October 2 and 3 issues of Yediot Ahronot, 26 deal exclusively with Palestinian and Arab Israeli violence, and with its Jewish Israeli victims. The main front page headline on October 2, in huge white letters on a red background, reads: FIRE SPREADS TO ISRAELI ARABS. On October 3, the front page headline is: RIOTS IN HAIFA, SHOOTING IN ACRE, SETTLEMENTS BLOCKADED. Other headlines read:

INTIFADA IN THE GALILEE AND JAFFA

WOUNDED SOLDIER WAITED 5 HOURS FOR RESCUE—AND DIED

SETTLERS UNDER SIEGE

UNDER ARAFAT'S BATON

MURDER ON THE JOINT PATROL[2]

SHOOTING IN NAZARETH AND ACRE

SEVERE RIOTS IN HAIFA: "PALESTINE IS HERE"

ARAFAT TAKES HIS TIME

IDF SOLDIER KILLED IN PALESTINIAN POLICE AMBUSH

SOUGHT CHEAP CAR REPAIR IN SAMARIA, WAS SHOT TO DEATH FROM CLOSE RANGE

TARGET: OCCUPY SETTLEMENT

A few additional headlines address the political issues (U.S. BLAMES SHARON; MUTUAL RECRIMINATIONS BETWEEN BARAK AND ARAFAT) and other, relatively marginal issues (EMERGENCY DEBATE IN THE KNESSET). Only one headline deals with IDF operations in the first days of the riots: FIRST AIR FORCE ATTACKS IN GAZA. One headline deals with the dispute between the army and the government: IDF GENERALS: EVACUATE [settlers from] JOSEPH'S TOMB [in Nablus]. Two headlines introduce Op-Ed pieces written by prominent Arab Israelis: the headline of MK Azmi Bishara's article reads: BARAK'S FAILURE; the article by Lutfi Mashur, the publisher and editor of an Arab Israeli weekly, is titled: A MOST DANGEROUS TURN OF EVENTS.

The ratio of headlines in *Ma'ariv* is identical: 44 out of 70 headlines deal with Palestinian violence and its consequences. Here are a few examples:

NEAR WAR IN THE TERRITORIES—INTIFADA WITHIN GREEN LINE

DEATH TRAP AT JOSEPH'S TOMB

SHOOTING ON ROAD TO HAIFA

NEGEV BEDOUINS THROW ROCKS, FIREBOMBS

"DEATH TO THE JEWS" CALLS IN NAZARETH

OUTPOSTS[3] BLOCKADED: "WE WERE TOLD TO STAY HOME AND LOCK THE GATES"

YEFFET STREET, DOWNTOWN JAFFA: ROCKS AND FIREBOMBS

POLICE COMMANDER [Yair] ITZHAKI WOUNDED IN RIOTS

FIRST HE DRINKS COFFEE WITH YOU—THEN HE MURDERS YOU

A few headlines, in the back pages, do present a different perspective. For example:

SHARON'S VISIT TRIGGERED THE RIOTS

MOHAMMED DAHLAN:[4] "SHARON IS A WAR CRIMINAL"

DEATH OF A CHILD

Ha'aretz's general tone is more restrained, but the great majority of headlines published by the paper in these two days express the same alarm. A few examples:

ISRAEL: ARAFAT RESPONSIBLE FOR RIOTS. IDF DEPLOYS TANKS IN THE TERRITORIES

BEGINNING OF BLOCKADE: NETZARIM JUNCTION AND JOSEPH'S TOMB

ARAB MK'S SHARE RESPONSIBILITY FOR DIRE OUTCOME

PALESTINIAN SHOOTS PARTNER ON JOINT PATROL DURING COFFEE BREAK

APPROXIMATELY 70 POLICEMEN INJURED IN JERUSALEM CONFRONTATIONS

WESTERN WALL SITE EVACUATED THREE TIMES

IDF: ARAFAT INSTRUCTED TANZIM[5] TO ESCALATE RIOTS

Other headlines, again in the back pages, suggest a different point of view:

ARAFAT HAD NO CONTROL OVER EVENTS IN THE FIELD

PALESTINIAN CHILD AT NETZARIM SHOT IN STOMACH, DIES ON THE SPOT

WENT TO DONATE BLOOD; WAS KILLED BY ISRAELI POLICE

SHARON'S VISIT TO TEMPLE MOUNT INFURIATES PALESTINIAN AUTHORITY

In these two days, the number of Palestinian casualties makes front page news. As we shall see in chapter 4, these numbers vanish from the front pages a few days later.

One cannot overstate the importance of the unequivocal message carried by the headlines and pictures published in these first two days by the three newspapers. This message both reflected and reinforced the collective, traumatic outburst of fear, helplessness, anger, and sense of betrayal felt by the Jewish citizens of the state. Moreover, it cemented a factual reality (*who* did *what* to *whom*, *when*, and *why*) that informed the Israeli debate regarding the essence of the riots during the month of October. As we shall see, this factual framework contradicted not only what was actually happening in the field, but also the reports filed by the newspapers' own correspondents.

Sources and Headlines:
Arafat, Sharon, and the Riots

Let us begin, then, with the most fundamental topic the newspapers had to deal with: Why did the riots break out? This key issue consists of three interrelated questions: two of these are factual; the third deals with the broader political framework.

(1) What was the causal relationship between Ariel Sharon's visit to the Temple Mount on Thursday, September 28, and the outbreak of the riots the following day?

(2) Were the riots planned, orchestrated, and conducted by Arafat? Or were they a spontaneous outburst of Palestinian frustration over what seemed to be an Israeli threat to one of the holy sites of Islam—following the prolonged stalemate in the permanent status talks?

(3) What actually happened at the unsuccessful Camp David summit in July 2000, and how was this related to the outbreak of the riots?

The third question is addressed in chapter 7. The official Israeli answers to the first two questions are printed in large letters on the front pages of the three newspapers in the first days of October:

Ha'aretz: The main headline in *Ha'aretz* on October 2 states: **ISRAEL: ARAFAT RESPONSIBLE FOR RIOTS**. A special box on the front page, titled **THE MAIN FACTS**, provides the readers with the following information: "Last night Barak convened an emergency consultation in his home. He told Arafat that his 'immediate and personal' intervention is required. The U.S. is trying to stop the violence. The cease-fire agreement reached last night was not observed by the Palestinians. U.S.: Sharon's visit to the Temple Mount triggered the outburst."

The message is clear: Arafat is responsible for the violent outbreak and is doing nothing to stop it, and the claim that Sharon's visit to the Temple Mount caused the riots is an *American* claim. On October 3, *Ha'aretz* adds another piece of relevant information, under the same type of heading: "Sharon in a letter to Albright: The violence began before my visit to the Temple Mount."

Ma'ariv: The October 2 front page summary of the events deals with these questions:

ARAFAT'S ROLE—ANGER AND EMBARRASSMENT IN ISRAEL: ARAFAT IS BEHIND THE RIOTS; UNCLEAR WHETHER HE IS IN CONTROL OF EVENTS IN THE FIELD.

THE SHARON CONTROVERSY—THE U.S., THE PALESTINIANS, AND PART OF THE LEFT: SHARON'S VISIT CAUSED THE RIOTS. SHARON: THIS IS JUST AN EXCUSE.

Once more, it is Arafat who caused the riots, although it is not clear whether or not he lost control over them. The claim that connects the riots with Sharon's visit is associated with the U.S., the Palestinians, and the Left; it is not an "Israeli" position.

Yediot Ahronot: A sub-headline printed on October 2 below the main headline states: ISRAEL: ARAFAT INITIATED THE OUTBURST. The headline of the commentary written by Ron Ben-Ishai, the paper's senior military commentator, states: **ARAFAT SEEKS CONFRONTATION.** There is no mention of Sharon's visit on the front page. On the next day, *Yediot Ahronot* asks an expert witness to express his views on the matter in its front page—the witness is none other than Sharon himself. The headline of his article is **WHAT CAUSED THE FIRE**, and the article itself, quite obviously, lays the blame at Arafat's door. As far as *Yediot Ahronot* is concerned, the causal relationship between Sharon's visit and the outbreak of the riots never surfaces as a newsworthy topic.

Let us now take a look at the reports filed by the newspapers' reporters, and at some of the headlines printed in the internal pages:

Ha'aretz: In addition to the defense establishment's official version, *Ha'aretz* presents the views of two senior commentators. Military commentator Ze'ev Schiff reports:

The riots on the Temple Mount broke out following an Israeli provocation. . . .
The overall impression is that Arafat had no control over events in the field,
perhaps not even over the Tanzim's actions. Later, Arafat embraced the grass-
roots activity and did not act to stop it.

Dani Rubinstein, a senior commentator and expert on Palestinian affairs, writes:

> Many members of the Palestinian leadership approached their senior Israeli acquaintances and tried to prevent Sharon's visit to the Temple Mount. . . . The response was negative. On many occasions in the past, the Israeli government has prevented MKs from all factions from making ostentatious visits to East Jerusalem or the territories, because such visits could have sparked riots. This time, Barak and his ministers did not do this. They were worried about angry reactions from Sharon and the opposition parties, and perhaps about the reaction of Israeli public opinion as well.

The headline of Schiff's article is: ARAFAT HAD NO CONTROL OVER EVENTS IN THE FIELD; of Rubinstein's: SHARON'S VISIT TO TEMPLE MOUNT INFURIATED THE PA. Paragraphs from the two articles appear on the front page, but without headlines. This is common practice in Ha'aretz, but the fact remains that the insights of the two commentators did not find their way to the front page headlines.

Moreover, in the *sixth* paragraph of its lead article, Ha'aretz states:

> The incidents began on Friday on the Temple Mount, in protest against the visit there on Thursday of MK Ariel Sharon, chairman of the Likud Party. The PA holds the Israeli government fully responsible for the clashes, first and foremost for the fatal clash on Friday at El-Aqsa. The PA claims that witnesses who were praying in the mosque at the time testified that the Israeli police behaved in a provocative manner, and were quick to use rubber-coated metal bullets from short range.

Reporter Amira Hass writes on page 8 that

> on Thursday, when the PA and the Fatah called on the population to protest against 'Sharon's provocation,' the response was lukewarm; no more than a thousand people came to the mosque. Again, as many times before, the PA proved incapable of mobilizing tens of thousands of people for violent and dangerous clashes with the IDF.

These factual reports did not find their way to the headlines either.

Ma'ariv: As we have seen, the front page attributes the link between Sharon's visit and the outbreak of the riots to the U.S., the Palestinians, and "part of the Left." On pages 16–17, however, it brings an identical claim—this time from senior sources *inside the Israeli police*. Here is the opening paragraph of the report:

> "Sharon's visit led to the riots," said police officers. The PA, they said, was not pleased with the relatively minor opposition during the visit and "wanted

another round to improve performance." "The street was quiet. There was no reason for riots to break out and it did not appear that the Palestinians were headed for confrontation. Sharon's visit set fire to the street," said the police officer.

This unequivocal statement, coming from an Israeli defense source, captured the headlines of pages 16–17 but did not make it to the front page. Why? Perhaps because the Israeli reader, who can dismiss U.S., Palestinian, and Leftist claims as biased or irrelevant, would probably find the words of a police officer more credible; or perhaps because the lead article, on pages 2–3, opens with the "defense establishment"'s claim that "it was Arafat who ordered the riots in the territories, but subsequently he lost control"; or perhaps because the most energetic denial of Sharon's role in the incidents came not from him, but from the prime minister's entourage: "Senior members in the prime minister's circle said that 'the riots did not erupt because of Sharon's visit to the Temple Mount.' The minister of tourism, Amnon Lipkin Shahak, also rejected claims that it was Sharon's visit that triggered the riots." Why did these senior sources find it so crucial to deny a claim that now seems to have been corroborated by the U.S., the Palestinians, the Left, police officers, and at least two senior commentators? We shall get back to this question shortly, after we take a look at *Yediot Ahronot*.

Yediot Ahronot: In the seventh paragraph of its lead article, on pages 2–3, *Yediot Ahronot* writes: "Last night, sources in the defense establishment accused the PA of inciting the riots." This report does not mention Sharon's visit to the Temple Mount at all. This event is mentioned, as a news item, only on page 14, under the headline U.S. BLAMES SHARON. In this short article, Sharon himself is quoted as claiming that the riots had been planned ahead of time and had no connection whatsoever with his visit. Sharon's comments are followed by quotes from the American State Department, the Egyptian foreign minister, and MK Yossi Sarid. At the very end appears a short quote from Chief of Staff Shaul Mofaz—the most senior source in the defense establishment, whose words routinely make front page headlines. He says: "There is no doubt that part of the escalation was the result of the events on the Temple Mount."

Senior commentator and reporter Ron Ben-Ishai publishes a commentary article on the front page of the paper. Note how he manages, in the space of one paragraph, to shift from the assertion that "the eruption was instigated" to the statement that "the Palestinian street exploded on its own":

The eruption was instigated and spread like wildfire. It started on the Temple Mount, the focal point of the conflagration, with occasional shooting in the territories, until, on the first day of Rosh Hashana, the fire reached what the IDF calls "friction points": the army posts at Netzarim Junction and Rafiah, on the Egyptian border, at Joseph's Tomb, and in Hebron. On the third day, Israeli Arabs joined in and formed a third combat region. Arafat did not have to exert himself. He did not even need to instruct the Tanzim to set fire to the area. It was enough that he did not put his foot down and order his security forces to snuff out the violent confrontation from the outset. The Palestinian street, restless already since the Camp David summit, was inflamed by Arafat's comments about Jerusalem and the holy sites of Islam, and exploded on its own. The Tanzim did not need explicit instructions in order to confront the IDF.

What, then, is Ron Ben-Ishai trying to tell us? Was the conflagration instigated or not? Were there explicit orders issued? Did Arafat initiate the events or did he not? The only reading of this text that could corroborate the official Israeli version of the events would be that Arafat initiated the riots by not putting his foot down to stop them after they broke out.

In his commentary on page 11 of the same newspaper, Roni Shaked, one of the reporters who contributed to the lead article, says:

> The actions of four Israelis have led, in the past decade, to bloody riots on religious grounds. In October 1990 it was the leader of the Temple Mount Custodians movement, Gershon Salomon, whose attempt to enter the Temple Mount triggered a bloody confrontation in the course of which twenty-one Palestinians were killed. In February 1994 Baruch Goldstein broke into the Tomb of the Patriarchs [in Hebron], massacred twenty-nine Palestinians, and caused serious rioting in the territories and in Jerusalem. In September 1996 Prime Minister Benjamin Netanyahu opened the Western Wall Tunnel, leading to widespread and bloody riots in which some sixty people were killed. Last week it was MK Ariel Sharon who fueled the anger of Muslims with his visit to the Temple Mount. These four events show that the Palestinian street's religious feeling is much stronger than its nationalistic feeling. In all cases the Palestinian leadership first lost control over the masses, which were led by religious leaders in the mosques. Later, the Palestinian leadership "joined in the party" to reap the political benefits. The current wave of violence fell into Arafat's lap like a ripe fruit. The bloody events of Rosh Hashana, which have already engendered condemnations against Israel, will consolidate his political position, unite his divided people, and once again focus international attention on the Palestinian problem. Arafat demonstrated his control of the streets and ordered the escalation of violence when he wanted it. He knew that in the end he would return to the negotiating table reinvigorated and would explain how the bloody events following Sharon's visit demonstrate that sovereignty over the site must be in Muslim hands. Have any lessons been learned from past mistakes? The Zamir Commission, which investigated the Temple Mount events in 1990, recommended that security maintenance in so sensitive a place requires planning

at the state level. Had the government of Israel implemented this recommendation, it is likely that Sharon's visit would have been prevented and the bloody events avoided.

What is the appropriate headline for such a clear-sighted commentary, which describes the dynamics of the outbreak in the Palestinian street, out of PA control, and considers the authorization of Sharon's visit a mistake made by a government that did not learn from the past? The editors of *Yediot Ahronot* chose the following headline:

UNDER ARAFAT'S BATON

The importance of this choice can hardly be overstated: Hundreds of thousands of people probably browsed through this copy of *Yediot Ahronot*. Most of them glanced at the headlines and looked at the pictures. A minority read the lead articles, and maybe the more personal ones, for example the tragic story of the injured border policeman Yusuf Madhat, who waited at Joseph's Tomb for five hours to be rescued before dying of his injuries. Of these, only a tiny minority paused to read Shaked's commentary; most read the headline and moved on. After all, the readers already "knew" that the riots broke out under Arafat's baton; this was the message they received from television newscasts throughout the holiday. The fact that the commentary tells a different story from its headline sank into complete oblivion.

Handling Complexities:
Between Ambiguity and Politics

Let us, then, take a closer look at the gaps between the different reports we have seen up to this point. According to the headlines, Israel determined that Arafat *initiated* the riots, which had been premeditated, and used Sharon's visit as an excuse. Ze'ev Schiff, Dani Rubinstein, and Roni Shaked tell us that the events began on the streets, *spontaneously*, and Arafat was quick to take political advantage of the opportunity. *Ma'ariv* writes that Arafat initiated the events but *lost control*. Ron Ben-Ishai tells us that Arafat did *not* initiate the events, but was in *complete control* of the street. These variations raise a natural question: Did *anyone* know with any degree of certainty what was actually happening in the field?

The simple fact is that during the first days of the riots no one in Israel knew what was really happening in the PA. Opinions were divided not only among journalists, but also among what is termed the Israeli "intelligence community." The "defense sources" that the newspapers quoted, who reported that Arafat initiated the events and was in full control of their development, were senior officials of the Defense Department and senior IDF (especially army intelligence) officers. All of them indeed believed that Arafat was the key to understanding the events, although, as we have seen, opinions within the IDF differed in this regard. Others in the defense establishment, notably the General Security Services (the Shin-Beth), viewed events differently. In his article in Section B of *Ha'aretz* on October 6, Uzi Benziman says the following about the army intelligence and Shin-Beth analysis of events, as reported to Barak and to Internal Security Minister Shlomo Ben-Ami in the first days of the riots:

> The intelligence picture presented to Barak and Ben-Ami regarding the events leading up to the bloody outbreak was not unambiguous. There were differences between the army intelligence and the Shin-Beth. The IDF believed that the riots were premeditated and that Sharon's visit served as the excuse for carrying them out. The Shin-Beth thought that they were largely a spontaneous expression of passionate feeling that overwhelmed the Palestinians both in the territories and within the Green Line. The question regarding the extent of control Arafat had over the level of violence did not receive a clear answer either. The IDF believes that events hinge on the wishes of the PA chairman, while the Shin-Beth thinks that Arafat's orders do not necessarily carry much weight in all centers of Palestinian power.

The differences of opinion between army intelligence and the Shin-Beth are the subject of Yossi Melman's article in *Ha'aretz* on November 16. The army's opinion that Arafat is not interested in stopping the violence, writes Melman, follows from its assessment that the PA chairman initiated and controlled the violence. The assessment of senior Shin-Beth officials, however, is that "it is doubtful whether the shootings, the attacks, and the demonstrations would stop even if Arafat gave the order. Therefore, because of the fear that his weakness would be exposed, he is not willing to order a cease-fire." This appraisal is surprisingly close to that of *Ha'aretz* correspondent Amira Hass—the only Israeli reporter actually based in the territories. Senior army intelligence and Shin-Beth staff often discount each other's views. The army claims that the Shin-Beth has a close working relationship with the PA and therefore "feels comfortable accepting the assumption that Arafat has no control over events in the street. This absolves Arafat and the heads of his security apparatus from responsibility." The Shin-Beth, on the other hand, thinks that "the army is too square," as Ofer Shelach tells us in *Ma'ariv*'s weekend supplement on October 20: "They are addicted to simple and simplistic explanations and take the easy route of concentrating fire on one target." Either way, the plot thickens. It now appears that the official Israeli position, presented by the newspaper headlines, is contradicted not only by the U.S., the Palestinians, part of the Left, senior police officers, and several commentators—but by the Shin-Beth as well.

And there is more. Articles published in the *Ma'ariv* and *Yediot Ahronot* weekend supplements on October 6 inform us that various intelligence sources warned the political leadership that Sharon's visit to the Temple Mount was liable to cause an explosion. Nevertheless, the visit was approved. Ben Caspit explains this decision in *Ma'ariv*'s weekend supplement:

> On Tuesday of this week, the Knesset's Foreign Affairs and Security Committee met to hear reports from Minister Shlomo Ben-Ami and from Deputy Chief of Staff Moshe Yeelon. Ben-Ami spoke first. He said that no unusual problem had been identified with respect to Sharon's visit to the Temple Mount. According to one intelligence report, he said, the visit was to take a peaceful course. This was based on, among other things, contacts with senior Palestinian officials. "As long as Sharon does not walk into the mosques themselves, it will be possible to live with it," they said. This was the assessment in Ben-Ami's words. . . . [Then] it was the deputy chief of staff's turn to speak. General Yeelon voiced almost the reverse opinion. He said that IDF analysts and intelligence staff had estimated that the field was saturated with gunpowder liable to explode. Yeelon said that any "deliberate action" could set off such an explosion and the ensuing heavy rioting. Sharon's visit, he said, provided the pretext for the events.
>
> MK Zahava Gal'on from [the moderate left-wing party] Meretz, who noted the discrepancy between what the minister and the general had said, asked how that was possible: "If you judged that Sharon's visit was liable to ignite the area, why did you not bring the assessment to the attention of the political leadership? This is a serious intelligence failure." Yeelon tried to calm everyone down: "There was no failure. I don't think such terms are warranted."
>
> Whether or not there was a failure, it is clear that the possibility of riots following Sharon's visit to Temple Mount had been taken into account and brought to the attention of decision makers, who decided nevertheless to allow the visit. Barak and Ben-Ami knew that they had no chance against a possible appeal to the High Court of Justice by Sharon. In the meantime, they would lose important political and diplomatic ground. They hoped that it would all blow over quietly. This hope was deceived. According to yet another hypothesis, Barak believed that there would be violence following the visit, and still did not stop it. It is possible that Barak, as well as Arafat, knew that only a shock could jolt the stalemated process. He knew that his attempt to stop the Likud's leader from visiting Temple Mount could become the sharp edge of an election campaign against him, and he chose to gamble. He knew that the violence would yield some type of dividend: he would get either Arafat—or Sharon.

And here are Ron Ben-Ishai, Roni Shaked, and Alex Fishman in *Yediot Ahronot*'s weekend supplement:

> Wednesday, September 27: The plans of Likud chairman Ariel Sharon to visit the Temple Mount are causing a stir. Palestinian VIPs and Arab MKs warn about the consequences of the visit. Gibril Rajub, head of Preventive Security in the PA, says in an interview: "There will be rioting. I cannot, and actually do not want to, prevent that." But the Shin-Beth and the Israeli police have no knowledge of anything beyond a big demonstration. The assessment is that there will be no serious deterioration, and therefore there is no legal ground for canceling Sharon's visit.
>
> This assessment sits well with Barak, who believes that Palestinian pressure should not prevent a legitimate visit to Temple Mount by a senior Israeli politician. Barak does not want a confrontation with Sharon, because he sees that Sharon is interested in bringing the Likud into a national unity government, primarily because of his fears of Netanyahu's return [to politics].

If the reports in the weekend supplements of *Ma'ariv* and *Yediot Ahronot* were not true, their statements to the effect that Barak and Ben-Ami chose to allow Sharon's visit out of ulterior motives would be tantamount to libel. If, however, they turned out to be true, the papers would be dealing with a scandal of national proportions: Could it be that despite assessments indicating that it would be preferable to prevent Sharon's visit to Temple Mount, the prime minister and the internal security minister chose to "gamble" because (among other reasons) they detected an interest on Sharon's part in joining a national unity government, "primarily because of fears of Netanyahu's return"? Could the prime minister's parliamentary weakness have played a part in this decision? As Chemi Shalev, a senior commentator for *Ma'ariv*, writes on October 2, if indeed "the proper authorities, from Prime Minister Ehud Barak down, knew that the field was on the verge of an explosion . . . and nevertheless approved Sharon's visit, they demonstrated a lawless combination of cynicism and weakness." And if these reports were indeed true, what would that say about the official Israeli version regarding the course of events? Was there any connection between all this and the fact that "senior members of the prime minister's entourage" were quick to deny any connection between Sharon's visit to the Temple Mount and the outbreak of violence, and to place the blame exclusively on Arafat's shoulders?

The answers to these questions remain obscure, but remember: We are dealing not with the events themselves but with their newspaper coverage—and as far as this coverage is concerned, there is hardly any place for doubt. Each one of the facts that appeared on the previous pages, facts rescued from the depths of back pages and supplements, could have served as noteworthy, revealing, and relevant main front page headlines. The statement of police officers that Sharon's visit led to the riots deserved a front page headline; so did the disagreements between the Shin-Beth and army intelligence about Sharon's visit, about Arafat's masterminding the outbreak, about his control of the field, and about his ability to reduce the level of violence. Above all, the approval given to Sharon and its connection with possible negotiations regarding a national unity government deserved an in-depth investigation and a series of front page headlines. None of these items, however, received a main front page headline or even a lesser headline on a front page. If claims reminiscent of these items appeared on the front page of one of the newspapers, they did so as American or Palestinian claims, or as claims revealing the leftist leaning of the speaker. Otherwise, the front page headlines of the newspapers broadcast the official version of the Israeli government: Arafat initiated the riots to wring new concessions from Israel, and he was in complete control of the field.

Toward an Explanation:
Bottom Lines, Sources, and Convictions

The question now is: Why did the newspapers act this way? The answer to this question is more complex than it seems at first. To a certain degree, it has to do with the general character of daily newspapers as information providers: Daily newspapers are impatient organizations; they find it difficult to deal with factual intricacies and with complex, ambiguous situations that contain contradictions and cannot be described in a simple and exhaustive manner. By definition, these situations do not have a "bottom line"; they do not yield concise headlines. Take a look, for example, at Alex Fishman's commentary published in *Yediot Ahronot* on October 26, dealing with the appearance of General Giora Eiland, head of IDF Operations, before the Knesset's Foreign Affairs and Security Committee. General Eiland presented the army's assessment of the situation nearly four weeks after the outbreak of the riots, having decided to share with the committee some of the disagreements among the officials in charge of evaluating the situation. Fishman writes:

> Such uncertainty, with no one really knowing where we are drifting, gives rise to vague and contradictory assessments of the kind the army presented yesterday before the Foreign Affairs and Security Committee. "There is no doubt that in the months ahead we face a serious risk that the situation will deteriorate," said the Head of Operations, General Giora Eiland, to members of the

committee. And in the same breath: "There is also the possibility that things will return to normal." When two such completely opposite views are constantly expressed, it is not surprising that in the end we receive obscure messages such as: things will take a turn for the better—or for the worse. For this you do not need to be head of Army Intelligence.

Fishman was looking for a "bottom line," and he finally found it: If the head of operations is not ready to provide an unequivocal assessment of the direction events are likely to take in the future, for the simple reason that "no one has a clear picture of where we are drifting," then Fishman and his readers have no use for his assessments. They want to know, here and now, once and for all, whether things will take a turn for the better or the worse. "You do not need to be head of Army Intelligence" to issue "obscure messages" that do not provide clear answers. The addictive need for simple answers may explain, to a certain extent, the contradictions between the headlines, the evasive statements, the clichés retrieved from the archives of the Israeli collective traumas, as well as the way in which complexity disappeared on its way to the headlines.

But this explanatory strategy can only take us so far. It *cannot* explain the fact that all the simple answers ending up on the front pages of the three newspapers converged with such unanimity around the same unilateral, narrow, catastrophic, and belligerent picture. As we saw, the newspapers were in possession of sufficient information from reliable sources indicating that Sharon's visit to the Temple Mount played a causal role in the course of events, and that Arafat did not give the order to ignite the conflagration. This depiction, whether accurate or mistaken, is in no way more complex than the other one.

Moreover, the suppression of those news items that did not tally with the official Israeli position *cannot* be explained by claiming that the newspapers, as commercial enterprises free from any ideological leaning, offered their readers what they wanted to read. According to this argument, bad news sells better than good news, and over-dramatization of events helps sell newspapers. A slightly different formulation of this argument has it that the readers would not have "bought" a better-balanced view of events: they wanted the newspapers to confirm their prejudices regarding Arafat's guilt, and they received what they asked for because, after all, the customer is always right. Indeed, it is fair to assume that a substantial number of readers on the traditional right found in the pages of the newspapers, in the first days of the Intifada, confirmation of their outlook—a spurious confirmation, to be sure. But other groups of readers, no less substantial, felt that the events portrayed in the Israeli media challenged their deepest convictions regarding the peace process: If Barak indeed "left no stone unturned" in search for peace, and if Arafat, on the eve of an agreement, responded with violence, the dream of a peaceful resolution was after all nothing but an illusion. These readers were not happy to receive the bad news, and the dramatization of events did not win their hearts. They would probably have preferred to receive a different, more balanced picture, and might actually have complained had they found out that the newspapers did not portray a true picture of the events.

The full explanation of the unilateral presentation of events in the newspapers should be sought elsewhere, in the complex combination of four factors: (1) the almost exclusive reliance of the papers on the flow of information from the prime minister's entourage and from senior officials in the defense establishment; (2) the automatic adherence of the newspapers to the task of national unity vis-à-vis what appeared as the clear and imminent danger of a "general conflagration"; (3) the systematic and complete disregard of the fact that the Palestinians in the territories still live under almost complete Israeli occupation, even after the implementation of the first stages of the Oslo agreements; and (4) the deep conviction that Barak did everything that could be done for peace, and therefore did not contribute, and could not have contributed, to the deterioration of the situation. We shall deal with these factors in the following chapters.

3

"Make No Mistake, Yasser"

Even the most pessimistic and militant opponents of the peace
process could not have invented the present nightmare. Unlike
the 1973 war, when two military fronts—both far from the center—collapsed for a short while, this time our most apocalyptic
and suppressed fears assail us simultaneously: diplomatic
conflict is derailed into a seemingly eternal religious war; Palestinian weapons are turned against us; clashes with the Hizballah occur right on our northern border; the new hostility of
Israeli Arabs, acting on the home front like a fifth column. And
to top all this, Hamas, and even Saddam Hussein, have reared
their heads, as if to suggest that terror—and perhaps even
missile—attacks on the hearts of our cities might complete this
nightmare.

—Doron Rosenblum, *Ha'aretz,* October 8

The two factual statements that came to dominate newspaper headlines
during the first two days of the Intifada—the "fact" that Arafat had initiated and planned the riots, and the "fact" that he used Ariel Sharon's visit
to the Temple Mount as an "excuse"—remained at the core of the news
coverage of the Intifada throughout the entire month. During the next five
days, from October 4 to Yom Kippur eve on October 8, the newspapers presented their readers with a new, catastrophic explanatory frame for these
freshly minted contentions: They took their readers on a dramatic, pathos-
ridden, almost frantic tour along the roads of Israel's traumatic history
(these were, after all, the Terrible Days[1]), and brought back to life all the
old national clichés, which had lost some of their attraction in the Oslo
years. As the holy day of Yom Kippur was approaching, the interpretive
metaphor of the War of Independence—a metaphor of fear, frustration, and
helplessness—was gradually substituted by the equally traumatic metaphor
of the 1973 war. Back then, on Yom Kippur itself, Israel was surprised by a
joint Egyptian and Syrian attack, because of the fixation of its military intelligence on what came to be called "the conception": the idea that the

Arab countries' awareness of their comparative weakness would prevent them from initiating an attack on Israel.

Now, the papers explained, Israel was forced yet again to realize that its "conception"—the Oslo conception—had collapsed. Unlike the dramatic War of Independence metaphor, this metaphor was presented as a piece of sober reasoning: Israelis had no choice, the newspapers claimed, but to look reality in the face and understand that nothing had changed since that Yom Kippur, almost thirty years ago. "Yom Kippur 2000 and Yom Kippur 1973 are all of one piece," wrote senior reporter and commentator Nachum Barnea on *Yediot Ahronot*'s front page. "The circle of Arab hostility surrounding Israel seems as tight as ever. This siege-feeling comes along with the realization that our partner is no partner, that understandings are not really understandings, and that any retreat only whets the other side's appetite, in the territories as well as in Lebanon." On the same day, on *Ma'ariv*'s front page, chief editor Ya'akov Erez published a text that is probably the best representation of the sense of catastrophe projected by the papers, perfectly defining the role the Israeli press took upon itself in the new situation:

> Twenty-seven years ago—counting back from tomorrow—on Yom Kippur noon, the Egyptian and Syrian armies simultaneously attacked the IDF formations in the Suez Canal and the Golan Heights. The enemy had surprised our forces, thus putting them in a difficult position and gaining the upper hand. Nevertheless, fighting ended with a victorious IDF defeating the aggressors and reconquering the land they had occupied. The sense of necessity, the understanding that we had no choice, was then a central factor of the national mood felt by the people back home as well as by soldiers on the front. We knew we had no alternative but to fight and win. In the days preceding the present Yom Kippur, the reasons that led great parts of the Israeli public to believe that there would be no more war, and that eternal peace would reign between us and our neighbors, have disappeared. Thus, the public must regain this sense of necessity, this sense of togetherness.

Within this new perspective, the week's news was framed in catastrophic, almost mythical terms, far beyond its concrete significance. On Wednesday, when Barak and Arafat met in Paris in an attempt to reach a cease-fire agreement, the papers informed their readers that French President Jacques Chirac had decided to revert to his "traditional pro-Arab diplomacy," and was "inciting" Arafat against Israel; once again, they claimed, "the whole world rallied against Israel." Later on, during the weekend, it "became apparent" that Israel had forever lost its ability to deter Arab hostility: The IDF was forced into a "shameful retreat" from Joseph's

Tomb in Nablus, and Palestinian policemen had "conquered" the Temple Mount and "raised the Palestinian flag" on the Dome of the Rock. Then, as in the worst of nightmares, three soldiers were kidnapped by Hizballah forces on the northern front, and the newspapers promptly announced that a "regional conflagration" was just around the corner. As we shall see, these events, taken by themselves, in no way warranted the new perspective. Nevertheless, they came to be used as the ultimate proof for the new frame, and the transmutations they went through, in order to fit this role, provide some of the most dramatic examples of hands-on, ideologically driven framing processes to be found throughout the month. Let us then consider them one at a time.

"Humiliating Conditions" and "Brutal Demands": The Paris Summit

On Wednesday, October 4, the main headlines dealt with Barak's departure to the Paris summit. *Ha'aretz*'s headline read: CRISIS ON THE WAY TO SUMMIT: BARAK THREATENS TO STAY HOME BECAUSE OF CONDITIONS SET BY ARAFAT. *Yediot Ahronot*'s headline was SUMMIT UNDER FIRE. *Ma'ariv* chose a more dramatic formulation: SHOOTING—AND TALKING. Thursday's headlines reported that an agreement had been reached, but on the same morning it turned out that they were wrong: Negotiations had been disrupted on the previous night, after the papers were printed. Friday's headlines, then, dealt with the "reasons" for this disruption. *Ha'aretz*'s headline announced:

BARAK ACCUSES CHIRAC OF UNDERMINING AGREEMENT AND
ENCOURAGING ACTS OF VIOLENCE

Ma'ariv's headline read:

BARAK BLAMES ARAFAT: DEMAND FOR
"INTERNATIONAL INVESTIGATION COMMITTEE"—AN
ALIBI FOR AVOIDING PEACE DECISION

Yediot Ahronot "exposed" backstage details from the summit:

ALBRIGHT CRIED, ARAFAT SHIVERED, BARAK SHOUTED AT CHIRAC

More than anything else, these headlines reflect the rage felt by Barak's entourage in Paris. *Ha'aretz*'s reporter Aluf Ben, who accompanied the Israeli delegation to the summit, wrote that Arafat had presented Barak with

"humiliating conditions" before the summit, "the chief one being the demand to set up an international investigation committee, with Egyptian
and French representatives, to investigate the events [of the first days of the
Intifada]." According to Ben, Barak had intended to demand an immediate return to the permanent status negotiations, but having been handed
Arafat's "humiliating" terms, he "probably felt he had been giving Arafat a
message of weakness, and so he announced that the purpose of his trip to
Paris was to stop the violence" rather than to resume negotiations. Barak
was adamant in his opposition to an international investigation committee; after all, according to the story he had impressed on Israeli public opinion, with the newspapers' help, Arafat had *initiated and planned* the riots in
order to force further political concessions from Israel—and for this very
reason it was absolutely impossible to let him have his way. Consider, for
example, the way *Ma'ariv*'s commentator Oded Granot defined Arafat's position on Wednesday, October 4:

> As far as he is concerned, continued clashes in the territories, an ever-in-
> creasing number of casualties on the Palestinian side, and maximal exposure
> of the pictures of the dead boy from Gaza in the international and Arab
> media will guarantee that the American diplomatic effort shall start bringing
> in the dividends he expects to reap from the present conflict.

On the same day, *Yediot Ahronot* quoted sources in the defense establishment, who flatly contended that "Arafat does not have enough Israeli
corpses on his hands for his meetings in Paris and Sharm el-Sheikh. The
level of panic in Israel is still not high enough for him to use these meetings in order to pressure Barak on the Jerusalem issue." This appeared under
the headline SEARCHING FOR A SOLUTION IN PARIS, next to pictures of
Barak and Arafat: Barak talking, raising his fist; Arafat covering his ears
with his hands, as if refusing to listen.

What actually happened at the summit? According to the papers, the
main story of the summit was the behavior of French president Jacques
Chirac. According to *Ha'aretz*'s Aluf Ben, Chirac decided to change the
"French policy back to the old pro-Arab line," after "a period of grace in his
relationship with Barak." Guided by this seemingly arbitrary decision, "the
French president charged Israel with the responsibility for the outburst of
violence, talked of the Likud chairman Ariel Sharon's 'provocative' visit to
the Temple Mount, and said that it seemed as if this visit had been coordinated with Barak." *Yediot Ahronot*'s Shimon Shiffer reported that Chirac had
decided to humiliate Barak completely: "He set aside all rules of diplomatic
etiquette . . . and immediately launched a massive attack on the prime min-

ister." He "was all fire and brimstone," he "turned toward Barak, as if trying to actually touch him, and blamed him." Barak, wrote Shiffer, "spoke politely," and "his little smile never left his face." According to Ma'ariv's Oded Granot, Chirac "brutally demanded that Barak explain the disparity in the number of Israeli and Palestinian casualties." Barak, says Granot, answered in no uncertain terms: "You, Mr. President, would probably want us to kill a few Israeli soldiers to make sure the numbers are equal."

Chirac's purported attack on Barak came to dominate the news pages of both Ma'ariv and Yediot Ahronot, which painted it in stark colors of insult and humiliation. Ma'ariv's headline reported a **DIFFICULT MEETING WITH CHIRAC**. One of Yediot Ahronot's major headlines actually let it be known that

**THE FRENCH PRESIDENT DID NOT EVEN
OFFER BARAK A GLASS OF WATER**

At a certain point, according to the reports, it seemed that Arafat himself was considering the option of signing a cease-fire agreement without an international investigation committee. It was then that Chirac "decided to intervene." Here is Shimon Shiffer's description:

> Chirac turned to Arafat and asked him whether it had been decided to create an international investigation committee. Arafat said no. "Why?" asked Chirac, and then declared that "the violent events in the territories should be checked by an international body sponsored by the UN." Arafat nodded agreement. Barak refused. The atmosphere was tense. They all had their picture taken, but no one except Chirac smiled. At the palace door, Chirac whispered to the Palestinians, "Don't settle." Barak was standing apart, alone.

Encouraged by Chirac's support, Arafat now adamantly refused to sign the agreement. Midnight passed, and "Barak retired to his room, where he spent some time browsing through art books." He went to sleep and woke up at 4:30 A.M., asking whether "something new had come up." Nothing new had come up. Barak "blamed Chirac and said he was responsible for the fact that the agreement had not been signed." He then admitted: "The worst is yet ahead of us. Things are escalating. In a matter of weeks we shall know whether we have a partner on the other side." The delegation returned to Israel. The following day, just as predicted, "the situation deteriorated."

This, then, is the official version of the Paris events, the version presented by the "senior source" in the prime minister's entourage and then adopted wholesale by the three papers: A chronically manipulative Arafat had tried to corner Israel; a consistently brutal Chirac had decided to revert to France's traditional pro-Arab line, his very behavior "encouraging violence" (according to *Ha'aretz*'s editorial on October 8); a persistently peace-oriented Barak had desperately tried to reach a cease-fire agreement, but would not cave in to humiliating dictates.

What is missing here? Well, to begin with, the papers do not in any way acknowledge that the Palestinians may have had a different perspective on the Paris events. On Thursday and Friday, when the reports from the summit were published, none of the newspapers had a single news story quoting Palestinian sources. (A single color piece in *Ha'aretz* indicates that the members of the Palestinian delegation actually felt that Barak had managed to "captivate" Chirac.) *Ha'aretz* offers two commentaries, both by Dani Rubinstein, the only writer who consistently tried to explain the Palestinian dynamics without relying on the Israeli defense establishment, and these maintain that "the conditions set by Chairman Yasser Arafat before the summit in Paris, as well as the postponements of the summit, were no tricks or games on his part. He is under severe pressure from different quarters to avoid a meeting with Prime Minister Ehud Barak." Rubinstein also writes: "Yesterday it turned out that Arafat did not sign mainly because he did not want to be perceived as signing an agreement with Prime Minister Barak while the number of casualties in the territories keeps rising." These insights did not find their way to the news stories or their headlines, which relied exclusively on Barak and his people. Thus the papers totally ignored the possibility that Arafat—just like Barak, in a way—was not busy "reaping dividends from the conflict," but was actually looking for some way to extricate himself from a messy situation, without caving in to his own people's pressure on the one hand, and without accepting Barak's dictates on the other. This interpretive option was already "blocked," so to speak, by the papers' acceptance of Barak's basic premise that Arafat initiated the Intifada in the first place.

Moreover, the papers neglected to mention the fact that all of Chirac's "brutal" statements were actually consistent with statements made by senior Israeli officials during those same days: Chirac had described Sharon's visit to the Temple Mount as a provocation, he had claimed that the visit was coordinated with Barak, he had complained that the IDF responded to the Palestinian demonstrations with excessive force. None of this was uniquely French. The all-important fact, mentioned by *Ha'aretz*'s Aluf Ben, that American Secretary of State Madeleine Albright had also pressured Barak to accept the idea of an international investigation committee—even this was forgotten. The newspapers uncritically presented their readers with a bitter story about France's sudden change of heart and did not even consider it necessary to actually *ask* Barak whether his refusal of the investigation committee was in any way connected to the fact that he was then a prime minister on his last leg, fighting for political survival, and groping for a way to create a national emergency government—*with Ariel Sharon*.[2] None of the journalists who joined Barak's entourage asked any of these questions, or if they did, the questions—let alone the answers—never made their way to the news pages. As a result, then, the diplomatic failure at Paris came to be perceived as the ultimate proof of Israel's isolation and lack of international support.

Reporting Anxiety:
All-Out War Just around the Corner

Once the summit was over, the newspapers directed their attention to the coming weekend, basing their perspective once again on senior sources in the defense establishment—the same sources that had consistently claimed that violence would continue even during the summit and now were proved right. This, to be sure, is one of the deepest ironies in the dynamics of the Intifada coverage: The defense establishment issues evaluations saying that Arafat has the exclusive power to shape future events according to whim and that he has not yet "exhausted" the use of violence; thus Israel cannot actively influence the turn of events, and therefore has to "respond with restraint" and patiently await some change in the chairman's position; the "restrained" response involves closures, blockades, and other harsh measures of collective punishment, resulting in dozens of casualties every week (fifty-eight Palestinian dead had been counted by that Friday morning); then a Palestinian "response" follows, seemingly proving that the original evaluation was right on the mark: Arafat has not yet "exhausted" the use of violence. At this point, as reporter Amos Harel writes that morning in *Ha'aretz*, "the army's upper echelons can note with satisfaction that they have not lost control and have not made the situation worse"—and continue to the next evaluation. We shall return to the topic of response and restraint in the following chapter.

On Friday morning, then, the three newspapers concentrated on the security forces' preparation for the Palestinian "Day of Rage" planned for that day. *Ma'ariv*'s main headline says: COMPLETE CLOSURE; TOP ALERT ON TEMPLE MOUNT. *Yediot Ahronot*'s headline is: TOP ALERT TO CONTAIN PALESTINIAN "DAY OF RAGE." *Ha'aretz*'s main headline reads: SPECIAL PREPARATIONS FOR "DAY OF RAGE".[3] The weekend's events, of course, "proved" once again that the defense establishment's assessments were right all along, and the papers did everything they could to make it clear to their readers that nothing would ever be the same again. The soldiers' kidnapping on Mount Dov, near the Lebanese border, the "conquest" of the Temple Mount by Palestinian policemen, and the destruction of Joseph's Tomb by the Palestinians all seemed to support the feeling that Israel was indeed engaged in a battle for its very existence, with an all-out war raging on all fronts.

On Sunday, October 8, the papers project this sense of distress in every headline, every picture, every commentary. "A few years from now," writes *Ma'ariv's* commentator Chemi Shalev, "people will still remember exactly where they were and what they did on this black Saturday. They will still vividly feel the bitterness they feel now. . . . They will tell their grandchildren about a weekend when a triple punch hit Israel's softest spots—the Temple Mount, Mount Dov, and Joseph's Tomb." And Ron Ben-Ishai, *Yediot Ahronot's* commentator, offers his readers the following chilling analysis:

> The deterrence factor [which Israel relies on] has been eroded over the past twenty-four hours to such an extent that things might deteriorate into an all-out regional war. The evacuation of Joseph's Tomb, the arson of the police checkpoint at Lions' Gate in Old Jerusalem, and the kidnapping of three soldiers on the Lebanese border give rise to the feeling—in the Arab world and in the territories—that our public's sensitivity to casualties, the Barak government's political weakness, and the pressure of international public opinion are checking the IDF's military power. Should this process be allowed to continue, it will lead to active conflict on the borders as well as in the territories.

The tabloids' front pages express the anxiety in dramatic graphics. *Yediot Ahronot's* main headline, printed in enormous white letters on a black background, is

ATTEMPT TO AVOID REGIONAL CONFLICT

Above the headline, in two symmetrical boxes, we find two headlines in yellow and red:

WARNING TO SYRIA AND LEBANON: RELEASE THE THREE
KIDNAPPED IDF SOLDIERS IMMEDIATELY

WARNING TO PALESTINIANS: STOP FIGHTING WITHIN TWO DAYS
AND RETURN TO NEGOTIATIONS

Next to pictures of two of the kidnapped soldiers we find an appeal by one of their fathers: "DO EVERYTHING TO RELEASE MY SON." Right below, the following headline appears in a yellow box—FOR THE FIRST TIME: RADIO BROADCASTS ON YOM KIPPUR. The significance of this fact would be immediately clear to any Israeli reader: The country was in a state of war.

Ma'ariv's main headline—again, in gigantic letters on a black background—is this: CAPTURED BY HIZBALLAH. Above this headline, we find another one, in slightly smaller letters: BARAK IN ULTIMATUM TO ARAFAT: YOU HAVE 48 HOURS. (We shall return to this ultimatum in the next chapter.) Two additional pictures appear under the photos of the kidnapped soldiers. One of them shows policemen rescuing an officer caught in the burning station at Lions' Gate in the Old City of Jerusalem. The headline above it says:

POLICEMEN CALLED FOR HELP IN BURNING STATION;
UNDERCOVER UNIT RECONQUERED TEMPLE MOUNT

The second picture shows Palestinian youths in a group photograph on the dome of Joseph's Tomb. One of them is holding a Palestinian flag. The headline:

PALESTINIANS CELEBRATE, DESTROY JOSEPH'S TOMB;
YESHIVA STUDENT MISSING—CONCERN FOR HIS WELFARE

Ha'aretz's main headline says: BARAK IN ULTIMATUM TO ARAFAT: CALMER FIELD BY TOMORROW, OR NEGOTIATIONS WILL STOP. The banner says: HIZBALLAH KIDNAPPED 3 SOLDIERS AT MOUNT DOV; BARAK CONSIDERS EXCHANGING PRISONERS DIRANEE AND UBAYED. Next to these headlines, on the upper left side of the page, Yoel Markus's commentary carries the catastrophic headline: YOM-KIPPUR CALAMITY.

Back to the Six-Day War: The "Battle" for the Temple Mount

Let us, then, take a look at each of these events, starting with the Temple Mount. *Ma'ariv* allotted this story an entire double-spread (pages 10–11), and their graphic design is fascinating. At the very top, in large letters, we find the logo TERRIBLE DAYS: THE FIGHT FOR TEMPLE MOUNT. A huge picture of the Dome of the Rock—not a picture of the El-Aqsa mosque, or of the Temple Mount compound, but of the dome itself—covers most of a page. The following headline, in huge black letters, is spread across the picture:

PALESTINIAN FLAG ON THE DOME OF THE ROCK

Where is the flag? Looking closely, readers may detect a tiny flag, along the Dome's rim, somewhere in the lower left corner of the picture. *Ma'ariv*'s graphic designers actually marked it with a circle, to make it more conspicuous. The size of the gigantic picture now makes sense: the flag—which grates so on Israeli sensibilities—would have been almost invisible on a smaller picture. On the opposite page we find the following headline:

"HELP!" CRY OFFICERS CAUGHT
IN BURNING STATION AT LIONS' GATE

And next to it, again, the picture already seen on the first page: policemen evacuating one of their men from the station.

Yediot Ahronot also allocates a double-spread to the Temple Mount events. The banner says: REGIONAL CONFLICT FEARED—THE BATTLE FOR TEMPLE MOUNT. The page's headline reads:

TEMPLE MOUNT WAS NO LONGER IN OUR HANDS

Note the peculiar formulation of the headline. Ron Ben-Ishai's report "explains":

> On the morning of June 7, 1967, the parachutists' force, headed by commander Mota Gur, made its way to the Temple Mount compound. Shortly afterwards his thrilled and excited voice was heard on the communication system: "the Temple Mount is in our hands." Day before yesterday, for the first time in thirty-three years, the responsibility for security in the Mount compound passed from Israeli hands to the hands of the PA. On the morning of the Palestinian "Day of Rage" the police and border police forces retreated from the Mount, and for many hours Palestinian flags were raised on the mosques. Control of the Mount returned to Israeli hands as late as 6 P.M., after the raging Palestinian mob attacked the Lions' Gate police station, set fire to it, and confronted border policemen on the streets.

Next to the text appear two pictures: One of them, spread on two thirds of the page, shows Palestinian youths—some of them masked—throwing stones. The caption reads: "Palestinian youths throwing stones on the Temple Mount. The Israeli policemen retreated, and the rioters gained control of the area." The smaller picture is the same one we saw in *Ma'ariv*—the policemen victimized by the rioters.

The headlines, captions, and pictures, then, tell a frightening story: Israeli security forces were forced to retreat from the Temple Mount following Palestinian riots, and the site was reconquered only after the Israeli policemen were almost burned alive in their station. Note, however, Ron Ben-Ishai's unusual wording, according to which responsibility for security on the Mount "passed" from Israeli to Palestinian hands. This surprising choice of words becomes perfectly clear if—but only if—we read on. We then discover a completely different state of affairs. It turns out that on the night between Thursday and Friday senior Israeli officers met with the heads of the Palestinian security apparatus in the West Bank, Gibril Rajub and Taufik Tirawee. They reached an explicit agreement: The Palestinian police would be in charge of the Temple Mount during Friday's prayers. According to Ma'ariv's Amir Ben-David, this decision was authorized by Prime Minister Ehud Barak. And so, reports Ron Ben-Ishai, Rajub and Tirawee deployed their people on the Temple Mount early in the day. The imam of the El-Aqsa mosque asked worshippers to conduct their prayers while "avoiding confrontation and violence," and the prayer was held in a completely peaceful manner. Israel did not lose control of the Temple Mount, then, and Israeli forces certainly did not retreat as a result of stone-throwing. Rather, the event started out as a pragmatic attempt to avoid unnecessary friction, with Palestinian security forces supervising the prayer. This was actually a case of *collaboration*, based on meetings and specific measures authorized by the same prime minister who during those days repeatedly declared that the peace process was dead, and that "at this moment in time" Israel had "no partner for peace."

Once the prayer was over, however, things did get out of control: Many worshippers started throwing stones at the Wailing Wall, and the Israeli security forces hastened to evacuate Jewish worshippers from the site—such an attempt to prevent unnecessary friction also being part of the agreement. A group of Palestinian worshippers later moved to another side of the Temple Mount and attacked the police station at Lions' Gate. Seven policemen were inside at the time. The Palestinians tried to force the door, and a few youths threw burning rags through the barred windows.

At this point, says Ben-Ishai, the policemen realized "that the Palestinian security forces were unable to restore peace and decided to intervene." They evacuated the officers from the station and entered the Temple Mount. Only after the station was evacuated did the Palestinian youths set fire to it. As *Yediot Ahronot*'s reporter Zadok Yehezkely wrote, the police gained control of the Temple Mount "with almost no need for fighting. . . .

One by one, the Palestinian youths made their way home." It becomes quite clear, then, that the police did not "reconquer" the Temple Mount, and there was no "battle" even remotely reminiscent of the one in 1967. The policemen caught in the station did of course go through a stressful experience, but as commander Yair Itzhaki, of the Jerusalem precinct, told journalists, "their lives were not in danger at any point." From the point of view of the police, the cooperative strategy proved useful. As former Police Commander in Chief Assaf Hefetz told *Yediot Ahronot*'s reporter: "When I was police commander we used a similar strategy to prevent casualties."

In the papers, however, all this disappears completely under the flood of hysteria. Consider, for example, the report of *Ma'ariv*'s Amir Ben-David:

> In the afternoon hours, when stones and firebombs became more frequent, and it turned out that a few dozen youths had re-entered the Temple Mount, the police decided to regain possession of the Mount. The police, incidentally, claim there was no breaking in and reconquering, but a "return to routine arrangements."

The police, then, "claim" that the entire event amounted to a "return to routine arrangements," but the papers seem to know better: As far as they are concerned, the pragmatic decision was actually a "retreat." The positive collaboration between Israeli and Palestinian security forces was hidden deep inside the news stories' middle paragraphs; the understandable difficulties of the Palestinian police in controlling events and the "return to routine arrangements" that followed became a "battle for the Temple Mount" —and the entire event was taken as proof that Israel's military power no longer deterred Arab violence.

Another "Shameful Defeat":
The Retreat from Joseph's Tomb

The story of Joseph's Tomb is in some ways similar. Joseph's Tomb—a site with only a shaky claim to holiness, as we shall see—is located at the center of Nablus. According to the Oslo agreement, this area should have passed to Palestinian hands long ago. For about a year and a half before the Intifada, the IDF repeatedly asked the prime minister to evacuate the tomb: Securing the site and the safety of settlers living nearby had become an operational impossibility. Besides, the place had become the focus of constant friction between the Palestinians, who considered it a thorn in their side, and the IDF and the settlers. The Shin-Beth, as well as the border police,

supported this IDF request. Barak refused. On the second day of the Intifada, a border policeman was killed in a fierce battle at the tomb. From
the IDF's point of view, this proved that its original demand was totally justified. The top echelons of the security forces appealed to Barak yet again.

As *Yediot Ahronot* revealed six weeks later (on November 15), the head
of the IDF southern command, Brigadier-General Yom-Tov Samia, threatened resignation should Israel hold on to the tomb. At a meeting of the
IDF operational command, Samia had said that the holding on to the tomb
was "patently illegal." Finally Barak agreed to comply with the IDF request,
and the tomb was indeed evacuated. Clearly, this was a rational decision to
evacuate a site that had become the focus of completely unnecessary friction—even from the point of view of those opposed to an Israeli withdrawal from the occupied territories.

Once again, however, the newspapers seem to have had a wholly different interpretation of the event. They framed the evacuation of the tomb
in terms of a humiliating defeat. On page 9 in *Ma'ariv*, under the logo RE-
TREAT FROM JOSEPH'S TOMB, we find the headline EVACUATION—AND
DESTRUCTION. Above the headline is a huge picture of "inflamed" Palestinian youths destroying the tomb. The story opens with the sentence: "A
few hours after its evacuation by the IDF yesterday, Joseph's Tomb was ran-
sacked and burned by Palestinian demonstrators." Other pictures, on pages
8 and 9, show Palestinians setting fire to the tomb's grounds and breaking
the entrance door, which was engraved with a Star of David. The headline
on page 8 reads: AHMED TIBI: "RACHEL'S TOMB COMES NEXT." The implied link between the huge headline and the picture is clear: Swept along
on the "inflamed" youths' wave of violence, Arab MK Tibi was now calling for the destruction of Rachel's Tomb as well. Actually, Tibi was calling
on Israel to evacuate "all the sites that create friction between Israel and
the Palestinians," including Rachel's Tomb. The military logic of the evacuation is discussed only in a small box on the lower part of page 9. The
headline reads: HOW THE DECISION WAS MADE: IDF AND SHIN-BET
PRESSURED; BARAK GAVE EVACUATION ORDER.

Yediot Ahronot handled the event in a similar way. The headline on
page 6 states: IDF EVACUATES TOMB; PALESTINIANS BREAK, WRECK,
AND BURN IT. Page 7 consists almost entirely of pictures—the same pictures that appeared in *Ma'ariv*—as well as one showing the ceremony held
in Joseph's Tomb in 1997, when a Torah book was introduced to the site for
the first time, and another showing two Palestinians holding holy books left
there after the evacuation. One of them, in a white shirt, is standing on the
tomb's roof and browsing through one of the books.

A box on page 9 presents the readers with the history of the site. The story clearly explains why the Palestinians came to regard Joseph's Tomb as one of the prominent symbols of Israeli occupation: The site is actually the tomb of Sheikh Yussef Dwikhat, and until 1974 Muslim believers were the only ones who considered it a place of worship. At this point, Jewish settlers started to frequent the site, brought in a Torah book, and turned the place into a synagogue and a yeshiva, "to the dismay of the Palestinians."

"Over the years," we are informed by the text, "Jews came to consider the place as holy." In other words, the settlers took a Jewish tradition, which places the tomb Jacob bought for his son Joseph in the town now known as Nablus, and attached it to the Sheikh's tomb. Under IDF protection, the settlers then turned out the Muslim worshippers who had been praying there for years. By granting Joseph's Tomb the status of a "holy site," the Oslo agreement actually sanctioned this situation, enabling the settlers to keep up their persistent, provocative, and violent presence within the Palestinian town of Nablus.[4]

Does all this help explain the destruction of the tomb by Palestinian youths? Certainly. One cannot understand the nature of occupation, and Palestinian life under this occupation, without understanding the full meaning of the settlers' violence, carried out under IDF protection, in Hebron, in Netzarim, at Joseph's Tomb, and at many other sites. The Palestinians did indeed celebrate the evacuation of Joseph's Tomb—but this evacuation should have also been a great moment of celebration for all those Israelis who purportedly supported the peace process during the last years. The newspapers, however, told the story in injured, bitter tones, and completely blocked the option of a more rational interpretation. (Incidentally, French president Jacques Chirac condemned the destruction of the tomb on Saturday and "expressed his outrage at this act of desecration." This stand, taken by the man who only a few days earlier had "encouraged Palestinian violence with his brutal statements," was only mentioned by *Ma'ariv*, and even there it did not merit a headline, appearing as the last paragraph of the story opening with MK Tibi's call to evacuate Rachel's Tomb.)

Ignoring Military Blunders:
The Soldiers' Kidnapping

Let us move on, then, to the third event that the newspapers and their commentators perceived as cataclysmic: the kidnapping of the three soldiers on the Lebanon border. Unlike the two previous cases, this one was a truly troubling event. On Saturday noon, a few months after the IDF re-treat from South Lebanon, Hizballah warriors broke through the border's barbed-iron fence near the IDF outpost on Mount Dov and opened fire at an IDF patrol vehicle. They captured the three soldiers on patrol and trans-ferred them to an unknown destination in Lebanon. According to IDF evaluations, the operation was preceded by a decoy ruse—a violent demon-stration next to the fence of nearby Zar'it (according to the international press, two Lebanese were killed during this demonstration, and thirty were wounded). Hizballah leader Sheikh Nasrallah announced that he would be willing to exchange prisoners—the three soldiers in return for the Lebanese held in Israeli jails and detention centers.

The kidnapping operation was indeed a valid reason for concern—but not quite the type of concern expressed by the newspapers, which immedi-ately and unequivocally spoke of the danger of a "regional conflagration." The natural, reasonable concern should have focused primarily on the sol-diers' safety, and then on the military blunders that made the kidnapping possible in the first place. The investigation carried out in the coming days revealed the following: No electronic fence had been erected in the area after the IDF retreat, as elsewhere along the border; the patrol vehicle was not an armored one; the army had forbidden transit in the zone where the soldiers were kidnapped; the soldiers did not open fire when attacked; there were only three soldiers in the vehicle, and not four as required by regula-tions; and too much time passed until the commanders in the field under-stood that the soldiers had indeed been kidnapped. According to Yoav Limor's report, printed in *Ma'ariv* on Yom Kippur eve, military intelligence had given out constant alerts about Hizballah's intentions to kidnap sol-diers in order to negotiate a prisoner exchange, and "the main concern had to do with a kidnapping operation in the Mount Dov area, where the elec-tronic fence had not yet been completed." A senior military source told Yoav Limor that there were "serious shortcomings" at the brigade level, and even the chief of staff, General Shaul Mofaz, said that this was "an event that could have been prevented." Senior officers, then, expressed concern about the fact that the forces on the border had not proceeded appropri-ately. In normal times, such a fact would have merited main headlines. But on Yom Kippur eve, as part of the overall attempt to "regain this sense of necessity, this sense of togetherness," the military blunders were given short shrift. This was not the type of concern the newspapers cared for on such a day. *Yediot Ahronot* did not even mention them on its front page; *Ha'aretz* did not include them in the front page news material, although they are briefly mentioned in Yoel Markus's commentary; and *Ma'ariv* chose to tell its readers, toward the end of a long sub-headline: THE IDF REGARDS THE EVENT AS A BLUNDER. This phrasing sends a clear message: The IDF might regard the event in this light—but this perspective is not necessarily shared by the newspaper.

In his analysis in *Yediot Ahronot*, Alex Fishman asks readers to ignore the military failure. "We must not in any way search the soldiers' conduct for an explanation," he says. Why not? Because "the kidnapping of the three soldiers is an example of the impossible situation that has developed on the northern border ever since the IDF retreated from Lebanon without a signed agreement." According to Fishman, Hizballah had been stationed next to the border fence ever since the IDF retreat, and the army lacked a "security net." Here, then, was an additional cause for concern: The kidnapping of the soldiers could be indicative of Israel's inability to solve the Lebanon situation unilaterally, without an agreement with Syria. Given this state of affairs, the sense of surprise and injury expressed by the newspapers seems quite inappropriate—especially when considering the fact that Israel was—and still is—holding seventeen Lebanese prisoners and detainees (two of them, Sheikh Abd-el-Kareem Ubayed and Mustafa Diranee, have been detained for years *without trial*, after being kidnapped by Israel in Lebanon).

All this is certainly complex, and quite unpleasant from the Israeli perspective. But this complexity—just like the military blunders on the border—did not find its way to the newspapers' front pages. These focused on a single point: The kidnapping, and the events on the Temple Mount and Joseph's Tomb, were taken to indicate that escalation to all-out regional war was just around the corner, since Arabs everywhere now realized that Israel's deterrence was diminishing. "The first problem we face," writes Nachum Barnea in *Yediot Ahronot*, "is the loss of deterrence. The battle zone does not end on the slopes of Mount Dov or at Netzarim junction. It stretches between Teheran and Baghdad, reaching both Damascus and Cairo. Each blow Israel takes in the field increases the danger of regional war."

Convictions and Suppression: The Occupation Is Over

What is the basis for Barnea's statement? Why does Yoel Markus declare, on *Ha'aretz*'s front page, that "this is the pessimists' big day?" We shall touch upon the newspapers' war panic further on, but let it be said at this stage that there was no manipulation involved: The newspapers' analysts, as well as their editors, were truly alarmed, truly offended—and this was why they all clung to the Yom Kippur metaphor, as if by common accord, hoping to find the key to some sort of explanation. Thus, for instance, Doron Rosenblum, who was quoted at the beginning of this chapter—for years one of the most creative voices of the Left—considers "the present nightmare" worse than the 1973 war, when Israel was surprised by the military forces of two countries and lost thousands of soldiers in the battlefield. The existential fear reflected in these texts as well as in the graphic design of the front pages is completely genuine.

The point, however, is that this fear, this sense of injury, of isolation, was not only sincere but also tragic: The papers were really trying to make sense of the events, to find reasons for the sudden cataclysm and consider possible remedies, but at the very same time they completely and systematically ignored the role Israel itself played in the situation. Except for Amira Hass's stories in *Ha'aretz*, the news pages of the first week of the Intifada, including Sunday's news pages, had not a word to say about the causal link between the uprising and the daily hardships of three million Palestinians living under occupation for decades (including seven long years since the Oslo agreement), constantly humiliated by soldiers and settlers on the roads, at roadblocks, in their own houses. The newspapers had not a single word to say about the fact that the Palestinian youths, those "rioters" who posed an "existential threat" to the State of Israel, had been born under occupation and spent their whole lives under its yoke; or about the fact that for all practical purposes, the Oslo agreement perpetuated this state of occupation.

One may certainly ignore all these elements of reality—most Israelis have done so successfully for many years—but it is impossible to ignore them *and* understand the October 2000 events. Consider Nachum Barnea's commentary on Tuesday, October 3: "The images of the past days—the stones, firebombs, rubber bullets—are similar to the images of the [first] Intifada. But the essence is different. The 1987 Intifada was an uprising of a people under occupation, a people left with no choice but to try to attain freedom by force. The riots at the Wailing Wall tunnel four years ago were a response to an Israeli move that was perceived as an attempt to change the status quo on the Temple Mount. The last days are something completely different. They came about after an Israeli government agreed to negotiate all territories conquered during the Six-Day War, including the Old City [of Jerusalem] and the Temple Mount." From Barnea's point of view, then, the fact that Barak agreed to negotiate these points—a fact certainly significant as such—automatically cancelled, as it were, the state of occupation: This was no longer the "uprising of a people under occupation." In his article quoted as the epigraph for this chapter, Doron Rosenblum does at least mention the fact that there were serious problems with the way Barak had conducted negotiations, and that "every negotiation he carried out reached a dead end, as if by some subconscious programming." But even Rosenblum immediately adds that Barak "did indeed turn stone after stone, only to find a venomous scorpion under each and every one of them."

Given such systematic suppression of the most essential elements of reality, it is hardly surprising that the newspapers portrayed the situation in apocalyptic tones, unavoidably reaching the conclusion that the whole world had turned against Israel, that the Arabs were only waiting for an opportunity to crush the Jewish state, and that Israel was gradually losing its ability to deter the enemy. This seemed to be the only conceivable conclusion. And from this conclusion, the "factual" reports in the newspapers ensued as necessary corollaries: If Israel had no share in the crisis, if indeed it was simply *there*—as passive as the soldiers in the photographs, peacefully sitting on their armored vehicles, watching the rioting Palestinians—then it was only natural to perceive Arafat as someone determined to "collect corpses" on his road to Palestinian independence, and to feel that a Palestinian flag on the Temple Mount posed an existential threat to the State of Israel.

Given such an emotional state, it was also only natural for the papers to send threats to Arabs all over the region—Palestinians, Syrians, Lebanese—and call on Barak to act "more forcefully." Thus, we find Ma'ariv's editor Ya'akov Erez prodding Barak "to land a hard and painful blow on Lebanon"; Nachum Barnea telling his readers on Sunday that "Barak took off his gloves yesterday," and stressing that "this is not enough"; and Ron Ben-Ishai explaining that only "a ground operation initiated by the army" will extricate Israel from the unfortunate position in which it is trapped, since "such type of action, with which the IDF is familiar since Lebanon, will keep armed Palestinians away from our communities and army positions, and eventually the fire will peter out." And in Yediot Ahronot's Sunday edition, we find an article by Sever Plotzker, Yediot Ahronot's economic analyst and one of the most persistent representatives of the moderate left. The article—under the title MAKE NO MISTAKE, YASSER—is probably the most striking example of the tectonic shift experienced by the Israeli public, and especially the moderate Left, during the first week of the Intifada. Here is the last paragraph of this memorable piece:

> The events of the past week have revived the atmosphere of the days before the Six-Day War, and have revived forgotten expressions: "the enemy has risen to annihilate us," "few against many," "the whole world is against us,"

"there is no one to talk to," "a no-choice war." Once again we fear for our very existence. This is an ancient Jewish fear. But make no mistake, Yasser: this fear does not paralyze us. It unites and rallies us. Israel is a democracy, and democracies are slow to move. They do not rush into war before making sure they have turned every stone on the way to peace. Democracies prefer fair compromise to bloodshed. They must ensure the support of public opinion, which is not automatically granted to any elected government. Thus, on the face of it, democracies appear to be weak. But this is a mistaken perception. When a democracy joins battle, it does so with the force of conviction of all its citizens, and therefore it wins. History is strewn with the skeletons of defeated non-democracies. Make no mistake, Yasser. Make no mistake, Nassrallah. No terror organization has ever defeated a democratic state. Not us, not on the threshold of our home.

4

"The Limits of Restraint"

A difficult period awaits us in the coming days and weeks. Confrontation will escalate. The Palestinians will attempt to inflict injuries on Jews and provoke Israeli atrocities and massacres. Israel, on the other hand, will have to muster IDF sophistication and restraint to prevent them from achieving their goals.
—Ron Ben-Ishai, *Yediot Ahronot,* October 10

On Saturday evening, October 7, Prime Minister Ehud Barak held a news conference and presented Arafat with a forty-eight-hour ultimatum:

> I call on the Palestinians to stop violence immediately, and to consider accepting Clinton's invitation for continued talks. Israel will not conduct negotiations as long as the violence continues. Until now I have called for restraint—the IDF does not act, but only responds. But if we do not see a change in the coming two days, we shall consider Arafat responsible for the end of negotiations, and will instruct the IDF and the security forces to use all the means at their disposal to stop violence.

As we have seen in the preceding chapter, Barak's ultimatum captured the Sunday papers' main headlines. The main front page headline in *Ha'aretz* is: BARAK'S ULTIMATUM TO ARAFAT: CEASE FIRE BY TOMORROW OR NEGOTIATIONS ARE OFF. Under another front page headline—ISRAEL PLANNING A SERIES OF SANCTIONS—the newspaper writes:

> The defense establishment has prepared a "package" of punitive measures against the PA, in case it does not accept the ultimatum set by Israel to stop violence within forty-eight hours. These are the sanctions that have been prepared for the eventuality of a unilateral declaration of a Palestinian state, but it now appears that some of the steps will be taken sooner.

According to the article, the plans included, among other steps, a freeze on the transfer of payments to the PA, complete and prolonged closure of the territories, stopping the entrance of Palestinian workers to Israel, capturing key positions close to Palestinian villages, and a wider deployment of heavy military equipment.

The main front page headline in *Ma'ariv* reads: BARAK IN ULTIMATUM TO ARAFAT: YOU HAVE 48 HOURS. On page 5, a huge headline reads: ULTIMATUM. Above the headline is a picture of one of the tanks stationed the previous night in Gilo, the neighborhood/settlement at the south of Jerusalem, which had been disturbed by continuous shooting from the nearby Palestinian town of Beit Jallah. Next to the picture is a smaller headline: JERUSALEM: TANKS IN HA'ANAFA STREET IN GILO. The opening paragraph of the article, under the huge headline, reads:

> Yesterday, Prime Minister Ehud Barak issued an unequivocal ultimatum to Yasser Arafat: If you do not stop the violence in forty-eight hours, I will instruct the IDF to use all the means at its disposal to do your job for you. A diplomatic source said yesterday that the prime minister's statement constitutes a declaration of war, because Barak has come to terms with the fact that there is no real partner for peace on the Palestinian side.

Finally, *Yediot Ahronot* publishes the following overline above the main front page headline: WARNING TO PALESTINIANS: STOP FIGHTING WITHIN TWO DAYS AND RETURN TO NEGOTIATIONS. The huge headline on page five reads: DECISIVE 48 HOURS. Under the headline is a picture of a thoughtful and concerned Barak at the news conference. The caption says: BARAK YESTERDAY AT NEWS CONFERENCE: "WE ARE FEW, BUT WE HAVE STRENGTH AND COURAGE."

Barak's dramatic ultimatum to Arafat—based, of course, on the assumption that the chairman of the PA was in complete control of events in the field—raises a series of questions concerning the newspapers' coverage of the prime minister's general political and diplomatic strategy, and of the deployment of the IDF in the territories throughout the Intifada. The coverage of the diplomatic angle is discussed in chapter 7. The current chapter focuses on the military and operational aspects of Barak's ultimatum, and on the key terms he used to describe the deployment of the IDF in the first week of violence, namely, "restraint" and "response." As we shall see, these two terms dominated the coverage of events by the two so-called "popular" newspapers, and to a very significant degree by *Ha'aretz* as well. During the entire period under investigation, the newspapers systematically suppressed factual data showing that the restraint slogan did not correspond to the IDF actual operations; and they provided partial and censored information on the results of the Israeli actions and on their causal contribution to the deterioration of the riots into a full-fledged war of attrition. This is extremely important: It is simply impossible to understand the course of events, and how and why they took the turn they did, without grasping the full impact of the Israeli actions and the resulting Palestinian suffering— but the great majority of Israelis were never exposed to the relevant facts. In a survey published in *Ma'ariv* on November 10, 38 percent responded that the Israelis suffered more than the Palestinians in the first five weeks of the Intifada. In light of the factual reporting they received from the newspapers, especially from the two large ones, this was an entirely rational conclusion.

Patterns of Suppression:
The Number of Palestinian Casualties

Let us begin, then, with the concept of restraint. Ehud Barak officially announced his policy of restraint at the beginning of the first week of the Intifada. As reported by *Ha'aretz* on Tuesday, October 2,

> the prime minister decided to follow a policy of restraint in response to the violent outbreak in the territories and to abstain from threats or punitive measures against the PA. Barak decided that Israeli action will be limited to local responses by the IDF to events, and that Israel will wait for the restoration of calm and the resumption of diplomatic negotiations.

The policy thus combined two principles: First, the IDF would refrain from using all the means at its disposal to quell the uprising; second, Barak would refrain from punitive action of the type called for by Israel's political right: reconquering territories that had been transferred to the PA, demolishing rows of houses in refugee camps, and so on. No such action was taken, and it is possible that Barak and senior IDF officers considered their conduct mature and responsible; having such an arsenal on their hands, and not making free use of it, they may indeed have felt they were showing impressive restraint.

However, the fact of the matter is that the concept of restraint never applied to what actually took place *in the field*. First and foremost, it was never consistent with the steadily increasing number of Palestinian casualties. On the first day of the Intifada 7 people were killed; the next day, 13; the following day, 10. By the end of the first week, 59 Palestinians had been killed. By the end of October, 130 Palestinians had been killed in the territories, and thousands were wounded. These astounding numbers, in and of themselves, should have made the newspapers critically examine the concept of restraint already in the first week of the Intifada and ask the decision makers the same tough questions that the army itself, as we shall see shortly, asked a few months later. But during the first week of the Intifada, and throughout October, the newspapers showed little interest in the Palestinian casualties and reported them in a way that confirmed the claim of restraint.

To begin with, the newspapers mentioned only a small number of Palestinian casualties on their front pages. The rest of the casualties were mentioned, if at all, in the middle paragraphs of back page articles. The dynamics of suppression are fascinating: In their first Intifada issues, on October 2, all three newspapers mention the Palestinian dead on their front pages. *Ma'ariv* writes: THE BLOODBATH SINCE FRIDAY: 2 ISRAELIS DEAD; TENS INJURED; APPROXIMATELY 30 PALESTINIANS DEAD AND HUNDREDS INJURED. *Yediot Ahronot's* overline says: BORDER POLICEMAN AND OFFICER DIED. 29 PALESTINIANS DEAD AND HUNDREDS WOUNDED. *Ha'aretz's* overline declares: 30 PALESTINIANS AND 2 BORDER POLICEMEN KILLED IN RIOTS IN THE TERRITORIES.

A day later, on October 3, the Palestinian dead disappear from *Ma'ariv's* front page. (The Arab-Israeli casualties are still mentioned, as we shall see in chapter 5.) They are first mentioned, rather casually, toward the end of a line on page 8. The headline of the page reads:

FOR THE FIRST TIME, THE IDF SHOT MISSILES
FROM HELICOPTERS AT THE PALESTINIANS.

The sub-headline says:

ANOTHER DAY OF HEAVY FIGHTING AT NETZARIM JUNCTION; HUNDREDS OF PALESTINIANS THREW ROCKS AND FIREBOMBS AT THE OUTPOST. MORE THAN 10 PALESTINIANS DIED IN THE EXCHANGE OF FIRE, AND TENS WERE INJURED. NO IDF CASUALTIES.

More than ten Palestinians were killed in one day, then, but this dramatic fact is not mentioned on *Ma'ariv's* front page, nor in any of the back page headlines. The importance of this editorial decision cannot be overstated: Most readers probably finished browsing through the paper with the impression that the previous day had ended with no Palestinian casualties.

At this stage, *Yediot Ahronot* and *Ha'aretz* still make a point of mentioning the Palestinian casualties on their front pages. *Yediot Ahronot's* front page sub-headline says: YESTERDAY'S CASUALTIES: 2 ISRAELI DEAD, 4 ISRAELI ARABS KILLED, 8 PALESTINIANS DEAD. *Ha'aretz* says in a front page headline: IN THE TERRITORIES: 2 ISRAELIS AND 15 PALESTINIANS KILLED. (The difference between the numbers mentioned in these two headlines tells us something about the intensity of the events; as Amira Hass reports on October 5, even the Palestinians themselves lost count of their casualties during the first week of the Intifada.)

And so it continues, throughout the first week: *Yediot Ahronot* and *Ha'aretz* mention the number of Palestinian casualties on their first pages— while *Ma'ariv* persists in ignoring them. On October 5, for example, *Ha'aretz* reports in its MAIN FACTS box: 7 PALESTINIANS KILLED YESTERDAY. One of *Yediot Ahronot's* front page headlines says: YESTERDAY IN TERRITORIES: FIGHT-ING AT NETZARIM, 7 PALESTINIANS DEAD. In sharp contrast, *Ma'ariv's* first mention of the Palestinian casualties appears in the *text* of the article on page 6: "Despite the official cease-fire and diplomatic talks in Paris, fight-ing continued yesterday in the territories. Three soldiers and two civilians were injured in the rioting. A few Palestinians were killed, and many were injured."

So far so good. But after the weekend that ended with Barak's ultima-tum, the Palestinian dead vanished from the front pages of *Yediot Ahronot* and *Ha'aretz* as well. In the remaining three weeks of October, the Pales-tinian dead are mentioned only five more times on the front page of *Ha'aretz*. On the 11th, a front page headline reports: IDF APOLOGIZES FOR FATAL SHOOTING OF 12-YEAR-OLD CHILD[1] BY SNIPER IN RAFIAH (the accompanying picture shows the child transported to an ambulance); on the 12th, the MAIN FACTS box reports the death of a Palestinian in Nablus; on the 22nd, the overline on the front page reports: ESCALATION IN THE TERRITORIES; 12 PALESTINIANS KILLED DURING WEEKEND; and on two occasions, on the 23rd and the 29th, picture captions on the front page mention the death of 4 Palestinians. On all the other days, the dead are mentioned in internal pages, sometimes in headlines. On October 15th, for example, a headline on page 4 says: 2 PALESTINIANS KILLED DURING WEEKEND. On the 16th, the last paragraph of a story on page 7 reports the death of a Pal-estinian injured a week earlier. On the 17th, a headline on page 4 reports that a thirteen-year-old Palestinian died of his injuries. The article adds that another Palestinian was killed, and that "according to Red Crescent data, 187 Palestinians were injured yesterday, 6 of them critically, and 13 ambulances were hit by IDF fire while trying to evacuate the wounded." In the remaining three weeks of October, then, the front page of *Ha'aretz* mentioned 22 of the 76 Palestinians killed.

Yediot Ahronot mentions Palestinian casualties on its front page only *twice* throughout the rest of the month. On the 24th a sub-headline reports that A PALESTINIAN WAS KILLED AND HIS CHILDREN INJURED BY IDF FIRE IN HEBRON. On the 30th the sub-headline reports: 4 PALESTINIANS DEAD IN ANOTHER DAY OF FIGHTING. On all other days, Palestinian casualties appear in the text of internal pages, in many cases as "accidents" and Palestinian "reports" of dead and wounded. During these three weeks, *Yediot Ahronot's* front page mentions 5 of the 76 Palestinians who were killed.

And there is more: On three different occasions, *Yediot Ahronot* publishes graphic summary boxes on pages dedicated to the Intifada. Diagrams published on the 22nd and 23rd of October, under the headline WAR CHRONICLE, chart the events of the previous day—hour by hour. The diagrams list firebombs, exchanges of gunfire, the wounding of a border policeman, and so on, but the Palestinian casualties of the day are never mentioned. On November 1 the newspaper publishes a summary table of the first month of the Intifada, under the headline: ONE MONTH OF INTIFADA: SUMMARY IN FIGURES. The following figures appear: 600 shooting incidents; 1397 firebombs; 26 explosive charges; 184 Israeli injured; 12 Israeli dead; some 10,000 soldiers in the territories. That is all: The 130 dead Palestinians, and the thousands of injured, literally do not count. The caption reveals the source of the figures: DATA: IDF CENTRAL COMMAND HEADQUARTERS.

Ma'ariv continued its policy for most of the month. On the 18th, 20th, 22nd, and 23rd, a few Palestinian dead suddenly appear on its front page— 11 out of 130—but that is all.

It is a reasonable assumption, then, that readers who derived their factual information about the Intifada from the newspapers, and who did not carefully read every word in back page stories, had no real knowledge of the most basic fact regarding the Palestinian victims—their numbers. In her reports in *Ha'aretz*, Amira Hass made a point of tracking the number of dead Palestinians throughout the month, although this piece of data never made the headlines either. In *Yediot Ahronot* and *Ma'ariv*, the total number of dead Palestinians was discussed as a distinct topic only twice—and both times it was framed within the context of "the cynical use" Arafat supposedly made of the number of Palestinian casualties. On the 22nd, *Yediot Ahronot* dedicated an article on page 14, and an in-depth commentary on the front page, to the "morbid trick" Arafat pulled at the Arab Summit in Cairo. The article's headline reads: ARAFAT INFLATES THE NUMBER OF DEAD. The sub-headline says: AT CAIRO SUMMIT, 193 REPORTED DEAD, WHILE OFFICIAL FIGURES OF THE PA SHOW THAT 108 WERE KILLED.

Ron Ben-Ishai's commentary, under the headline THE MATHEMATICS OF DEATH, reveals a fraction of the PA chairman's supposed "intentions":

[Arafat's] present goal is to induce the United Nations to send an international force to the territories, as was done in Bosnia and Kosovo. . . . This is
why Arafat and senior PA officials now claim that Israel is carrying out a massacre of the Palestinian people and that the intervention of the international
community is required to stop it. To back his request and add credibility to
his claim, Arafat is playing a macabre game: he dramatically inflates the number of Palestinian casualties. . . . In its noon broadcast yesterday, the PA radio
announced that since the beginning of the "El-Aqsa Intifada" 100 Palestinians were killed by Israeli fire and the number of injured approaches 5000.
This did not deter Arafat from announcing two hours before, in a speech to
the Arab Summit, that the number of Palestinians dead since the beginning
of disturbances in the territories is 193, and that more than 7000 were injured, an addition of nearly one hundred percent to the real count. It should
be emphasized that Arafat knows the real numbers. The data published by
the Palestinian department of health match almost perfectly the scrupulous
tracking by *Yediot Ahronot* of casualties on both sides. . . . It might have been
possible to disregard the inflated number of casualties supplied by Arafat, but
experience proves that a lie repeated time after time becomes fact. . . . It is
thus obvious that the IDF cannot forgo its policy of restrained response at this
time. Responding with massive fire and the capturing of territories, as the settlers demand, would result in dozens or even hundreds of dead on the Palestinian side, and the United Nations would hurry to give Arafat exactly what
he wants.

What is Ben-Ishai trying to tell us in this passage? If the inflated numbers—193 dead and 7000 injured—warrant talk of a "massacre," how can
100 dead and 5000 injured prove that Israel's "policy of restrained response"
is justified? How can one claim that a "massive response" is liable to cause
"dozens or even hundreds of dead on the Palestinian side," when this is exactly what happens when Israel is conducting a policy of "restraint"? And
what about the "scrupulous tracking" by *Yediot Ahronot* of the number of casualties on both sides? The fourth paragraph of the news story on page 14
informs us that "only this last weekend, which was especially violent, fourteen Palestinians died of IDF fire." It was indeed a particularly fatal weekend, but this was not mentioned on the front page of the newspaper—and
did not merit a headline. Next to the story is the **WAR CHRONICLE** mentioned above, in which the Palestinian dead are not listed. If indeed *Yediot
Ahronot* kept a scrupulous count of casualties, it did not choose to share it
with its readers.

Ma'ariv, for its part, first discussed the number of Palestinian casualties
as a distinct topic in early November. On November 1 a summary table appears on page 3 containing, among others, the number of Palestinian dead.
But a story on page 5 tells us that the police suspect that "hospitals in

Jerusalem and in the territories 'fabricate' X-rays and medical certificates . . .
to support the claim that more Palestinians were injured by IDF fire than
actually were." The headline reads: PALESTINIAN PHYSICIANS FABRICATE
CERTIFICATES TO INFLATE THE NUMBER OF CASUALTIES. From the
point of view of both large newspapers, then, the high number of injuries
was nothing but a propaganda tool used by the Palestinians. They never
stopped to check whether these numbers cast a shadow on the definition of
the IDF policy in the territories as one of restraint.

The Circumstances of Death
and the Allocation of Responsibility

The newspapers misled their readers not only as far as the number of casualties was concerned, but also in the manner in which the *fact* of these
deaths was reported. Generally speaking, the reports fall into two cate-
gories. In most cases, the newspapers laconically mention the fact, or the
Palestinian *claim*, that so and so many Palestinians were killed. Occasionally, a few details are added: the location of the incident, the weapons used
by the IDF, and, less frequently, the identity of the victims. In all cases, the
newspapers make it quite clear that the death of the Palestinians was the
direct result of their own conduct. This is what Ron Ben-Ishai predicted in
his commentary, quoted in this chapter's epigraph: "The Palestinians will
attempt to inflict injuries on Jews and provoke Israeli atrocities and massacres. Israel, on the other hand, will have to muster IDF sophistication and
restraint to prevent them from achieving their goals." Here is one example,
selected for its exceptional detail. The story appeared on October 4, on
page 14 of *Yediot Ahronot*.

> The day's fighting began when a Palestinian resident, Mohammed Fahmi
> Abu Omena, 26, climbed on the roof and tried to hurl a propane gas tank and
> a firebomb at the outpost. A sniper shot and killed him before he managed to
> throw the gas tank. According to Palestinian sources, the young man's head
> cracked open and pieces of it were scattered about. Inflamed youths, accord-
> ing to these sources, grabbed what appeared to be parts of the head and in-
> cited the crowd that gathered there. At this point the crowd went wild and
> began throwing rocks and burning tires. The Palestinian policemen, who first
> tried to prevent the riot, gave up, and in short order armed individuals joined
> the crowd and began shooting toward the IDF outpost. Because the outpost
> came under fire from several directions, an air force helicopter was called in.
> The helicopter shot at the rioting crowd and simultaneously fired a missile to-
> ward one of the focal points of shooting. In the course of the battle, three
> Palestinians were killed and dozens were wounded.

Note the causal chain: everything *began* with Abu Omena's attempt to *threaten the lives* of the soldiers. The sniper *responded* with fire and prevented the Palestinian from carrying out his scheme. Next, youths *incited* the crowd, which then *began* to riot, throw rocks, and burn tires. At this point, individuals *began* shooting toward the IDF outpost, again endangering the lives of the soldiers. *Because of the danger,* the IDF called in a helicopter that fired on the rioting crowd and killed three Palestinians. In other words, the Palestinians initiated the chain of incidents, step after violent step, and the IDF was acting in self-defense.

In a small number of other cases, the newspapers report the death of a Palestinian as the result of fire from an unidentified source—or as the result of an *IDF mistake*. In such cases—when it is clear, from the Israeli point of view, that the general method of operation of the IDF does not fall under any suspicion—the newspapers report the incident in detail, provide a headline, and even show the relevant pictures. On October 11th, for example, all three papers reported the mortal wounding of Sami Abu-Jazar, a nine-year-old child, by a bullet fired by a sniper in Rafiah. The IDF expressed its "regret" about the injury, and all three papers published the picture of the child being carried to the ambulance—seconds after being shot. *Ha'aretz,* as we have seen, outdid the other newspapers and even published a large photograph on its front page. *Ma'ariv* published the following headline on page 4: 9-YEAR-OLD PALESTINIAN CHILD SHOT IN RAFIAH, CLINICALLY DEAD. Abu-Jazar, to be sure, was not the only child to be shot by snipers during the month of October; others, for whom the IDF never expressed regret, did not receive the same sympathetic treatment from the press.

The most famous "mistake" of the Intifada is, of course, the killing of the child Mohammed al-Durra at Netzarim Junction. The October 2 front pages of all three newspapers show the picture of al-Durra weeping in his father's arms, then stretched dead on his father's knees. The two large newspapers dedicate their central two-page spread to the story. The headlines are DEATH OF A CHILD in *Ma'ariv,* and HORROR IN FRONT OF THE CAMERAS in *Yediot Ahronot.* The stories printed next to the photos report in great detail the tragic death of the child who was caught in the line of fire. In the following days, *Ha'aretz* and *Yediot Ahronot* sent correspondents to interview the father, a construction worker, who was hospitalized in Amman. The published interviews cover whole pages, receiving front page headlines. The headline in *Yediot Ahronot* reads: I BUILT TEL-AVIV, HAIFA, AND NAHARIYA FOR YOU, AND YOU KILLED MY SON. All this may seem quite impressive; no other Palestinian casualty, adult or child, received such sympathy from the Israeli press. But the sympathy was conditional—at least in the case of *Yediot Ahronot* and *Ma'ariv*—upon the acceptance of one of two alternate claims of fact: either the child was not killed by IDF fire, or his death was the tragic result of the Palestinians' own sinister decision to sacrifice their children in order to gain international sympathy and support. In *Ma'ariv's* October 2 issue, below the DEATH OF A CHILD headline, is another one that says:

COMMANDER OF THE GAZA DIVISION: HE WAS NOT KILLED BY IDF FIRE

Two days later, on October 4, after the prime minister had officially announced that Israel accepted responsibility for the death of the child, *Ma'ariv* mentioned this prominently on pages 10–11, but not on the front page.

Yediot Ahronot, on the other hand, adopted the second strategy. In the October 2 issue, the sub-headline of its two-page spread states that IDF sources believe the father and son were hit by IDF fire. But on the same page appears an article by playwright Anat Gov, an established spokesperson of the moderate left. The article's topic, CHILDREN UNDER FIRE, is printed under the author's name. The headline is THEY ARE ALL RIGHT. Gov complains about the sense of absolute right felt by all those involved in the first days of the Intifada. Sharon, according to Gov, "was right" when he went to the Temple Mount and detonated "the most explosive mixture of explosives in the world"; Israeli Arabs "are right to have become bitter and hateful after years of discrimination"; those who demand harsh measures against them "are also right because violence physically threatens the lives of citizens"; the soldiers who shot al-Durra "are right because when people are shooting all around you, you do not have time for in-depth analysis of where every bullet goes, especially if you too are a youth, and nothing is more right than defending your life when it is in danger" and, finally, the Palestinians "are right":

> The Temple Mount symbolizes for them everything they do not have—a country, freedom, dignity. It is right to fight for these things, and even to sacrifice the children. Because nothing makes better pictures than dying children, and in fighting for what is right you must also conquer the ratings. A dead child in his father's arms is a more efficient rating bomb than all the smart bombs of the IDF.

This is significant: All the newspapers report that al-Durra and his father arrived at the site by sheer accident, after leaving their home in the

El Burij refugee camp on their way to the market in Gaza—but Gov implies that the Palestinians "sacrificed" the child for high propaganda value. What is the source of this harsh statement? Is the author in possession of data substantiating this claim? Does she have information that the father and child were summoned to this place by someone on the Palestinian side, so that they might get hurt? Of course not. This is not a fact—it is the framing strategy adopted by formal Israeli sources. This, for example, is the communiqué the army spokesman issued after the incident:

> The Palestinians make cynical use of women and children by bringing them to places of violent confrontation in the territories. The incident photographed in the Gaza Strip began with live fire, explosives, and firebombs directed at IDF forces, and with hundreds of rioters charging the IDF outposts. There was heavy exchange of fire in the area. The picture focused on the father and son, who were caught in the line of fire at a time when it was not possible to identify the source of shooting. . . . In the situation that ensued, anyone who happened to be there could have been hurt, by either Israeli or Palestinian fire. The Palestinians and those who incited them are the ones responsible for everything that happened.

Note the outright contradiction within this text between the statement that "the Palestinians make cynical use of women and children by bringing them to places of violent confrontation" and the statement that al-Durra and his father "were caught in the line of fire." To be sure, the claim that al-Durra was "brought" to the location of the incident is entirely fictitious; the Palestinian people—men, women, and children—happen to live where the Intifada is taking place. But within twenty-four hours this fictitious claim became accepted as fact, the death of al-Durra underwent the ultimate cognitive reversal in the collective Israeli consciousness, and it ended up as the conclusive proof of the contrast between Israeli "restraint" and the "murderous nature" of the Palestinians: Not only do they kill Israelis—they sacrifice their own children.

Incidentally, toward the end of October, the IDF commissioned an inquiry of the shooting incident. The inquiry was carried out by two civilians, the physicist Nachum Shachaf and the engineer Yoseff Doriel—who had made a name for themselves a few years before by claiming they possessed "dramatic photos" that cast a "new light" on the murder of Prime Minister Itzhak Rabin. The inquiry ended up with the conclusion that the IDF did not kill al-Durra. On October 27 *Yediot Ahronot* published this conclusion on its front page, under the headline: "**CHILD MOHAMMED AL-DURRA NOT KILLED BY IDF FIRE.**" *Ha'aretz*, however, chose to check these conclusions more closely and on November 7 published the results of its investigation under the front page headline: ODD WAY FOR IDF TO INVESTIGATE DEATH OF CHILD AT NETZARIM. In its editorial on November 10, Ha'aretz criticized the inquiry in harsh terms: "It is difficult to overstate the foolishness that prompted this bizarre investigation. . . . The fact that an organization as disciplined and capable as the IDF acts in such amateurish fashion, in an investigation of such sensitivity, arouses consternation and concern." Thus Ha'aretz handled the army's belated attempt to dissociate itself from al-Durra's killing in a different way than the other two newspapers did. As far as they were concerned, every incident, including al-Durra's death, simply demonstrated IDF restraint and Palestinian guilt.

Warning Bells and Muffled Questions

A few basic facts, however, could have made it clear to the newspapers, already in the first week of the Intifada, that the naïve picture of reality presented above did not stand up to empirical and logical examination. For example, the fact that the IDF chose to use snipers against demonstrators should have sounded a warning bell. The sniper's rifle allows shooting from as far as 800 meters—way beyond the range of the demonstrators' stones and firebombs. Questions could have also been asked regarding the official shooting guidelines the IDF issued to its soldiers, especially regarding the circumstances under which they may open fire. For example, as early as October 4 the soldiers at the Netzarim junction received "less stringent guidelines for opening fire": they were allowed to fire on vehicles *approaching* the outpost (for fear of car bombs) and on anyone climbing the roofs of two neighboring buildings, known as the "Twin Towers" (to prevent shooting at the outpost from the roofs). The papers laconically reported all this in their back pages, but never used the information at their disposal to ask the relevant questions: Is preventive shooting consistent with the criteria of restraint? Does the use of snipers result in unnecessary casualties? What about firing missiles from helicopters? And even if the guidelines issued by the high command actually specified the general need for restraint, have these guidelines been observed punctiliously in the field? As the experience of the first Intifada taught us, young soldiers, scared and confused, at times eager for battle, who receive changing and sometimes contradictory instructions about when to open fire, are not engaged in exercising restraint—they want to get home in one piece.

Amira Hass tried to deal with these issues from time to time in Ha'aretz. On October 3, on page 6, she reported, under the headline PHYSICIANS: THE NATURE OF PALESTINIAN INJURIES INDICATES INTENT TO KILL, that most of the Palestinians killed in the first four days of the Intifada were in-jured in the upper half of their bodies, primarily in the head but also in the chest and stomach—in direct contradiction to the order to shoot demon-strators, when they pose a direct threat to soldiers, in the lower parts of their bodies. Amos Harel, a senior reporter for *Ha'aretz,* addressed the same issue in an article published on October 23 under the headline: NOT ONLY RESTRAINT HAS DIMINISHED—BUT ALSO SOLDIERS' PATIENCE. Harel claimed that in the first three weeks of the Intifada "the guidelines regard-ing restraint were strictly observed," but he went on to say that "by the end of the last week . . . the number of casualties rose sharply." The reasons for this, among others, were "tougher methods of response by the IDF, relax-ation of the guidelines for opening fire in the West Bank, and what seemed to be a loss of patience by some of the forces in the field." As noted above, it is doubtful that the restraint was strictly observed even in the first three weeks, but *Ha'aretz* nevertheless took Harel's report seriously and published his story on its front page.

This is significant. The two other newspapers did not broach the sub-ject at any point and did not investigate it. Occasionally, they sent re-porters to spend time with the soldiers—and heard from them and from their commanders that "everything was okay." *Yediot Ahronot's* reporter Roni Shaked, for example, visited a group of soldiers from an elite battal-ion called Duchifat at an army post near the Psagot settlement, and told their story in the daily supplement of October 10:

> Three days ago, I walked through the outpost's communication trenches. Stooping the whole time, I glanced through the embrasures towards Ramal-lah, from where enemy fire was raining uninterruptedly. Running between the positions, I heard calls from soldiers who had already experienced this: "Look out and get the hell out of here. Put on a helmet. Don't take off your flak-jacket." I met Dudi Benita, 20, from Kiryat-Yam in a concrete trench. He was sporting a flak-jacket on his chest, a helmet on his head, and a smile on his lips. On his left and right, along the trench, was a squad he had trained for seven months. "I am proud of them," he said, offering me a bottle of warm Coke. "They are doing a wonderful job." Dudi and his soldiers spend many hours in the positions between the embrasures, with one eye peering con-stantly through the sight of the rifle. Every now and then they raise their heads to obtain a broader view of the field. They are ready for the shooting—and more than that, they are looking for the enemy in order to shoot and hit. The positions are manned continuously, in the morning, at noon, in the evening, and at night. Dudi's soldiers are tense, alert, and determined. Eli Ochana from Kiryat-Gat is a professional sniper. Lying flat in his position, he is very tense. He has little time to talk to us. "It began with shooting toward the remote houses [of the settlement]. Then there was shooting at us," he

says. "We responded. It was the first time I fired at the enemy. We try to keep our heads down and remain behind cover at all times. We are not tired. We do shifts, take turns, and are well protected. We help each other. No arguments, no yelling. Everyone understands the situation." The fighting was as much of a surprise to Eli Ochana as to the others in the platoon. But in a few days they have become professional soldiers in every sense of the word.

What does Roni Shaked mean when he says that Dudi Benita's soldiers "are looking for the enemy in order to shoot and hit"? Shaked's description makes it clear that the soldiers themselves were not in any danger. How many of the Palestinians who were shot directly threatened the lives of the Psagot settlers? How many Palestinians have the soldiers killed altogether? What are their guidelines for opening fire? Shaked does not ask—and does not provide answers.

Only once in the course of October did a reporter of one of the large newspapers get caught in the middle of real fighting—on the Palestinian side. It happened during the first week of the Intifada. On October 6, Zadok Yehezkeli of *Yediot Ahronot* found himself on the Temple Mount, on the Palestinian side, before the Israeli police "reconquered" the site. According to Yehezkeli, these were "five hours in which you find yourself not behind the barrels of the guns but in front of them; not facing a shower of rocks but behind them; five hours of feeling like David, not like Goliath." This is how he describes the experience:

> In fact, the scariest moment was during one of the Israeli assaults of the occupied site. I found myself, along with a few other journalists and photographers, in a structure that served as a toilet, which had just changed hands. The policemen who burst in and pointed their guns at us were not sure of our identity. Their eyes were wide open, in a mixture of dread and tension. They relaxed for a moment—but only for a moment—as we waved our IDs. A policeman was hit by a stone, and he went crazy. In a fit of rage he started to smash the facilities with his club. This wounded Israeli policeman was the most frenzied person I met in these five hours.

Of all the Israeli reporters, then, only two found themselves "facing the gun barrels" on the Palestinian side. Amira Hass was there on a regular basis; she kept claiming that the "restraint" policy was an empty slogan. Zadok Yehezkeli was there by accident, only once, and brought back the story of the frenzied policeman. All that was needed in order to obtain a more reasonable picture of reality, then, was to spend more time in the field—and on the Palestinian side—rather than in briefings with IDF officials. Throughout October, the two large newspapers simply did not do this.

In the following months, the three newspapers published three stories that cast a heavy shadow on the image of restraint and should have made it clear to the editors that IDF's conduct called for serious investigation. This did not happen, and at least one of the reporters, Yoav Limor of *Ma'ariv*, later testified that he was under heavy pressure to keep the story to himself. His article appeared in the newspaper's daily supplement on December 12, under the headline:

RESERVE OFFICERS WHO SERVED RECENTLY IN GAZA AREA CLAIM: "IDF SOLDIERS 'HEAT UP' AREA ON PURPOSE"

Yoav Limor writes:

> Since the beginning of the riots, the PA has been claiming that the IDF uses excessive force in confrontations in the territories. They bring the high number of Palestinian casualties as proof. The IDF vigorously rejects this claim, stating that it is merely responding to Palestinian aggression and does not initiate the fighting. . . . But the testimonies of enlisted soldiers and of reservists in the Gaza Strip paint an entirely different picture. *Ma'ariv* has evidence indicating that soldiers in two field units act in defiance of guidelines and conceal the fact from the high command. . . . "The only thing they care for is shooting," says one of the reservists. "At times it happens in a perfectly quiet area, with almost no enemy activity. The soldiers contact the sector commander and report that they are under fire, and ask for permission to respond."

One of the reservists told the reporter about an encounter between soldiers of one of the units and a Palestinian squad that was "setting up an explosive charge on the road adjacent to the electronic fence":

> The soldiers arrived at the site, opened fire on the terrorists, and succeeded in killing them. But the shooting did not end there. The soldiers continued to fire indiscriminately in the direction of the nearby village and did not stop when women and children began fleeing in panic. One of the soldiers in the ambush, who was among those shooting, later boasted that he shot at the ambulance that came to evacuate the Palestinian wounded and chased it away.

The reservists also told Limor about a position in the Nahal Oz area, manned by a battalion of the regular army, "where there was constant fighting."

> A few weeks later a reserve force relieved the battalion, and suddenly there was perfect quiet. Not a single incident. Not a single bullet was fired at them. Then the regular force returned, and the fighting started again the very same

day. A few weeks passed, the reservists returned, and all was quiet again. This is either an astonishing coincidence or something much more serious.

The army spokesman responded to this story with the following statement:

> The army spokesman does not respond to gossip. The unit in question performs its duties with tenacity and dedication. The unit plays an important part in providing security and defense to Israeli citizens in the Gaza district and beyond it.

On the same day, *Ha'aretz* published a story by reporter Amos Harel, under the headline ARMY BEHAVES LIKE BLINDFOLDED BOXER. The overline says: DEFENSE ESTABLISHMENT BELIEVES TOO MUCH FORCE IS USED IN TERRITORIES. Amos Harel writes:

> Over the past few weeks, on his own initiative, a former senior official in the defense establishment has begun a series of talks with IDF regiment commanders in the territories. His purpose is to persuade the commanders to refrain from using excessive force against the Palestinians. . . . The IDF invested a huge effort, destined to fail from the start, to show that it did not spill the blood of the child Mohammed al-Durra. But who is examining the dozens of other deaths? "No one can convince me that we did not kill dozens of children unnecessarily," says the senior officer. There was no malice, most likely. But in many cases there was certainly breach of guidelines as well as faulty judgment.

Harel's story deals with the way formal IDF policy was implemented in practice. It explains that the policy "passes through many hands until it reaches the last link, the soldier on patrol or at the checkpoint, who adopts its most severe interpretation. Simultaneously, regiment commanders, worn out by prolonged fighting, are eager to show quick results in the fight against terrorism, and especially to provide some sense of security to the threatened population of settlers. This is how the constraints and initiatives of the tactical level are forging the strategic reality."

A month later, on January 19, military analyst Alex Fishman published an article on this subject in *Yediot Ahronot*'s weekly supplement. The headline says: IDF PRESENTS: THE X-FILES. The overline states: SOLDIERS SHOT AN ELECTRICIAN, A HANDCUFFED MAN, A BISHOP, AND AN AMERICAN PHOTOGRAPHER— AND NO MILITARY POLICE INVESTIGATION WAS STARTED.

In the article, Fishman writes about a Palestinian electrician who was using a drill at a construction site and was shot by a soldier who mistook the drill for a weapon; about a Fatah activist shot by soldiers while handcuffed; and about a soldier who opened fire on a Palestinian cab and killed two of its passengers, after passengers in another car that drove past earlier had fired at him. At least two of the incidents involved soldiers of the Nahal battalion serving in the Hebron region. Fishman writes:

> Perhaps there is a problem in this battalion, and perhaps thorough investigation of their operations would reveal deficiencies in the soldiers' value systems, or discipline problems, or individual breaches of discipline. But who knows, and who cares? The top brass of the Central Command believe that the "problems" stem from the Nahal soldiers' lack of experience; that is all. The incidents [mentioned above] are those that reached the media. How many more were not publicized? Who knows? And who's counting? Who is reporting and how is it being reported? And what does the high command know about what is happening in the trenches? Four months into the Intifada, even the high command is finally beginning to realize that something is wrong.

It may have indeed taken the high command four months to realize that "something was wrong," although no detectable measures were taken to remedy this state of affairs; but the signs were already there, for anyone who wanted to see them, in the first month. Most of these signs, as we have seen, were routinely reported by the field reporters. The newspapers could have investigated, asked the tough questions, and published the findings. They did not.

Out of the Frame:
Settlers' Violence and Collective Punishment

Two additional important points should be made here. First, the IDF is not the only Israeli element active in the territories. The settlers themselves played a crucial role in the events. During the forty-eight hours of Barak's ultimatum to Arafat, for example, groups of settlers went on a violent, intimidating campaign in the territories. According to various reports, the settlers stopped Palestinian cars on the Cross-Samaria Highway, beat passengers, and damaged the vehicles. According to Palestinian sources, settlers entered seven villages and shot at buildings and vehicles. Palestinians reported that the settlers killed three residents, and in one case blocked the road and prevented an ambulance from reaching one of the injured. In one of these cases Israel claimed that the Palestinian was killed in a traffic accident, but even if this particular case was indeed an accident, the significance of the settler violence during these days cannot be overstated. Under such circumstances it is simply impossible to claim that *Israel* exercised restraint—even if the IDF itself did.

How did the newspapers deal with these reports? On October 10, *Yediot Ahronot* published on page 14 an article about what the paper termed "the settlers' rage," following the murder of Hillel Lieberman, a resident of the settlement Elon Moreh. The headline reads: SETTLERS THREATEN: "WE'LL TAKE LAW IN OUR HANDS." The implication, of course, is clear: the settlers are *threatening*, but have yet to do anything. The Palestinian claims, mentioned in the article's last paragraph, are immediately and forcefully denied by the police and by the Council of Settlements. *Ma'ariv* mentions the topic at the bottom of page 18, in a brief article headed: CONTROVERSY ABOUT THE DEATH OF A PALESTINIAN. The opening paragraph says: "The PA uses the death of a resident of Um Tsafa in the Ramallah area in a road accident for savage incitement against settlers and IDF forces, say sources in the defense establishment." The other incidents are not mentioned at all.

Ha'aretz, on the other hand, reports the topic in an article at the top of page 2, under the headline: WAVE OF SETTLER VIOLENCE AGAINST PALESTINIANS. The story is also mentioned in the MAIN FACTS box on the front page. This is indeed significant. But even *Ha'aretz* regularly falls into the conceptual trap posited by the settlers' conduct: Official government sources, who viewed every violent Palestinian action as direct indication of PA policy, nevertheless referred to the settlers as an independent element whose activities were not indicative of official Israeli policy. Amos Harel writes about this "double standard" in a commentary published on page 2 of *Ha'aretz* on October 12: "The IDF claims all along that everything depends on the Chairman [Arafat], but when we asked a senior officer about settler violence this week, he answered: 'We will act to reduce anarchy, but we cannot control every individual.'" All three newspapers consistently adopted this double standard in their reports from the territories. Thus, the actions of the settlers did not affect the Israeli self-image of restraint.

The second point is this: The exercise of Israeli force in the territories was not limited to active fighting, but also included a long series of collective punitive actions: general closure, the closure of individual Palestinian towns, blockades around villages, preventing people from getting to work or obtaining medical treatment, and so on. These measures made the lives of millions of Palestinians unbearable, and in many cases took their toll in human life. In an article published in *Ha'aretz* on October 18, under the headline COMPLETE CLOSURE HOLDS UP MEDICAL SUPPLIES AND ASSISTANCE, Amira Hass writes:

> The West Bank and Gaza Strip were put under complete closure on Thursday, October 5. A week later, on October 12, the closure was tightened and

became an internal blockade throughout the West Bank. Since then, heavily reinforced IDF checkpoints surround the main entrances to towns, preventing direct access to them and severing the connection between the towns and the surrounding villages. Nablus is under complete internal blockade for the second week. Passage through the Rafiah and Allenby border crossings is limited. Some forty thousand residents of Old Hebron, home to a few hundred Jews, have been under full curfew for nineteen days. The closure disrupts all forms of activity, first and foremost the provision of medical treatment. . . . Various medical organizations report enormous difficulties in providing medical services to the sick. Physicians cannot reach their clinics throughout the West Bank because of the internal blockade, and the sick in the villages cannot reach the hospitals and clinics in the towns.

The following day, October 19, Hass once more reports the deadly consequences of the internal blockade:

There is a serious shortage of medicine in the villages. In most villages there are no pharmacies, and the chronically ill cannot reach the towns to purchase the drugs they need. . . . The physicians' organization reported two cases of death: Naim Ahmed, 37, from the village Zawia in the Kalkilya region, a dialysis patient who received treatment twice a week at the hospital in Nablus, was not able to make his way through the checkpoints or to negotiate roundabout ways to reach the hospital last week. His condition deteriorated and he died on October 16. The second case is that of Alaa Abu El-Aziz, a ten-year-old girl from the village Sawia in the Nablus region, who suffered stomach pain for two days and was not able to reach a physician in Nablus. A physician took her to a clinic in Qablan, a neighboring village, but she died on the way there.

On October 31 Hass sent the following story from Old Hebron:

It is Friday morning. At this hour the marketplace is generally bustling. But for more than a month, some thirty to forty thousand Palestinians are under complete curfew, round the clock, imprisoned in their homes in Old Hebron in the area under Israeli control—where some five hundred Jews reside as well. The curfew does not apply to the Jews. . . . The eleven members of the "M" family live in a rented three-room apartment. Nine children, six of school age. Their first complaint—shared by their mother—is that they have been prevented from going to school for a month. The thirty-four schools are closed because of the curfew. From their rooftop they can see the Jewish children driven to school and everywhere else, while they are wandering between the kitchen, the bedroom, the guest room, and the staircase. . . . In the first fifteen days they could not get out at all. Twice during those two weeks, people she did not know came and delivered basic food items. In the other two weeks, the curfew was lifted five times, for a few hours each time.

None of this ever appeared in *Yediot Ahronot* and *Ma'ariv*. Throughout the month of October, the two large newspapers did not devote a single article, let alone a headline, to this topic. Here we are not dealing with facts being printed in the less prominent parts of the newspapers, or in remote paragraphs. This is complete, self-imposed censorship: The suffering of millions of Palestinians simply did not exist for the two large newspapers. To be sure, this suffering was, and still is, a news item of utmost importance: It is impossible to understand this Intifada without grasping the levels of suffering and despair, of hatred and vindictiveness, produced by such systematic treatment of an entire population by an army of occupation.

In this respect, then, *Ha'aretz* is in a league of its own. During October, it published thirteen articles by Amira Hass, a weekly article by Gideon Levy, who has been following human rights violations in the territories for years, and one story by Daniel Ben-Simon, reporting from the towns of the West Bank. Still, two comments are in order. First, the suffering of the Palestinians was mentioned on the *front* page of *Ha'aretz* only once throughout the month, on October 6, in an article by Amira Hass appearing under the headline: CHILDREN IN GAZA TERRIFIED BY MOHAMMED AL-DURRA'S DEATH. All the other components of Palestinian hardship not mentioned in this one article were simply absent from the newspaper's front page. Second, the newspaper never used Hass's reports for a critical examination of its general perspective, especially regarding the concept of restraint. *Ha'aretz* did provide ample space for Hass's articles, so as to bring to its readers the "Palestinian perspective," but it did not assign to these reports the same factual weight assigned to stories based on Israeli security sources. The November 15 issue of *Ha'aretz* provides an almost amusing example. The main front page headline reads: BARAK CONVENES CABINET. NO CHANGE EXPECTED IN POLICY OF RESTRAINT. The editorial that day states:

> The Prime Minister wisely decided not to respond [to Palestinian violence] in accordance with the wishes of extremists, and he intends to continue the policy of restraint. This policy is liable to lead to frustration and be subject to sharp public criticism. But as long as even a glimmer of hope for the resumption of the diplomatic process remains, this is the only appropriate policy.

But right beside its editorial, *Ha'aretz* printed Amira Hass's article under the headline: THIS IS NO RESTRAINT. Hass describes in detail the Palestinian deaths in the two previous days, the thousands of people who fled their homes at night for fear of shooting and missile attacks, the policy of closure, and the economic hardships. The contrast between Hass's article and the newspaper's main headline and editorial—which officially represent the paper's viewpoint—demonstrates the degree to which *Ha'aretz* was cut off from the picture of reality its own reporter in the territories sent in day after day.

Reporting Israeli Suffering:
The View from Gilo

To be sure, the Israeli disregard for Palestinian suffering was not the product of the current Intifada. But this disregard acquired a special meaning in October 2000, in light of the press's intense concentration on the Israeli suffering resulting from Palestinian violence. This is best illustrated by the newspapers' coverage of the events in Gilo.

Palestinians started shooting at Gilo on October 4. The next morning, a headline on *Ma'ariv*'s front page reads: LAST NIGHT: SHOOTING AT HOMES IN THE GILO NEIGHBORHOOD IN SOUTH JERUSALEM. The newspaper devoted all of page 7 to the shooting. The sub-headline announces: PANIC ON HA'ANAFA STREET IN GILO: WINDOWS SHATTERED, PROPERTY DAMAGED. The sub-headline in the corresponding page in *Yediot Ahronot* reads: HEAVY GLOOM IN ISRAELI TOWNSHIPS CLOSE TO THE RIOTS. On October 6, the sub-headline on page 2 of *Ma'ariv* reports: SEVERAL RESIDENTS LEFT THE NEIGHBORHOOD. OTHERS DEMONSTRATED: "WE FEEL AS IF WE WERE IN LEBANON." A few days later, the suffering of Gilo's residents became the central news item in the papers. On October 18 the main headline of *Ma'ariv* reports the injury of a border policeman in the neighborhood, and the huge headline on pages 4–5 reads: WAR IN GILO. Under another headline—ANGRY GILO RESIDENTS: "DO SOMETHING"—the newspaper reports: "Gilo residents are shocked and angry. Yesterday they recalled the moments of fear they experienced while shots were being fired at their homes. 'Death to the Arabs,' they called, as they protested against IDF restraint." The reporter Yehuda Golan adds his personal impressions of the neighborhood's situation under the headline LEBANON GETTING CLOSER TO JERUSALEM.

The next day, *Yediot Ahronot* published a front page picture of the concrete wall built on Ha'anafa Street to block the bullets, devoting the opening page of its daily supplement to this topic. The picture that appears on this page shows a young girl peering over the concrete fortification. The headline announces:

NEIGHBORHOOD UNDER FIRE

The sub-headline reads:

CONCRETE FORTIFICATIONS DEPLOYED YESTERDAY IN GILO DID NOT REDUCE THE
RESIDENTS' ANXIETY. WHAT KIND OF LIFE IS IT WHEN YOU MUST STOOP TO GET
INTO THE KITCHEN?

The headline on pages 2–3 of the supplement says: "A CONCRETE WALL
CANNOT DRIVE OUT FEAR." One of the picture captions quotes a neighborhood resident explaining that "we hide behind stones, and the Palestinians are walking about fearlessly."

On October 24 the topic captures the main front page headline in
Ma'ariv:

ANOTHER NIGHT OF SHOOTING IN GILO AND PSAGOT

The headline on pages 10–11 says:

"WE FEEL AS IF WE WERE IN A GHETTO"

Two boxes on these pages offer advice from a psychiatrist ("CONVEY A
SENSE OF SECURITY TO CHILDREN") and general guidelines (DO NOT
STAND ON BALCONY, NEAR OPENINGS OR WINDOWS). The opening
page of *Yediot Ahronot*'s supplement of the same day shows a photo of two
sisters, ages six and twelve, leaning on a windowsill of their house, with the
concrete wall on Ha'anafa Street behind them. The headline is:

CHILDREN ON THE FRONT LINES

The sub-headline reads:

VOLLEYS OF GUNFIRE, ARMY HELICOPTERS, MISSILES AND THE SOUND OF
EXPLOSIONS HAVE BECOME ROUTINE IN THE LIVES OF CHILDREN IN THE GILO
NEIGHBORHOOD IN JERUSALEM. HOW TO COPE WITH THE CHILDREN'S TENSION
AND ANXIETY?

And so it went on for the rest of the month and afterwards, almost
daily. Let us be clear: There is no doubt that the Palestinian shooting created great hardship for the residents of Ha'anafa Street, whose apartments
face Beit Jallah. It is also likely that the sound of the shooting and the Israeli shelling disturbed the children's sleep in the area. A few of the residents were injured, most of them lightly. But it is still a fact that the
neighborhood, as such, was never "under fire," and that "war" was never
waged in Gilo. This is what Dina Ofek, a Gilo resident, says in an article by
Arie Dayan, published in section B of *Ha'aretz* on October 22:

Whoever claims that Gilo is under siege is wrong. I do not feel besieged or
threatened. They shot at Ha'anafa street from Beit Jallah, but there are thirty-

five thousand residents in Gilo whose lives go on as usual. One would think, by reading the newspapers, that the residents of Gilo are being constantly bombarded by rocks and shot at from Beit Jallah and Bethlehem. This is not true. Only Ha'anafa street is in the line of fire. By the way, I heard about the shooting there on television. If I had not watched TV, I would never have known that they shot at Gilo. . . . Anyone reading the newspapers and watching television could think that the residents of Gilo are lying under their beds all night.

Of course, it was no secret that most of Gilo's residents learned about the Palestinian shooting from the media—but the two large newspapers never took this into account. They were also indifferent to the data their own reporters collected concerning the scope of the Palestinian forces shooting at Gilo. On October 24, the day *Ma'ariv*'s main front page headline is devoted to the shooting in Gilo, reporter Yossi Levy writes the following lines in a story published on page 3:

> The shooting at Gilo in the past two weeks has been carried out by two squads of two or three people each. They have few weapons. This was the assessment of a senior defense official last night. The same official said that these were probably Tanzim squads, who came to Beit Jallah from outside, equipped with a machine gun and two or three Kalashnikov rifles.

And the following article by Nachum Barnea appears in the *Yediot Ahronot* supplement on October 27:

> On Sunday the chief of staff visited the Ezion regiment, which covers the area stretching from south of Jerusalem to the entrance to Hebron. The regiment commander, colonel Marcel Aviv, brought up the name of Abdallah Abu-Hadis, a Tanzim man, who shoots at Gilo every night. The name caused some excitement among the officers. "He arrives at the house, shoots, then runs away," says one of them. "We recognized him. We saw how he tried to get into a house and the residents threw him out."
>
> Night after night the IDF searches for Abdallah Abu-Hadis. They are looking for him from the turrets of tanks and from sniper positions. "We are in the dark," says the commander. That evening I asked [reporter] Roni Shaked whether he had heard of Abdallah Abu-Hadis. "Let's check him out," he said. He called Issa Karaka, the commander of the Fatah in the Bethlehem area. Karaka was happy to bring the press up to date. "Correct," he said. "Abu-Hadis is a Tanzim man."
>
> "Is it true that he is the one shooting from Beit Jallah?"
>
> "He poses as a great hero," said Karaka. "But he is very far from it. Besides, he's an invalid; he can barely move. You know what? Ask him yourself. Here is his cell phone: 051-714786."
>
> We dialed. In flawless Hebrew, a woman's voice said: "The party you called is not available." Roni Shaked said: "He must be at work."

Just then, another volley came from Beit Jallah. He is indeed at work (if it is him).

The shooter operates an old Russian machine gun, known in the IDF by the initials R.P.G. It handles the range of 780 to 900 meters with difficulty. When the slugs reach their target, they are weary, lacking momentum. This is why, in most cases, the thin pumice-block walls of Gilo managed to prevent the enemy's penetration.

This, then, is where the newspapers' policy showed its colors most clearly: all these huge headlines and double-spreads, all this rhetoric of fear and anxiety, dedicated to "weary" slugs shot toward a few houses on Ha'anafa Street in Gilo by a few Palestinians, possibly only one, armed with a machine gun and maybe a few rifles. And in contrast—not a single headline, throughout the entire month, dedicated to the daily suffering of millions of Palestinians. This imbalance cannot be attributed to the newspapers' natural and understandable inclination to feel more sympathy for their own people. This is an obsessive aggrandizement of the proportions of Israeli suffering and a total suppression of Palestinian suffering.

The Vicious Cycle:
From "Restraint" to "Helplessness"

This imbalance, to be sure, contributed to the sense of victimization felt by so many Israelis throughout the beginning of the Intifada, to the common feeling that the Palestinians were "walking about fearlessly" and were not "paying the price" for the suffering they inflicted on the Israelis. But it did more than that: To begin with, it obscured the fundamental fact that in this two-sided war of attrition, conducted within the continuous framework of occupation, the rhetorical distinction between "action" and "response" does not in any meaningful way reflect the violent dynamics on the ground. Throughout the entire month, the newspapers completely ignored the obvious link between the Palestinian suffering and the fact that they continued to demonstrate on the streets, throw firebombs, and shoot at IDF outposts. This fundamental fact—that Palestinian actions were as much of a "response" as Israeli actions—never entered Israeli consciousness. On October 23, after Israeli helicopters fired missiles at Beit Jallah in response to the shooting in Gilo, Ma'ariv commentator Chemi Shalev wrote that "from Israel's point of view, helicopter fire is an adequate response to repeated attacks on Gilo, but it must be remembered that it immediately creates a need for an appropriate Palestinian response. This negative cycle is far more important than any political calculation." This was the *only* time, throughout October, that this basic insight was expressed on the papers' news pages.

Moreover, this pattern of suppression prevented the newspapers from asking the necessary questions about the logic of IDF actions in the territories, and from reminding their readers, as well as the decision makers, that military action has its operational limitations. After all, from the defense establishment's point of view, IDF actions were supposed to send a deterring message to the Palestinians, persuading them to stop the violence. But throughout the long weeks and months of the Intifada it became clear that the strategy did not work: Israel "responded" with "restraint," and the Palestinians did not stop the violence; Israel responded more harshly, and still the Palestinians refused to desist. After the October 7 ultimatum lapsed, Barak announced the first intensification of the response. Four days after the Lynch in Ramallah (to be discussed in chapter 6), Barak announced that "from now on we will not just sit and take it and then respond." Israeli helicopters attacked in Ramallah and Gaza, and the mayor of Haifa, Amram Mitznah, generally a spokesman of the moderate left, published the following words on page 7 of *Ma'ariv*: "IDF restraint has come from strength, not from weakness. Now that all limits have been exceeded, Arafat and all the Tanzim heroes will have a taste of the IDF's strength, and believe me—all the 'tigers' of the Tanzim will return to being alley cats."

The "alley cats" of the Tanzim, however, continued to shoot even after they had "a taste of the IDF's strength." Therefore, the IDF was "forced" to intensify the response again, and then again, and again: At the beginning of the third week of the Intifada, the guidelines for opening fire on rock throwers became more flexible. At the beginning of the fourth week, the IDF "escalated the means of response in some areas." The same week, helicopters and tanks used missiles and machine guns to fire at civilian homes in Beit Jallah, and a senior military official told journalists that "the rules of the game have changed." By the end of October, helicopters attacked Fatah headquarters in PA areas. At the beginning of November, senior sources in the IDF announced: "The games are over, the time has come for some really serious response." Barak declared that from now on the IDF "will act firmly, but without letting itself be drawn into adventurism." A week later Hussein Abayat, a Fatah activist in Bethlehem, was assassinated by the IDF—the first in a long series of assassinations. But all along it was becoming clear that the Israeli actions were not bringing about "a calmer field." Some began to understand this even within the IDF. On October 23, for example, the day after helicopters fired missiles at Beit Jallah, *Ma'ariv* quoted security sources claiming that "the Palestinians are finding it difficult to understand our messages." The sources explained that "over the past days the Palestinians got 'unambiguous messages' that the IDF would respond sternly if the shooting from Beit Jallah to Gilo continued. Since these messages were not heeded, there was no alternative to the helicopter attack."

But the Palestinians did not "get the message" even after the helicopter attack. Senior officers quickly drew the conclusion: If the Palestinians are not listening, our response must have been too mild. On November 1, two days after IDF helicopters bombed the Fatah headquarters in Ramallah, Nablus, and Han Yunes, *Yediot Ahronot* published a story under the headline: FRUSTRATION IN THE IDF: THE ATTACK IS WEAK AND NOT DETERRENT. The article quotes senior officers who complained that "what is actually being done is very little, it's too weak, and it does not deter the Palestinians." One of the officers said: "The IDF keeps threatening that it will respond to Palestinian attacks. But the Palestinians know that they have nothing to fear." In a commentary published next to the article, Ron Ben-Ishai explained:

> Field commanders in the IDF say that the attack achieved no military goal, and it is clear that it did not contribute to the IDF's and Israel's deterrence capability. Anyone willing to sustain deaths and injuries day after day will not be deterred by the destruction of a few walls. The Palestinians are fully conscious of the IDF's enormous technological advantage. . . . They have also learned to use their military weakness and the Israeli demonstrations of force to their advantages in the media. . . . It is likely that Barak, and those who had a share in the decision about the helicopter attack, knew in advance that this would be the result. But they had to deal with other considerations: on the one hand, the need to satisfy the angry public in Israel following the recent murders, and to disprove the claims that the politicians are tying the IDF's hands; on the other, the American pressure to avoid dramatic measures that would escalate the fighting, and the secret contacts between Barak and Arafat intended to restore calm. The symbolic attack was the compromise between these opposing considerations, and the only damage it caused was in the field of public relations.

Ben-Ishai finds no fault with the helicopter attack—intended, by his own account, to "satisfy the angry public in Israel"—except for the fact that it was not sufficiently severe and hence did not act as a deterrent. He goes on to recommend that Israel should stop sending "warning signals" to the Palestinians, and he is pleased to report that the IDF has begun "using its forces in a pattern similar to methods used in Lebanon." Of course, these methods too failed to achieve the desired ends (as they failed also in Lebanon).

Throughout this entire period the newspapers never raised one of the most fundamental questions: What was the basis for the defense establishment's assumption that the steady escalation in military response—more dead and injured, more bombings and assassinations—would eventually subdue the Palestinians? On October 24, in an article published in section B of *Ha'aretz*, Amira Hass quoted an anonymous Palestinian youth, a resident of Beit Jallah: "Israel's weapon is its ability to kill. Our weapon is our ability to die. I am optimistic. I know that we will defeat you, because our ability to die is stronger than your ability to kill."

One need not be a Palestinian, or even to sympathize with Palestinian suffering, in order to understand this chilling statement, and to see that the youth from Beit Jallah was actually right: One only needs to know something about modern history, national liberation struggles, the limits of force, the collective identity that a national group can develop when subjected for years to occupation by another people. None of this ever appeared in the papers. Whenever the newspapers criticized IDF policy in the territories, the criticism came from the *opposite* direction. The front page of *Ma'ariv*'s weekend supplement on November 17, for example, featured a large picture of a demonstration organized by the settlers in Jerusalem that week. The headline under the picture, in large red letters shaped like bloodstains, reads: **THE LIMITS OF RESTRAINT.** Above the picture appears the following unsigned text—an emotional appeal coming directly from the newspaper: "The experts and commentators support Ehud Barak's policy of restraint, but the heavy price paid in blood strains the people's nerves and makes them wonder: how long can we take it quietly? What is the red line beyond which it is no longer possible to sit there and take it?"

In the lead article, Yoav Limor reports that politicians are willing to allow the IDF to initiate action, but the army "now hesitates more than ever to take chances"—since the army is concerned about regional escalation and wants to avoid mistakes in the operations it initiates. According to a senior officer quoted in the article, "Arafat is sitting there waiting for a shell to misfire and kill 50 Palestinian children in a schoolyard. That would win the battle for him." Beyond that, however, senior officers in the field told Limor that "in this game the IDF has no way of winning—military victory is simply impossible." Note, then, the dramatic gap between the reality in the field, the commanders' grasp of this reality, and the newspapers' views. On the one hand, at that point Israel had already killed 204 Palestinians, but the army still complains about "hesitation." On the other hand, even the IDF understands that it could not win this war—but the newspaper still asks, "What is the red line beyond which it is no longer possible to sit there and take it?" The newspaper does not even offer an operative plan of action. It merely expresses what the editors believe to be the feelings of the angry public, whose nerves are already overstrained.

The fact of the matter is that the IDF operations in the territories not only failed to restore calm but actually played a crucial causal role in exacerbating the situation. Throughout the Intifada, sources in the PA repeatedly said that the only chance of restoring calm was an entire week without funerals, a week in which the IDF would exercise *real* restraint in dealing with the demonstrations. "You do not understand what's going on," said the anonymous youth from Beit Jallah in the third week of the Intifada. "People go to funerals, they mourn the dead, wash their hands, and go to the next confrontation, to become, perhaps, the next casualty." If the price paid by Israel marked the red line beyond which "it is not possible to sit there and take it," how could anyone believe that exacting a much heavier price on the Palestinian side would lower the level of violence? If Barak and the IDF had to send helicopters to bomb Palestinian towns to "satisfy the angry public in Israel," how could anyone expect Arafat to order his people to lay down their weapons—even if one assumed, quite mistakenly, that he had complete control of events in the field? These are some of the most fundamental questions that needed to be posed by a responsible media from the very outset of the Intifada. They simply were not asked.

Finally, toward the end of October and the beginning of November, various sources in the IDF began speaking openly about a causal relationship between the increasing feeling of hardship of the Israeli public (a feeling that had been systematically encouraged by the newspapers) and the actions initiated by the army against Palestinian targets. On November 2, for example, Amir Oren writes the following lines in *Ha'aretz*:

> Had the resilience of our citizens remained steady, the IDF could have carried on . . . at the level of activity it had drilled and prepared against Palestinian violence. . . . In the year 2000, in a country that has become accustomed to the good life, the military commanders and political leaders do not have this luxury. What may appear to the Palestinian side as frustrating Israeli sophistication is perceived as impotence by Gilo residents and anyone watching the broadcasts from that neighborhood.

On November 10, one day after the assassination of Hussein Abayat in Beit Sahur, Amir Oren writes that the assassinations also had "an internal dimension," having to do with Ehud Barak's relations with the army military command and the public at large:

[The assassination] was forced upon Barak directly by the chief of staff and his generals, who are not willing to take deadly blows passively because this erodes the military's prestige and encourages further aggression, and indirectly by the growing dissatisfaction in the public with the political and military policy, which until now seemed to indicate helplessness.

It is difficult to overstate the importance of this vicious cycle, involving Ehud Barak, the defense establishment, the newspapers—and that mysterious thing called "public opinion." When Barak defines his policy as one of restraint; when the press systematically suppresses the fact that the restraint slogan does not correspond with the conduct of the IDF in the field; when the press, at the same time, obsessively exaggerates the dimensions of Palestinian violence, and does not report the dynamics of violence, with Israeli action triggering Palestinian responses and Palestinian action triggering Israeli responses; and when the press does not remind readers of the limits of power and does not ask decision makers the really meaningful questions—then it turns out that public opinion shows "growing dissatisfaction" with the "helplessness" indicated by Israeli "restraint," and the IDF has to act to protect its eroding prestige; and IDF actions in their turn trigger Palestinian responses, demanded by Palestinian public opinion—and so on and so forth. It could be expected from the newspapers, as organizations wishing to play their independent role properly, that they would identify this vicious cycle—and not be sucked into it.

5

"A Fifth Column"

And so it turns out, to everyone's dismay, that the pessimists and extremists were right. Throughout the years they upset us all, insisting that the Arabs within Israel were the real problem. Now, they can give themselves a medal. While a violent confrontation between two unequal armies unfolds in the territories, the Intifada has erupted in the most unexpected of places —within the country. Israeli citizens have turned against Israeli citizens. Arabs against Jews.

—Yoel Markus, *Ha'aretz,* October 6

On Yom Kippur eve, October 8, about twelve hours after the apocalyptic morning newspapers hit the stands, thousands of Jews throughout Israel took to the streets. They had decided to deal personally with what Yoel Markus had called, in the above paragraph, "the real problem." In Nazareth, Karmiel, and Tiberias, in Hatikva neighborhood in Tel Aviv, in Jaffa, Jerusalem, Hedera, and Dimona, Jews beat up Arabs, set fire to their stores, offices, and apartments, burned car tires and blocked roads, violated a Muslim cemetery, and tried to set fire to several mosques.

Although Arab rioters also hurled firebombs at synagogues in Jaffa and Ramallah, and although there were some stone throwing incidents, Yom Kippur 2000 will be remembered for the outburst of Jewish hatred, and especially for the bloody events that took place in Nazareth. Early in the evening, hundreds of Jews from the Jewish town of Upper Nazareth marched down to the Arab city and started a real riot. The Jewish rioters beat up passersby, started fires, and vandalized property. The police force rushed to the scene, applying the same strategy used in all the Arab towns within the Green Line: Jewish rioters were handled with tear gas, while the Arab residents of Nazareth were treated with live and rubber-coated metal bullets. Two Nazareth residents were killed. In an op-ed piece published in *Yediot Ahronot* on October 10, Zohir Andreus, the editor of the Arabic newspaper *Kul El-Arab,* wrote that for the Arab citizens of Israel, Yom Kippur was the ultimate proof that "the State of Israel has cut off its Arab citizens. . . . The members of the Arab national minority in Israel are not citizens of this country."

The October 10 newspapers, edited and printed twenty-four hours after these events, once Yom Kippur was over, reveal an acute sense of distress—the distress of a people whose deepest fears keep shifting at an uncomfortable speed. Only two days earlier, as we have seen, the prospect of "regional conflagration" was the overwhelming cause for anxiety; now it was substituted by the fear of civil war. Only two days earlier, Israel's Arab citizens were "the real problem," a veritable fifth column; now, all of a sudden, it seemed that the very fabric of Arab-Jewish coexistence was crumbling. The newspapers thus rallied to the task of reconciliation.

Under its front page headline, CIVIL WAR FEARED, Ma'ariv displays a picture of the Jewish demonstrations in Tel Aviv's Hatikva neighborhood, several pictures of the mosque and synagogue the rioters had tried to burn down, and an article by the country's chief rabbi, Israel Lau. "I call on the public—Jewish and Arab alike—not to get carried away by provocations," wrote Rabbi Lau. "We must all come to our senses and put our trust in the security forces. They—and only they—will restore order and secure personal safety." The appeal probably elicited a bitter smile from Arab readers: As we shall see, it was quite obvious that during the riots the security forces were almost exclusively concerned with the safety of Jewish citizens.

Yediot Ahronot's front page features a huge picture from the riots in Hatikva neighborhood: A Jewish teenager stands on top of a turned-over car, his torso bare, his appearance threatening. Behind him, hundreds of demonstrators are smiling. The main headline is STREET FIGHTS. As part of the reconciliation effort, the paper publishes on its front page an article by senior reporter Sima Kadmon: For the first time since the outbreak of the riots, a woman's voice reaches the front page. "The Jews who attacked their Arab neighbors on Yom Kippur eve," writes Kadmon, "proved . . . that we have nothing to be ashamed of as far as mobs are concerned: ours is as much of a mob as theirs."

On pages 12–13, the newspaper publishes reports from two funerals—one Jewish, one Arab—under the headline PAIN ON BOTH SIDES. The reports are completely symmetrical: on the right side we find the pictures of Nazareth's Omar Akawee and Ussam Yizbek, and a picture from their funeral procession; on the left side, the picture of Bhor Zhan, killed late Saturday when a stone hit his car on the coastal highway, and a picture from his funeral. The following day, both tabloids carry lengthy stories about a group of Israeli writers who visited the mourning families in Nazareth. A picture of this visit appears on *Yediot Ahronot*'s front page; *Ma'ariv* presents the story, in great detail, on its center pages, under the title **RECONCILIA-TION DUE**.

Thus, following the Yom Kippur events, the newspapers temporarily set aside their sense of betrayal and the apocalyptic perspective concerning Israel's Arab citizens that had dominated their coverage during the previous week. This, however, was too little, too late. Too little, because in spite of this quest for reconciliation, the newspapers continued reporting the events of Yom Kippur and the days that followed in the same one-sided way on the *news* level. They still based their information almost exclusively on police sources and scandalously distorted the meaning of the events. And too late, because the Arab citizens had already been "cut off" during the previous week not only by the rioters, and not only by the state (Prime Minister Barak, Internal Security Minister Shlomo Ben-Ami, the police, and the border police), but by the Israeli press as well. We have already seen some of this in previous chapters: In chapter 1 we discussed the local newspaper supplement *Tel Aviv*, which unequivocally stated on its front page that **IN CASE OF WAR—JAFFA'S ARABS WILL ATTACK TEL AVIV**; in chapter 2, we looked at some of the relevant front page headlines from the first two days of the Intifada. The overall picture, however, is more interesting, and more troubling, because during the first week the newspapers were already swinging between these extreme moods: between biased, frightened, virulent reports, avoiding the red-hot iron of police violence as well as the deep causes for the outburst of Israeli Arabs' rage, and dramatic visits of worried, peace-oriented reporters from Tel Aviv to Arab restaurants and stores, which had lost their entire Jewish clientele; between messages verging on incitement, and sentimental, somewhat paternalistic gestures of reconciliation and understanding; between "those Arabs" and "our Arabs." This jittery, nervous combination actually created an even harsher view of the situation: Arabs were rioting and inciting, while Jews were showing restraint—to the point of actually sharing Arab grief.

Let us return, then, to the newspapers of the first days of October, and follow their coverage of events within the Green Line.

Layers of Misrepresentation: Headlines, Sources, Questions

Arab Israelis started demonstrating on Sunday, October 1, almost two days after the beginning of the violent clashes in the territories. As we have seen, *Yediot Ahronot* and *Ma'ariv* dedicate their main headlines of October 2 to this latest development: *Yediot Ahronot*'s version is FIRE SPREADS TO IS-RAELI ARABS; *Ma'ariv*'s is NEAR WAR IN THE TERRITORIES; INTIFADA WITHIN THE GREEN LINE. The message is clear: Palestinian violence has crossed the Green Line and is now threatening to strike Israelis not only "on the threshold of [their] home," in Sever Plotzker's memorable words, quoted at the end of chapter 3, but also within the home. The headline of a front page commentary in *Yediot Ahronot*, written by Haifa's mayor Amram Mitznah, gives the official explanation for the outburst of the rioting: MK INCITEMENT. Ron Ben-Ishai's commentary makes the same point: "Yesterday, Israeli Arabs joined the violence for two reasons: the first is their accumulated anger with the northern police commander, Alik Ron. But the real reason is systematic, unbridled incitement by Arab MKs." We will return to this "real reason" in detail later on.

The sub-headlines of the front pages and the headlines on the inner pages elaborate the story along the same lines. *Yediot Ahronot*'s sub-headline, for instance, tells its readers: YEFFET STREET IN JAFFA WAS CLOSED YESTERDAY BECAUSE OF STONE THROWING, and adds: RIOTS IN ARAB COMMUNITIES IN THE GALILEE AND THE CENTER CUT OFF ACCESS TO THE NORTH. *Ma'ariv*'s sub-headline says: ISRAELI ARABS BLOCK HAIFA–TEL AVIV ROAD AT FARADIES JUNCTION; RIOTS IN THE GALILEE, CENTRAL JAFFA AND BEDOUIN SETTLEMENTS IN THE SOUTH. *Ma'ariv*'s sub-headline also reports one Arab Israeli killed in the riot. Here is a selection of headlines from both newspapers' inner pages:

INTIFADA IN GALILEE AND JAFFA

POLICE COMMANDER: THOSE RESPONSIBLE WILL STAND TRIAL

LIVE FIRE ON ROAD TO HAIFA

OUTPOSTS UNDER SIEGE: "WE WERE TOLD TO STAY HOME AND LOCK THE GATES"

"DEATH TO THE JEWS" CALLS IN NAZARETH

Beside the headlines, we find the obvious photographs: border policemen in full gear on Yeffet Street in Jaffa; youths waving the Palestinian flag in Kefar Kanna; hundreds of demonstrators blocking the Faradies junction, and so on. This, then, is the overall story reflected in the newspapers' headlines and pictures: Thousands of incited Arabs, all the way from the Galilee to Jaffa, took to the streets, blocked roads, cut the Galilee off from the center, besieged Jewish outposts, threw stones, and fired live ammunition. Intifada within, indeed.

Does this amount to a reasonable account of the events? Not quite. To get somewhat closer to such an account, we need to peel off at least three layers of misrepresentation. First, we have to deal with the misleading, almost hysterical wording of the headlines; next, we need to take a look at those elements of reality that appear in the reports but never make it to the headlines; then, we have to consider the facts that never even appear in the reports but could have easily been gathered in the field and should have featured prominently in any reasonable coverage of the events.

Let us start, then, with the wording of the headlines. Did the riots actually *cut off* access to northern Israel? Not quite. Many roads were indeed blocked, and vacationers returning to the center after the Jewish New Year were indeed stuck in traffic for many hours; but other roads in the north were completely clear throughout the day. Were the outposts in the Galilee *under siege?* Not quite. The police were concerned that Arab demonstrators might reach the gates of the outposts Yodfat and Hararit in western Galilee, and residents were asked not to leave their homes. Hararit's secretary, Avraham Segal, told *Ma'ariv*'s reporters: "We didn't really feel under siege. We were told to close the gates because there was trouble on Arava-Hararit road, and that's what we did." Segal thus explicitly says that there was no siege, and the reporter says there was no siege—but the headline simply states: OUTPOSTS UNDER SIEGE. This is more than a systematic attempt to frame the events in a certain way. This is simply distortion.

Moving on to the next layer, let us take a glance at the sub-headline on *Yediot Ahronot*'s page 4. Here we find a fact that somehow lost its way to the headlines: In the town of Um-el-Fahem, an Arab demonstrator was killed. The text specifies the name of the demonstrator: Mohammed Jabarin, aged 23. Reading the story, we also discover that another youth, Ahmed Jabarin, aged 19, was critically injured. The following day it turned out that Jabarin died in the hospital. This is remarkable: The Israeli police killed an Israeli citizen and critically wounded another, and *Yediot Ahronot* does not even mention the fact on its front page or in its inner page headlines. *Yediot Ahronot* deals with Jabarin's death in one short sentence: "The worst incidents occurred in Um-el-Fahem, where one of the demonstrators, Mohammed Ahmed Jabarin, 23, was killed and another demonstrator suffered a critical head injury." The casualties are thus framed as an integral component of the events—a natural result of the "incidents."

Like *Ma'ariv*, *Ha'aretz* mentions the Um-el-Fahem casualty on its front page. But while it actually mentions the fact in the banner above its main headline, *Ha'aretz*—just like the tabloids—refrains from any investigation into the circumstances of Jabarin's death and never raises the obvious question: How did it come about that the Israeli police opened fire on Israeli demonstrators? *Ha'aretz* quotes Um-el-Fahem residents saying that "the police and the border police used live fire in some intense clashes that took place in town," and then goes on to state that "in the afternoon, a casualty was reported: Mohammed Jabarin, aged 23, who was killed by the security forces. According to the police, the circumstances of his death are unknown." Did the security forces indeed use live fire? Under what circumstances? *Ha'aretz* makes no such inquiries—and has no answers to offer.

Ma'ariv, on the other hand, is in a position to tell its readers about hundreds of youths who descended to the Um-el-Fahem junction "and started throwing stones, burning tires, and blocking the Wadi-Ara road." At this point, says *Ma'ariv*, the police arrived and "unsuccessfully tried to remove demonstrators from the junction, using guns, rubber bullets, and tear-gas." The newspaper quotes the paramedic who treated Jabarin, who said that Jabarin had "taken a bullet in his thigh and intestines." At what point exactly did the security forces start shooting rubber bullets? When did they move on to live fire? According to what regulations? Was Jabarin indeed one of the youths who blocked the junction? Again, we find no answers. *Ma'ariv* reports other incidents in which security forces opened fire: In Jaffa, "policemen were forced to use large quantities of tear gas and rubber bullets." In Faradies, "usually a quiet and moderate village," demonstrators threw stones at policemen and passing cars, and "at a certain stage," the policemen "responded with live fire." Reporter Amir Gilat quotes Police Brigadier General Dov Shechter, commander of the coastal district, who had authorized live fire in the Faradies junction: "We were in a hard spot, and because we ran out of gas and rubber bullets and the crowd started attacking policemen and passing cars, and because there was no alternative, I let the officers use live fire. The bullets were fired by certain officers, who received meticulous instructions, and only shot at the legs of those rioters who directly endangered human lives."

In each one of these cases, then, the newspapers report that the policemen were in a tight spot, clearly had *no alternative*, and were thus obliged to shoot; and when they did finally shoot, it was only at the *legs* of those demonstrators who *directly* endangered human lives—the lives of the policemen themselves, or of citizens driving by.

All this sounds quite reasonable: One cannot really expect policemen to face a massive riot empty-handed and abstain from self-defense. But some basic facts, most of which could have been gathered that same day, describe a completely different state of affairs. Ahmed Jabarin, for example, was shot in the head, and Mohammed Jabarin was shot from behind—the bullet entered his body through the left buttock, then damaging internal organs. According to several witnesses, both youths were shot at a great distance from Um-el-Fahem junction, apparently by policemen positioned inside a house overlooking the junction. These witness reports make it appear probable that the youths were not part of the crowd blocking the junction and were not endangering the policemen (interestingly, the policemen withdrew from the house after the shooting and regrouped at the entrance to the town).

All the above facts were published about *a month and a half* later, in mid-November, as part of an extensive investigation by *Yediot Ahronot's* weekend magazine *7 Days*. We shall return to this important piece of investigative journalism, but for the moment let it be said that while an investigation of such scope might not have been possible during the first days of the Intifada, the newspapers could definitely have used the facts already apparent by the first weekend of the uprising to question the police version. Possibly they could not refute it the same day, but they could certainly confront it with the demonstrators' testimonies and then raise the obvious questions. Thus, for instance, Arab witnesses kept claiming, from the very first days, that the demonstrations became violent only after deliberate police provocation, and that live fire had been shot at demonstrators who were not endangering any policemen. The papers could have simply let them tell their version, instead of relying exclusively on the police version of the events. They could have also interviewed the doctors who treated the injured and the dead: They would have then discovered that some of the injuries appeared to be the result of live bullets, not rubber-coated ones. They could have paid attention to the repeated claims of Arab Israeli leaders in the months preceding the riots about systematic harassment by the northern police commander, Alik Ron. They could even have interviewed the policemen and border policemen themselves, and not only their commanders and spokesmen, and thus have heard first-hand testimonies of their experience. *Yediot Ahronot's* investigation, published in mid-November, quotes Tal Etlinger of the border police commando unit. She tells a story that leaves little room for doubt:

> I participated in the combat on the Temple Mount. I also participated in the shooting during the Um-el-Fahem riots. But the worst incident was the riot in Tiberias. Hundreds of violent Jews blocked the main road and threw firebombs at us. They almost set fire to our car—luckily, we were able to put it out in time. They threw stones and glass bottles, which crashed between our legs. They crossed every possible red line: my own people were attacking me

with tremendous force. It hurt. The violence there was just as bad as in Um-el-Fahem. According to regulations, we are allowed to shoot when firebombs were thrown. But we handled the Jewish riots differently. It was understood that we came to such demonstrations unarmed. The instructions came from high above. We only used gas.

Beyond the factual discrepancies between the police and the version told by the demonstrators, other questions might have been asked: If indeed the police's supply of gas and rubber bullets ran out as quickly as Brigadier General Dov Shechter testified, it could have been argued that the police failed miserably in preparing for events of this type. After all, dealing with demonstrations is one of the important tasks of the police. On November 17, six weeks after these events, on the same day when *Yediot Ahronot's* weekend magazine published its investigation into the deaths of thirteen demonstrators, the political supplement of the paper carried a related report about long-standing police negligence in preparing for such events. At the time the riots erupted, the police were not well supplied with the means usually used in such situations: water jets, helmets, shields, tear gas, and so on. In this case as well, no investigation was necessary in order to ask why the police had not used such means during the riots. One had only to remember the fact that democratic countries do not use live fire in dealing with demonstrators; that the roads of France were blocked for weeks during the gas strike, only a few weeks earlier, and no one was killed; that Jewish demonstrators—ultra-orthodox Jews blocking roads in Jerusalem on the Sabbath, settlers blocking roads throughout Israel, students demonstrating in Tel Aviv—were never shot. These are completely obvious facts—facts that certainly would have framed the newspapers' reporting if the demonstrators had been Jews. But in the apocalyptic atmosphere characterizing the papers' coverage during those days, and following the spontaneous verdict that had branded Israel's Arab citizens "the real problem," the newspapers had no use for such insights.

The newspapers might also have interviewed the relatives and friends of the deceased, as they regularly do when the victims are Jews. They could have learned a fact or two about their lives, their political stands and personal aspirations. An interview with Mohammed Jabarin's father, for example, would have revealed the fact that the night before he died Mohammed participated in an Arab-Jewish solidarity party. Such an interview would have also given the father occasion to say that Mohammed left home in his slippers to demonstrate with his friends at the junction after watching the television report about the death of the child Mohammed al-Durra. It may be safely assumed that such interviews would have added a more realistic dimension to the picture and would have made it harder for the newspapers to adhere to their one-dimensional vision of the demonstrators as a homogenous mass of incited rioters.

This is the crucial point: A more professional coverage of the events would have elicited the obvious insight that thousands of people do not confront armed policemen for absolutely no reason other than incitement by certain politicians. True, some reporters do mention this aspect of the affair—but their reports appear on the inner pages. In a commentary published on Ma'ariv's page 12, Amir Gilat writes about the Arab Israelis' "accumulated frustration and disappointment with Ehud Barak's policy." He then adds that "this time Arab leaders admitted that they lost control of their people." The newspapers also publish op-ed articles by leaders of the Arab minority—Zohir Andreus in Ma'ariv, Lutfi Mashur in Yediot Ahronot —but none of this percolates to the news items. Ma'ariv does carry a story with quotations from Arab Israeli leaders (on page 12), but in Yediot Ahronot Lutfi Mash'ur's article is the only chance Arab Israeli citizens ever get to express their voice. They are not quoted in any of the news items.

In Ha'aretz the situation is worse. At the bottom of page 3 we find a small item about the Arab leadership's decision to continue the general strike, but the newspaper does not have a single quote from an Arab Israeli leader—neither in the op-ed section, nor as part of any news item. The only writer who deals with the Arab leadership is Uzi Benziman, a veteran representative of the moderate Left. In his commentary, titled **ARAB MK'S SHARE RESPONSIBILITY FOR DIRE RESULTS,** he unequivocally states:

> The Israeli Arabs' parliamentary leadership, which took the lead in the protests against Ariel Sharon's visit to the Temple Mount, thus shares responsibility for the dire results of the bloody riots that ensued. MKs Ahmed Tibi, Abd Elmalek Dehamshe, and Taleb Assana should ask themselves whether they fulfilled their duty responsibly and maturely. No country allows live fire on its security forces, attempted attacks on its towns, blockades of main highways, and deliberate disruption of its daily life. This is what Arab Israelis did on New Year's Eve, and these serious misdeeds were effectively supported by Knesset members representing Arab parties. Such behavior cannot be understood, and cannot be tolerated.

A week later, after the Jewish riots on Yom Kippur eve, Uzi Benziman wrote the following lines:

> On Yom Kippur eve, Jewish hooligans rioted in Tiberias, Hedera, and Or-Akiva; hardly any of the Jewish leaders criticized this behavior. When Jewish hooligans set fire to a mosque in Tiberias, when Jewish punks attack Arab citizens, when youths riot in Tel Aviv, the heads of the state should sympathize

with the attacked minority. This did not happen, because of lack of awareness—which proves how justified the Arab population is in feeling alienated
toward the country and its institutions.

These two paragraphs provide one of the best examples of the newspapers' conceptual and moral confusion—the confusion shared by most
moderate writers. If indeed the Arab population's feeling of alienation is
justified, how can the Arab demonstrations just a week before be considered the simple result of incitement? And if the feeling of alienation is justified, why is it that their "behavior cannot be understood"? After all, the
Arab minority's sense of alienation was not born on Yom Kippur 2000; the
main source of this feeling was not the spontaneous violence of Jewish rioters but rather the institutional violence of the state—the humiliating, ag-
gressive attitude of the police and border police, as well as the systematic
discrimination by governmental institutions. The newspapers ignored all
this in the first week, until the Jewish hooligans took to the streets.

"Inflamed Youths," "Good Arabs":
Listening to the Other Side?

On Tuesday, October 3, the newspapers seemed to be struggling for more
balanced coverage, this time trying to tell the other side's story as well. The
result is complex, interesting, and troubling—mainly because all three
newspapers opted for the same strategy. On the *news* level, these issues
cover the previous day's events just as they did on October 2, relying almost
exclusively on police reports and concentrating on "Arab violence"—on a
day in which five Arab citizens were killed. But at the same time, all three
newspapers sent reporters to Arab towns for background stories about the
atmosphere on the other side. As we have seen, this combination does not
result in a balanced picture: The background stories do sound a different,
more attentive—if occasionally paternalistic—voice, but their insights do
not find their way to the news reports. The background, quite simply, remains in the background.

Unlike its Monday issue, *Yediot Ahronot* now mentions the Arab casualties on its front page. The paper dedicates most of its main headline to the
events within the Green Line: RIOTS IN HAIFA, SHOOTING IN ACRE, CLO-
SURE IN THE SETTLEMENTS. The message is clear: The Arabs are shooting, while Jews are under closure. The sub-headline specifies: YESTERDAY'S
CASUALTIES: 2 ISRAELIS DEAD, 4 ARAB ISRAELIS DEAD, 8 PALESTINIANS DEAD. The cum-
bersome wording is a devastating testimony of the intrinsic paradox involved in the ethnically based definition of Israeli identity: The word *Israeli*

actually stands for *Jewish*, since the "Israeli Arab" casualties are Israelis too. *Ma'ariv*'s banner reads: LIVE FIRE IN NAZARETH AND ACRE; 8 ISRAELI ARABS DEAD. Here the number of casualties includes those who died of their injuries, and an additional victim, a resident of the occupied territories. Note that the "live fire in Nazareth and Acre" refers to shooting by Arabs. *Ha'aretz*'s banner, above its front page headline, reads:

RIOTS ESCALATE: 5 ISRAELI ARABS KILLED YESTERDAY, ANOTHER 2 DIED OF THEIR INJURIES. TODAY: MEETING BETWEEN BARAK AND ARAB ISRAELI LEADERS.

The headlines of the inner pages once again tell the story of the previous day, and they all concentrate on "Arab violence." *Yediot Ahronot*'s headlines are:

LIVE FIRE IN NAZARETH AND ACRE

PREPARING FOR ANOTHER DAY OF BATTLE

SEVERE RIOT IN HAIFA: "THIS IS PALESTINE"

Ma'ariv's headlines read:

GALILEE ON FIRE: POLICEMEN SHOT AT IN ACRE AND NAZARETH

"DEATH TO THE JEWS" CALLS IN UM-EL-FAHEM

FAILED ATTEMPT TO "CONQUER" ROSH-HA'AYIN INDUSTRIAL PARK

COMMANDER RON: "THE DEMON MUST BE CONTAINED"

KEFAR YASSIF: 5 POLICEMEN SAVED FROM ANGRY MOB

"POLICE WILL QUESTION MK'S BARAKE AND DEHAMSHE TODAY"

STONES THROWN IN JERUSALEM AND IN JAFFA

Ha'aretz's headlines are:

ARAB DEMONSTRATORS IN ACRE
AND NAZARETH SHOOT AT POLICEMEN

FIREBOMB HURLED AT JAFFA SYNAGOGUE

JAFFA ALMOST OUT OF CONTROL DURING HOLIDAY

TWO DRIVERS WOUNDED BY STONES THROWN IN LYDDA

The pictures that go along with the headlines tell the same story: demonstrators in Kefar Kassem—5 MINUTES AWAY FROM PETAH-TIKVA—throwing stones; a wounded policeman receiving medical treatment in Um-el-Fahem; demonstrators hurling stones at the entrance to Kefar Kanna. There is not a single picture of the Arab casualties. The very fact that five people were killed merits only sub-headlines in *Yediot Ahronot* and *Ma'ariv*, while *Ha'aretz* only mentions it within the text of the news story. *Ma'ariv* also has a small headline, at the bottom of page 6, stating: 8 ISRAELI ARABS KILLED SO FAR. The report lists their names.

As usual, the stories report the previous day's events from the police viewpoint only: "Yesterday," reports *Ha'aretz*, "the surge of violence in the north increased—policemen were shot in several places, firebombs were hurled, and the incidents spread to the Segev area and the old town of Acre." In Nazareth, reports *Ma'ariv*, "police were forced to make massive use of rubber bullets and tear gas in order to push back rioters. One demonstrator was killed by police fire"; and in Um-el-Fahem, *Yediot Ahronot* reports quite flatly, "the police used snipers to try to paralyze the sources of stone throwing." These words merit a second reading. Snipers shoot at stone throwers, within Israel, and the killing of citizens is termed "paralyzing the sources of stone throwing." As in the other cases, no one raises the self-evident questions.

True, the newspapers do occasionally balance their police-based reports with quotes from some Arab Israeli leaders, who "claim" that the police did their share in provoking the crowds and exacerbating the situation and that the shooting was aimed to kill. But these quotes are no more than formal responses appended to the news items. The leads of all the news stories, as well as their headlines, carry quotes from senior police officers, presented as *factual* reports. Unfortunately, the Arab claims proved much more accurate than the supposedly factual reports of senior policemen. Thus, for example, according to *Yediot Ahronot*'s investigation in November, Iyad Lubani was shot in the chest between the houses of a Nazareth neighborhood, far from any main road, after he caught the tear gas grenade thrown at the demonstrators and threw it back at the policemen. Witnesses testified that he was shot by a sniper hiding behind a fence.

Walid Abu-Salah, a practical engineer, trained in Israel, was shot in Sachnin with live bullets, by policemen standing far from the reach of any stone. Just a few minutes later, in the same place, Imad A'naim took a live bullet in the head. Assil Asli, 17, a devoted member of the Arab-Jewish youth organization "Seeds of Peace," was killed by a live bullet that hit him in the neck. According to various witnesses, he was shot from close range by the police after they hit him with the butt of a rifle and threw him off his feet. In *Yediot Ahronot*'s investigative report, his father, Hassan Asli, described the murder that took place right in front of his eyes:

> Assil, my son, was not one of the demonstrators. He sat about forty meters away from all the rest, with his back to the policemen. He thought they couldn't see him. He was just looking at the demonstration, and wasn't endangering anyone in any way. But suddenly three policemen started running toward him. I shouted and told him to run away; he stood up and tried to get away, but they were already towering above him. They hit him in the back with a rifle butt, and he stumbled and fell. They kept beating him. He called out to me, Father, Father, but I didn't run. I was sure they would only arrest him. I didn't run because I was afraid. Then I saw them coming out of the woods without my son. Assil, Assil, I shouted—and then fainted. I later found out they had shot him there.

On Tuesday none of this appears in the news reports. But the papers do present their readers with a new kind of material: extensive background stories from Arab towns. *Ma'ariv*'s daily supplement features a "special project," under the title **INTIFADA IN THE HEART OF ISRAEL**, with reports from Faradies and Jaffa. *Ha'aretz* publishes a report from Um-el-Fahem along with interviews with Arab Israeli intellectuals. These stories occupy most of the printed material in the three pages *Ha'aretz* dedicates to the events within the Green Line. *Yediot Ahronot* features a story by Yaron London, who visited Um-el-Fahem and Nazareth. London found himself involved in the drama: At the entrance to Nazareth, demonstrators threw stones at his taxi and shattered its windows. With a good dose of self-irony, London writes:

> Shlomi, the skilled taxi driver, obeyed the roadblock commander's signaling and turned left into a side alley. But I was silly enough to direct an amused look at the youth. My look said something like—"I understand you, I too was young once, and have since grown wiser." He read disrespect into my glance, sounded the battle cry, and immediately chased us, together with one of his men, and hurled two rocks at the taxi's windows, which were completely shattered.

In his story, titled **PAIN ERUPTS**, London truly listens to his interlocutors, all "literate, sharp youths," who talk to him about police behavior, about Sharon's visit to the Temple Mount, about Barak, the discrimination, and the Jewish press. He also interviews his good friend Dr. Haled Diab, a Nazareth pediatrician, who points out that while Arab doctors in the world ostracize him as an Israeli, "here I'm a second-class citizen."

"Riots sound a single voice," London finally says. "But among Israeli Arabs there are different voices, and these will be heard again once the riots are over." This is important, but Yaron London's "penetration" behind the lines of violent conflict—the visits to what he terms "the quiet eye of the hurricane"—as well as similar stories from other reporters, all emphasize the fact that the voice of those who *participate* in the demonstrations is never heard. There is an age-based and class-based distinction at play (one may guess that the "roadblock commander" in Nazareth saw this distinction in London's smile), and despite the reporters' good intentions, this distinction helps entrench the traditional perception of Israeli liberals: The news items deal with violent clashes between the police and "youths," "inflamed rioters," and "hot-headed hooligans"—and in these stories, the demonstrators' voice is not heard. It is not considered legitimate. The background stories, on the other hand, generally reflect the voice of older Arab Israelis, professionals and prosperous businessmen. These are the "good Arabs": They criticize the government and the police, they complain about discrimination, but their words are more sedate, more moderate, easier to digest. Some of them implicitly, or even explicitly, point a blaming finger at the young demonstrators. The protagonists of Ma'ariv's story, for instance, are sorry that Jewish customers no longer feel safe to shop in Faradies. "Our inflamed youths have crossed the red line," one of them says; and another explains, "look who took to the streets—hot-headed youths."

These background stories, it should be noted, in no way interfere or connect with the news reports. The writers do not visit the families of casualties or their friends. They do not ask for detailed testimonies about police conduct throughout the events. All this makes life just a bit too easy for the reporters—as well as their readers. Certainly, the demonstrators are more bitter, more influenced by religious leaders; their views are more extreme; their words, as well as their actions, harder to digest. But ultimately, the real story that week was theirs. They were the ones who took to the streets, they were the ones handled by the police with such excessive force. In this sense, the newspapers do not tell the story as it should have been told, in spite of the profusion of background stories.

The Committee of Inquiry:
Between Reconciliation and Incitement

On Tuesday, October 3, Prime Minister Barak met with the Arab Israeli leaders for the first time since the outbreak of the riots. Wednesday's newspapers report this meeting in detail: It appears that Barak was equivocal, giving his interlocutors contradictory messages. He insisted that he would not create an *investigation* committee to check the grim events that had led (at that point in time) to the deaths of nine citizens; but he affirmed that he would be willing to create a "committee of inquiry," that would "clear up and investigate" the events. He expressed his regret about the casualties, sent his sympathy to their families, and announced that "the use of live fire is forbidden, except in case of immediate and palpable life-threatening situations." At the same time, he fully backed the police, especially commander Alik Ron. This was an ambivalent message, from a prime minister quite oblivious to the insult and alienation provoked by his sophisticated phrasing. But it was also the first sign that the state conceded that there was possibly a kernel of truth in the Arab Israeli leaders' consistent complaints.

The newspapers' response is fascinating. *Yediot Ahronot*'s Wednesday edition immediately deviates from its previous indifference to Arab claims: On page 7, we find pictures of six of the demonstrations' casualties and a photograph of one of their funerals. Above these pictures is an article by MK Mohammed Barake, under the headline WE ARE THE VICTIMS OF APARTHEID. Beside the picture appears a bold-lettered headline reading PAIN CROSSES FRONTIERS: TESTIMONIES OF VICTIMS ON BOTH SIDES. On pages 12–13, the story of Dr. Nassreen Assli, a Nazareth clinical psychologist who was beaten by the police, is reported in detail. Her story appears on the front page as well, and there we also find a sub-headline referring to the death of another Arab Israeli on the previous day. While the paper reports the death of Ramez Abas from Kefar Manda in the same laconic tone as on previous days, the overall picture does mark a significant change of heart.

Ha'aretz publishes the same pictures the following day, along with some information about the deceased. Above the pictures there is a long story by Gideon Levi, who attended Ramez Abass's funeral in Kefar Manda. The title is: DISAPPOINTMENT AT FUNERAL IN KEFAR MANDA: LEFT DIDN'T SHOW UP. The next day, Friday, *Ha'aretz* publishes a small item on page 6, under the headline FATHER OF ARAB CASUALTY: COPS KNOCKED MY SON DOWN AND SHOT HIM AT CLOSE RANGE. At this stage, then, *Yediot Ahronot* and *Ha'aretz* no longer insist on the clear-cut demarcation between "rioters" and other Arab Israelis, and some criticism of the police's conduct starts trickling into the news reports, whether implicitly or explicitly.

Ma'ariv's stance, on the other hand, becomes considerably more extreme. The newspaper does report the beating of Dr. Assli in Nazareth— after all, it was a *woman* who was beaten, and the incident had already been captured by the TV cameras—but it refrains from publishing the pictures of the casualties, keeps framing the demonstrations as nothing but illegitimate disturbances of order, and ostensibly sides with the police against the claims made by the Arab Israeli leadership. The cover of *Ma'ariv*'s daily supplement on Wednesday is probably the best example of this stance. Among all the pages in the press during October, it is definitely one of the most troubling. The page displays a text sent in by reporter Sa'id Badran—a harsh, angry declamation he heard from a young Arab Israeli demonstrator, an Um-el-Fahem resident.

> An eye for an eye, a tooth for a tooth. The policemen should beware of us. It was a child's game at first, we amused ourselves throwing stones. But once the police started using live fire, once they killed three of our youths, the rules of the game changed. They have gone one step further down the road—and so shall we. The police should beware of us. We've learned this from the children of the Intifada. We have nothing to lose. Palestine is our country and our land, and the Jews are temporary guests here. We've tried to live peacefully with them, but they have foiled these attempts, they've stolen our lands, they humiliate us over and over again. When a Jew fights with his wife at home, he starts calling "death to the Arabs," as if our blood were free for all. It is time for us to cry "enough!" We are not a minority, we are part of a great Arab nation. The Jews' behavior has determined their fate. Their end is near now, this land will not belong to two peoples. The Jews are no longer welcome here.

This is certainly a troubling statement, but the message it tries to convey is complex. The text does express a stark, nationalist ideology, but it also tells a story of pain, desperation, and bitterness, a story beginning with long years of discrimination and humiliation and ending with the deaths of three of this youth's friends, shot by the police. This demonstrator is actually trying to say something about the *dynamics* of escalation. From his viewpoint, what began as protest against long years of land expropriation by the state, against social, political, and economic discrimination, and against the perceived threat to El-Aqsa mosque, turned into something completely different once the policemen started shooting and killed his friends. This story was repeated by all the demonstrators: None of them expected to be shot by the Israeli police.

Ma'ariv's editors chose to put this text on the cover of their daily supplement. A photograph of the Arab youth's face, partially covered with a red keffiyeh, dominates most of the page. It is a low-angle shot: The demonstrator is looking at the reader from above; his eyes are harsh and narrow. From the reader's point of view, somewhere at his feet, he looks terribly threatening. His right arm is held up high, out of the picture's frame. What is he doing? Waving a fist? Throwing a stone? Holding the Palestinian flag? The alarmed reader can only guess. At the top of the page, in a black, grim box, we find the banner, a single sentence introducing us to the text. It reads:

A HATE-SUFFUSED MONOLOGUE BY A VEILED YOUTH WHO HAS BEEN BLOCKING THE ENTRANCE TO UM-EL-FAHEM WITH HIS FRIENDS FOR THE PAST THREE DAYS

Each and every word of this banner deserves careful reading: First, this is not a monologue of pain, or humiliation, or even pain and humiliation and hatred—it is simply about *hatred*. And it is *suffused* with hatred, just as a sponge is suffused with liquids: The hate has no source, no direction. It is a hate-suffused monologue of a *veiled youth*—not an Arab Israeli youth, not a veiled Arab Israeli youth, but a youth whose entire existence is defined by the veil hiding his face—the veil of Islam. And this youth has been *blocking the entrance* to Um-el-Fahem together with his friends: not demonstrating, or protesting, or even rioting, simply blocking the entrance to his own town, for three whole days.

Under this banner, beside the picture, we find this headline:

"THE JEWS' BEHAVIOR HAS DETERMINED THEIR FATE"

This harsh, nationalistic sentence, shouted by a passionate youth—not unlike the "death to the Arabs" calls of Jewish youths in Tiberias, Nazareth, Jerusalem, and Hatikva—here becomes a formal death sentence, given by an Arab youth, looking down at the frightened, defenseless Jewish reader. At this stage he is no longer an anonymous Arab youth from one town in the Galilee, who has just lost three friends and is swept off his feet by a wave of nationalism. As far as the Jewish-Israeli reader is concerned, he is now the official mouthpiece of the entire Arab nation. This carefully designed page has done away completely with the youth's despair, with his lost hopes and his sense of futility. His words have been used to formulate a devastating indictment against all Arabs wherever they may be—nameless, unidentified, their violent faces veiled. All of them, this page seems to tell the readers, are out to annihilate the Jewish nation.

All the issues that surfaced earlier in the week appear in this page in a condensed version: complete denial of discrimination and repression; racist generalizations; complete obliviousness to the fact that the demonstrations were handled by policemen using live fire; automatic rallying to the sense of siege of a frightened Jewish community; and a complete role-reversal between the sides—the Arab demonstrators are strong and threatening; the Jews are weak, under attack, their fate determined by the Arabs. And all this appears just as *Yediot Ahronot* and *Ha'aretz* publish pictures of the Arab casualties for the first time, just when both of them seem to realize that some alternative perspective is required.

Ma'ariv, moreover, goes beyond this incitement against Arab demonstrators. In Thursday's edition, two days after the government's decision to create a "committee of inquiry," the newspaper dedicates four pages—two news pages and two pages in the daily supplement—to the sense of injury among the police following this decision. The title on pages 8–9 says:

"POLICE LEFT OUT IN COLD."

The sub-headline elaborates:

SAID SENIOR OFFICERS YESTERDAY, IN RESPONSE TO THE PRIME MINISTER'S DECISION TO CREATE A SPECIAL COMMITTEE OF INQUIRY FOR THE VIOLENT CLASHES BETWEEN ARAB DEMONSTRATORS AND THE POLICE. "HUNDREDS OF POLICEMEN WERE UNDER FIRE, AND NOW THE LEGAL EXPERTS, SITTING IN THEIR AIR-CONDITIONED OFFICES, WILL COME AND CHECK THE EVENTS WITH THEIR SCALPELS"

The daily supplement expresses the identical position. The cover's headline reads:

POLICEMEN'S COMPLAINT

The headline on pages 2–3 is

"INSTEAD OF THANKING US, THEY'VE TURNED US INTO TARGETS"

The story, by reporter Amir Gilat, actually starts with the grievances of the residents of the Arab village of Jedida, about the police special order squads, which allegedly entered their village, smashed car windows, shot rubber-coated bullets at house windows and beat up civilians. The story then goes on to report that "as criticism of the police grows, so does their anger." A senior police officer is quoted as saying that "we were the last frontier before the complete collapse of law and order, and instead of thanking us, they've turned us into targets of criticism." The editors chose to feature this officer's words, rather than the complaints of Jedida's residents, in their headline.

There is another crucial point here. The police officers who spoke with *Ma'ariv*'s reporters and tried to shake off the accusations against them unwittingly pointed a finger at the government—thus corroborating some of the most bitter claims of Arab Israeli leaders. Talking about the new committee of inquiry, one of the police officers said: "This is lip-service to the

Arabs, at our expense. The government did not give Israeli-Arabs what they needed, and now the police will pay the price for the politicians' neglect." Another officer said: "These people are not frustrated because of the police, but because of years and years in which the government gave them nothing." These quotes, however, never made it to the headlines. Interestingly, the same points were also made in interviews with senior police officers conducted by the other newspapers, and on one occasion in a conversation with a senior Shin-Beth officer. On October 6, *Yediot Ahronot's* political supplement published an interview with commander Alik Ron, the chief protagonist of the events. Ron angrily asks his interviewer, Nachum Barnea:

> Will [the committee] check why the Rabin government's five-year plan for the Arab sector was never carried out? Will it check why nothing was done for the Arab sector during Barak's year and a half in government?

And this is what he says about the demonstrations:

> Someone must make the decision: where do you draw the red line? Is blocking the road a red line? Or attacking a security facility? Attacking a town? There were no red lines, we only got ambiguities. You finish a discussion with the prime minister, with the minister of internal security, and you just don't know. There are no clear instructions. They should specify the exact meaning of state security. There are no specifications. When the government makes no decisions, I make them. I decided to draw the red line at towns.

And on Thursday, October 5, a senior Shin-Beth officer told *Ha'aretz*:

> There is no entity directing activity in the Arab sector. Their anger erupted following the casualties on the Temple Mount and became a general venting of steam, after years of discrimination.

Six weeks later, in mid-November, a week after the government finally agreed to upgrade the "committee of inquiry" and turn it into a full-fledged "investigation committee," reporter Yoav Itzhak published the following item, hidden somewhere on page 21 of *Ma'ariv's* political supplement:

> Last week, the government decided to create an investigation committee for the events leading to the deaths of thirteen Israeli Arabs in the north. The committee was empowered to investigate both the security forces and the Arab demonstrators and rioters. . . . Over the past days, one man has dedicated every waking minute to preparing his defense: commander Alik Ron. It has come to my knowledge that Alik Ron is busily gathering material— very detailed material, to be precise—about Minister Ben-Ami's statements in different meetings with the police, private conversations he had with some

of the commanders, as well as larger meetings with all the commanders. Alik Ron intends to prove that the police in general, and he in particular, acted according to the policy dictated and/or indicated by the minister for internal security. He claims that the use of live fire—which led to the deaths of many, too many, demonstrators—was in accordance with regulations dictated by the minister, or at least according to clear and/or ambiguous understandings with him. Should Ron succeed in his quest, Ben-Ami might be facing quite a bit of trouble—not unlike the situation which was thrust upon Ariel Sharon (then Defense Minister) during the Sabra and Shateela affair, and which led to his resignation from office.

These statements and reports are dramatic not only because they stand in stark contrast to the official story as told by the newspapers on the first days of the riots, but because they provide the newspapers with the hottest, most relevant, most exciting material imaginable: senior security officials speaking about a systematic failure in the way the government handled the Arab minority, ongoing discrimination, dangerous ambiguity of the politicians' instructions regarding the demonstrations. Each one of the statements could have provided the newspapers with an ideal starting point for a real investigation into the meaning of the October demonstrations. Attempting to protect themselves, the officers let the papers take an inside look into the highest levels of the decision-making process. This, to be sure, is the stuff investigative reporting is made of: Highlighting the officers' statements would definitely be followed by the politicians' attempts to blame the police, and this struggle between the different interest groups would allow the papers to gradually tease out the truth from the web of concealment and disinformation. The opportunity, however, was never seized: The police criticism of the government's policy did not make a single inner page headline, let alone main headlines. The newspapers let the police and the government settle things among themselves without ever facing a single unpleasant question.

Yom Kippur in Nazareth: The "Dimension of Fear"

On Friday, October 6, both tabloids published their regular opinion polls. According to Ma'ariv's poll, 45 percent of the Jewish respondents maintained that the security forces had been "too soft" during the riots; 60 percent said all Arab Israelis should be deported; 32 percent were in favor of denying Arab Israelis the right to vote. According to Yediot Ahronot's poll, 74 percent of Jews defined the Arabs' behavior as treason. Ma'ariv's political commentator Chemi Shalev rightly pointed out that this hatred "was not born yesterday." A poll published a week earlier, before the riots, also revealed "profound hatred" toward Israeli-Arabs. But as Shalev pointed out, this deep hatred was now "compounded by a dimension of fear." Did the newspapers' inflamed, frightened coverage play a role in creating this new dimension, and thus in deepening the hatred? At the very least, it may be assumed that a more balanced, reasonable coverage would have enabled the readers to form a more rational view of reality.

Two days later, on Yom Kippur eve, thousands of Jews—their hatred now compounded with a "dimension of fear"—took to the streets. The newspapers, we have seen in the beginning of this chapter, were worried. But even on the day after Yom Kippur, when alarmed contrition was at its peak, the coverage of the clashes between police and Arab citizens was identical to the coverage of the previous week. *Yediot Ahronot,* for example, does not mention on its front page the two Nazareth residents killed on Yom Kippur eve. The inner page headline alludes to the fact—DEATH AND LOOTING ON THE HOLY DAY—but in order to actually read about the casualties one must reach the end of a long sub-headline. Note the wording: HUNDREDS OF UPPER NAZARETH JEWS DECIDED DAY BEFORE YESTERDAY TO TAKE THE LAW INTO THEIR OWN HANDS AND ATTACK THEIR ARAB NEIGHBORS. THEY WRECKED CARS, BURNED STORES, AND TRIED TO BREAK INTO HOMES. THE POLICE TRIED TO SEPARATE THE PARTIES WITH TEAR GAS AND RUBBER BULLETS, WHEN SUDDENLY LIVE FIRE SHOTS WERE HEARD, AND TWO ARABS WERE KILLED. POLICE: WE DID NOT SHOOT, CIVILIANS MIGHT HAVE DONE IT.

This is quite remarkable: Jews from Upper Nazareth *took the law into their own hands;* the police *tried to separate the parties;* the shots were heard *suddenly,* quite independently of what the police did; two Arabs *were killed.* The report itself quotes police officers denying any connection with the shooting; not a single Arab citizen is interviewed.

Ha'aretz mentions the Arab casualties in the MAIN FACTS box on its front page. The inner page headline is: TWO ARAB YOUTHS SHOT TO DEATH IN VIOLENT CONFRONTATION DURING JEWISH DEMONSTRATION IN NAZARETH. But the report, on page 8, tells the story from the police point of view, which, of course, holds everyone else responsible for the killing—not only the Jewish rioters, but even the Arabs themselves. According to the newspaper, commander Dov Lutsky, from the northern district's operations branch, "emphasized that the police did not shoot live bullets during the events in Nazareth. According to Lutsky, the police do not exclude the possibility that the citizens were killed by Jews or Arabs, who shot them by mistake." Note the phrasing—the police officer *emphasizes*, the police *do not exclude the possibility*—which frames the police as an objective party, asked for its opinion about the events.

Later evidence shows that the newspapers unconditionally accepted police disinformation: According to witnesses, Usam Yezbeq, age 26, was shot in the back of the head by policemen; witnesses said he was killed as he approached a group of youths and asked them to stop throwing stones. He was not even in the group of young people—he was one of the adults trying to restore peace after the Jewish riot. Omar Aqawee—age 42, certainly not a youth—was shot in the chest *after* the Jewish demonstrators left the Arab city.

Ma'ariv, as we have seen before, takes this approach one step further. Its daily supplement cover features the headline—FURY ERUPTS. The sub-headline "explains" the Jewish hooligans' behavior, actually sympathizing with the police:

"IF THE ARABS MAKE LIFE IMPOSSIBLE HERE, WE WILL NOT LET THEM BE, EITHER," SHOUTED MASSES OF RIOTING JEWS IN TIBERIAS AND BNEI-BRAK, AS THEY BLOCKED ROADS AND BEAT UP ARAB BYSTANDERS. THIS WAS THE LAST THING THE POLICE NEEDED: JEWISH RIOTS.

As it turned out, the outburst in Nazareth was the last event in the series of violent clashes within the Green Line, which saw thirteen Arab Israeli citizens killed. Once the level of violence decreased, the newspapers simply lost interest. From that moment on, they concentrated on the Intifada in the territories, which showed no signs of abating. As far as Israel's Arab citizens were concerned, however, the story was far from over. For many months Israel's jails were packed with dozens of Arab youths, many of them minors, arrested during the weeks after the riots on the basis of photos taken during the events. There was no real reason to assume that these youths would disturb the peace, but in a step authorized by the Israeli courts, most of them were arrested until their trials. The newspapers never dealt with this fact, nor with the deeper roots of the events—the entrenched social and economic discrimination against the Arab minority in Israel, and the discriminatory practices of the Israeli police. These, to be sure, were not dealt with by the government either. They are still there, waiting, as it were, for the next outburst.

6

"In All Their Murderous Ugliness"

"No more tears, no more bloodshed," said Itzhak Rabin, over seven years ago, on the White House lawn. "It is time for peace." But it now turns out that Rabin was wrong. We were all wrong. Between the sea and the Jordan River there is still great hunger for blood and tears, and there are those who are willing to provide the goods.

—Nachum Barnea, *Yediot Ahronot,* October 13

The second week of the Intifada—a short week that started the day after Yom Kippur, Tuesday, October 10—was burned into the Israeli collective memory as the week during which it finally "became clear" that the Palestinians had turned their backs on the peace process and were doing everything possible to drag Israel into a bloody war. On the evening of October 9, as the religious holiday ended, Prime Minister Ehud Barak convened a press conference and announced that Arafat had not complied with his ultimatum calling for cessation of all violence, and hence was no longer a "partner for peace." This perceived Palestinian obstinacy purportedly left Barak no choice but to order an escalation in IDF "responses."

The next day the papers claimed that Arafat had given his people the order to stop shooting, but had also released well-known terrorists from jail and had allowed Hamas and Islamic Jihad terror attacks against Israel. Finally, on Thursday, October 12, two Israeli reserve soldiers, Vadim Norzich and Yossef Avrahami, were murdered by a frenzied Palestinian mob at the Ramallah police station. The shocking murder, which came to be known as the Lynch, was recorded on camera by an Italian television crew. The images, broadcast on Israeli television all day long and printed again in the Friday newspaper editions, were appalling. But the Jewish Israeli collective consciousness, clouded with rage and frustration, also found a thrilling, captivating, almost pornographic element in these pictures: They offered a rare, chilling, yet vital glimpse into the "true nature" of the Palestinians—the "murderous," "cruel," "barbaric" core concealed for so long behind a thin veil of diplomacy. On the morning after the Lynch, *Ma'ariv* invited Ron Miberg, a journalist of the effusive type, to write its front page lead article. This is what he wrote:

> The Ramallah Lynch will be remembered as a turning point in the present conflict and a permanent stain on the entire peace process. Our negotiation partners were exposed in all their murderous ugliness, and they've set back the process to the days of [the 1970s terror attacks in] Munich and Avivim. Now we await Muhammad Def's explosives in the hearts of our towns, with stiff backs and clenched fists and jaws. There were those who wondered how we would be able to cleanse ourselves of the shame of that dead child [Mohammed al-Durra]. They will now find that this task is being taken care of by others. The Israeli establishment will do well to retain the images of the slaughtered soldiers. Our blood is boiling. The Apache bows are strung and the counter-pogroms are on their way. What the Palestinians did yesterday will not be forgotten or forgiven. The State of Israel was created so that Jewish corpses should never again lie on the streets.

A similar article by Nachum Barnea, published that morning in *Yediot Ahronot* and quoted at the beginning of this chapter, almost ceremoniously announced that Itzhak Rabin's dream of peace was an illusion.

Both of these emotional texts, as well as others we shall discuss further on, paradoxically convey a deep, almost solemn sense of relief—a feeling that started to take shape in the first days of the Intifada, and now, at the end of this week, became crystallized. The Lynch in Ramallah, Miberg and Barnea seem to be saying, finally made it possible for Israelis to go back, all together, with "stiff backs and clenched fists," to the good old conceptual framework of the pre-Oslo period. It offered the opportunity to find clarity again: Israelis may have *thought* that the time for peace had come, but it turned out they were wrong; the Palestinians, who until recently had *pretended* that the time for peace had come, had now been "exposed in all their murderous ugliness." On the Palestinian side there was still "great hunger for bloodshed and tears," and facing this innate barbarism, Israelis had to continue on course, "retain the images of the slaughtered soldiers," await "Muhammad Def's explosives," rebuild their deterrent power, and, mainly, neither forget nor forgive. At the Ramallah police station, Barnea and Miberg tell their readers, the peace process was finally exposed for what it was: not a diplomatic process of negotiation, but a cruel, sinister, hateful, irrational, unavoidable war. At the beginning of this week, Barak announced that Arafat and his regime were not worthy partners for negotiation; by the end of the week, the entire Palestinian people was declared "unripe for peace."

This chapter, then, tells the dramatic story of the week during which the newspapers completed the de-legitimization process of those who only weeks before were "negotiation partners." As we shall see, Barak's ultimatum, and his hasty announcement that Arafat was no longer a partner for peace, were more than anything else public relations maneuvers—heavy-handed attempts to appease Israeli public opinion and pressure Arafat to make concessions on the permanent status agreement. The newspapers, however, turned Barak's maneuvers into factual reports about Arafat's violent intentions. They then translated a series of half-baked assessments by the security establishment into a terrifying message, according to which Arafat had given terror a "green light." Finally, when the two soldiers were murdered in Ramallah, the newspapers provided their readers with a very partial account of the Lynch and the IDF's retaliatory bombings—thus in effect entrenching the feeling that the entire Palestinian people was implicated in the murder.

Barak's Ultimatum: Combative Rhetoric and Forgotten Facts

On Monday evening, October 9, as soon as Yom Kippur was over, Barak convened his cabinet for an emergency meeting and officially announced, in front of the cameras, that the chairman of the Palestinian Authority had not complied with his ultimatum calling for a complete cessation of violence. A very senior source in his office told the press: "Severe action will be taken." Most ministers supported such action. A senior minister said: "They must be shown their place, but escalation must be avoided." Later that evening, Barak reportedly had a tense phone conversation with the American president, Bill Clinton. He then announced that he had decided to give diplomatic efforts to negotiate a cease-fire "a last chance."

That evening, while printing was already under way, Ma'ariv replaced its main political headline (the newspaper carried two main headlines; the other, as we have seen, dealt with Jewish riots within the Green Line). The original headline had stated:

BARAK: ARAFAT UNRIPE FOR PEACE;
IDF PREPARES FOR FIRM ACTION

The new headline reads:

BARAK: LAST CHANCE FOR NEGOTIATIONS

The revised sub-headline elaborates:

AT A CABINET MEETING EARLY THIS MORNING, FOLLOWING APPEALS FROM
LEADERS WORLDWIDE, THE PRIME MINISTER ANNOUNCED THAT HE WILL ALLOW
MORE TIME FOR DIPLOMATIC EFFORTS TOWARDS A CEASE-FIRE

Other headlines in the newspaper, however, report that the escalation
in IDF operations had already taken place:

BARAK APPROVES HARSHER IDF RETALIATORY ACTION
AGAINST THE PALESTINIANS

IDF BOMBS "TWIN TOWERS"

Yediot Ahronot devoted its main headline to the riots within the Green
Line. The banner above the headline states:

ESCALATION IN THE TERRITORIES: IDF TAKES FIRMER ACTION;
SLIM CHANCES FOR AN EMERGENCY SUMMIT

Ron Ben-Ishai's analysis, published on the paper's front page, is titled:
ARAFAT WANTS ANOTHER KOSOVO. Other headlines in *Yediot Ahronot*
elaborate:

BARAK'S INSTRUCTIONS: HARSHER RESPONSE IN TERRITORIES

PLANNED STEPS: FULL CLOSURE, IMPROVING
IDF POSITIONS AND POWER CUTS

FIRST EVER: COMBAT CHOPPERS ATTACK HEBRON

Ha'aretz's main headline focuses on Barak's plans in this new situation:

BARAK OPTS FOR MEASURES OF "UNILATERAL
SEPARATION" FROM PALESTINIANS

The opening paragraph sums up things as follows:

Starting today, Prime Minister Ehud Barak intends to implement a series of
steps leading to a "unilateral separation" from the Palestinians; these measures will be implemented gradually, and they will become stricter if violence
continues in the territories and if the Palestinians choose to declare independence unilaterally, said a political source in Jerusalem yesterday. Accord-

ing to this source, Barak will also try to create a broad coalition government with the Likud. Barak's ultimatum to Arafat to stop violence in the territories expired yesterday. Israel has announced that the Palestinians have not met its requirements. Barak said: "We called for cessation of violence, but Arafat, who is responsible for the violence, has not put an end to it. We all want peace with the Palestinian people, but their leadership is unripe." Barak said he did not rule out a summit. The IDF now awaits government authorization for firmer action in the territories.

This, then, is what the headlines tell us: The ultimatum has expired, the Palestinians continue with their acts of violence, Barak has come to the conclusion that Arafat is unwilling to return to the negotiating table, and he has instructed the IDF to prepare accordingly. True to his quest for peace, however, he has also left an opening for an American mediation effort.

A closer look at the reports printed in the newspapers' inner pages, however, reveals a different story altogether. First, it turns out that Palestinian violence actually *decreased* during Yom Kippur. This was no coincidence: Early on Sunday morning, October 8, the commanders of the southern and central IDF commands, Yom-Tov Samia and Itzhak Eitan, met with senior PA officials and agreed to make a joint effort toward a cease-fire. After this meeting, the commander of the National Palestinian Forces, Abed A-Razek El-Majaida, announced that joint headquarters would be created with American and Israeli representatives in order to "handle irregular events." Following this agreement, and for the first time since the beginning of the Intifada, Palestinian police tried to prevent "disturbances of the peace" in Gaza. On page 7, *Yediot Ahronot's* reporters tell the story of the Palestinian policemen who actually attempted, if not always successfully, to "restrain demonstrators." They report an incident in which shots were fired at the IDF Judea and Samaria command, "just as a joint meeting of Palestinian and Israeli representatives was taking place there."

All this, to be sure, hardly accorded with Barak's feisty rhetoric. If indeed Israeli and Palestinian officers were holding joint meetings, and Palestinian policemen were trying for the first time, albeit unsuccessfully, to moderate the situation, this should definitely have been highlighted by the papers as one of the most important developments of those troubled days. It should have also raised a crucial question: If Barak knew of this development (and he probably did), why did he decide to make his dramatic announcement on that very day?

Second, a careful analysis of the news stories also reveals that the IDF had already begun to "escalate its response" before Barak's ultimatum expired, and that this new policy was continued after Barak extended the ultimatum, following his conversation with Clinton. We have seen some of this in the headlines: The IDF bombed the buildings known as the Twin Towers at Netzarim junction on Yom Kippur eve and later destroyed additional buildings in the area. The army also uprooted Palestinian orchards and olive groves. The next evening, on October 10, Barak accepted the IDF recommendations, and reportedly allowed commanders in the field to use combat helicopters. That same evening, IDF choppers attacked residential neighborhoods in Hebron. On *Ha'aretz*'s page 6, we find these words by analyst Amir Oren:

> An officer who plays a central role in the IDF operations in the territories said yesterday that the IDF is already at a "hot steel" stage—effectively if not yet formally. This stage implies a certain relaxing of the self-imposed restraint exercised by the army so far. Until now the army has operated according to normal security regulations, namely, exercising reasonable force when facing suspects. . . . In the new situation, regulations for opening fire at suspects are similar to those applying in times of war. Soldiers and commanders need not fear prosecution if it turns out that they innocently shot the wrong target. The IDF still prefers selective shooting at targets that endanger soldiers and civilians, but the clearing of strategic buildings in Netzarim junction will repeat itself in other arenas in the West Bank: the use of tall or dangerously contiguous buildings, which serve as positions for shooting at settlements, army bases, or main arteries, will be prevented. This will be done using fire and explosives.

The picture, then, is even more complicated: it turns out that the IDF was cooperating with Palestinian officers and at the same time releasing itself from its "self-imposed restraint." And, again, this complexity definitely does not accord with Barak's contention that the escalation in IDF operations was causally linked to the expiration of his ultimatum.

What was going on, then? Why did Barak choose to present Arafat with a public ultimatum, and why did he choose to declare him "unripe" for peace on the very day Arafat's forces seemed to start working to restrain demonstrations? Had he really concluded that the cease-fire negotiations were hopeless? Did he come to believe that a cease-fire agreement *could* be reached after all, following his conversation with Clinton? And why did he allow the IDF to "escalate its response" at the same time? How was all that related to the intense negotiations he was simultaneously conducting with Likud leader Ariel Sharon over the possible formation of a national unity government? These negotiations, after all, sent an unequivocal message to Arafat: "The greatest sanction Barak can impose on Arafat is a national unity government," a senior source in Barak's office told *Ma'ariv* on Wednesday. "If this happens, Arafat will understand that the diplomatic process is dead." The only writer who seemed to make an effort to solve this riddle was Aluf Ben, *Ha'aretz*'s political correspondent. This is what he wrote in an article published on Tuesday, October 10:

> As an additional step in his campaign to pressure Yasser Arafat, Prime Minister Ehud Barak decided yesterday to escalate the crisis in relations with the PA and implement a "unilateral separation." Unilateral steps suit the Prime Minister's nature, as he finds it hard to maintain dialogue and negotiation. Barak's ultimatum to Arafat and the threat of Ariel Sharon joining his government are supposed to encourage the U.S. and the international community to intervene and stop the crisis, thus achieving two goals: cooling down the territories and pressuring Arafat into accepting the American peace offer as a basis for the permanent status agreement.

Could this be? Is it possible that Barak decided to *escalate the crisis* in order to pressure Arafat? Is it possible that this had something to do with Barak's difficulties in "maintaining dialogue and negotiation"? At the very least it seems like a fairly reasonable hypothesis—definitely one the papers should have pursued. Take a look, for example, at what Barak himself had to say in the special cabinet meeting convened on Monday evening, October 9:

> We called for the cessation of violence. Unfortunately, Arafat, who is responsible for its outburst, has not done that. No government can agree to the prolongation of this situation. We all want peace with the Palestinian people, but at the present point—and in spite of our generous offers—their leadership is unripe for brave decisions. We must insist on our vital interests; peace will come only when our neighbors recognize the fact that for each side there are vital, non-negotiable points.

Note that Barak is speaking about the *permanent status agreement*, not about the cessation of violence. According to *Ha'aretz*'s front page lead story, he had set two conditions for another summit with Arafat: that Arafat should clearly call for the cessation of violence, and that he should also agree to the American mediation proposal regarding the permanent status agreement. It may be reasonably assumed, then, that Barak was attempting to achieve a very complex set of goals with his public declarations during these days: first, to force Arafat into accepting the American proposal for a permanent status agreement, using the threats of a national unity government, an escalation in IDF operations, and a unilateral separation plan; second, to regain public support and prevent the collapse of his government, with a militant declaration about the end of the diplomatic process and negotiations toward a national unity government; and third, to appease Clinton by agreeing to keep the peace process alive.

Barak, of course, was entitled to run his business as he pleased, but the simple fact is that his strategy (which, obviously, failed miserably) included, as a key component, the manipulation of public opinion—and the newspapers simply helped him along. They reported an "escalation in the territories" when their reporters in the field actually told a story of a *decrease* in Palestinian violence; they reported Barak's consent to continue negotiations "towards a cease-fire" when some of their reporters, and Barak himself, spoke of a clear linkage between the cease-fire issue and that of the permanent status agreement; they refused to acknowledge the significance of the negotiations with Sharon within this overall context; and most importantly, they flatly stated that Arafat had failed the test set by Barak, thus proving that he had turned his back on the peace process. Needless to say, as far as Barak was concerned, Arafat never stopped being a partner; he was in intense contact with him during those very days, and he continued negotiating with him until the eve of the 2001 elections. The newspapers, however, turned his declaration—a tactical, manipulative declaration attempting to further short-term goals on the political and diplomatic level—into a factual statement: Arafat was no longer a partner for peace; the prime minister had said so.

Ha'aretz is a special case in point, devoting its main headline, as we already saw, to the "unilateral separation" plan. This choice of headline is extremely significant, as it sends a clear message that *Ha'aretz* accepts Barak's contention that Arafat is no longer a partner for "bilateral" negotiations. The fact of the matter, however, was that the "plan" was nothing more than a media stunt. Anyone familiar with the topic, including mainstream journalists, knew that no such plan existed—not only because no one had actually planned it, but also because it was impossible to implement. This simple fact appeared again and again in the newspapers' *supplements*, but never in the news section. This, for example, is Nachum Barnea's report on the topic in *Yediot Ahronot*'s political supplement, on October 20:

> The newspapers spoke of a "plan"; actually, there is no plan. Not at the moment. There are wishes and questions, mainly. Separation is a solution acceptable to most of the public. The problem is implementation: How to separate [the Jewish settlement] Psagot and [the Palestinian town] El-Bireh, Pisgat-Ze'ev and Anata, Neveh-Ya'akov and Bet-Hanina . . . what about Kefar-Darom and Netzarim, two Jewish enclaves in the heart of the Gaza Strip; what about Palestinian villages near large settlements such as Ariel and

Beitar-Illit? There is no unilateral solution that can include all the settle-ments, except one: annexing all the territories that are under Israeli control.

Here is Ron Ben-Ishai's perspective, as expressed in *Yediot Ahronot's* politi-cal supplement on October 27:

> Surprisingly, the operative plan is not ready yet, even though the defense es-tablishment started working on it over a year ago, when Netanyahu was Prime Minister and the Oslo [interim] agreements were about to expire. Arafat had then threatened to create a Palestinian state by May '99. Since that period and until this very day, whenever Arafat brought up another date, the papers were pulled out of the drawers and work on the Israeli response was renewed. When the date passed, the papers were returned to their draw-ers. This happened again and again. Even the highly publicized transition to the plan's consolidation phase was—and is—part of Barak's deterring strat-egy vis-à-vis the Palestinians.

Finally, senior commentator Ze'ev Schiff wrote the following lines in an op-ed article published in *Ha'aretz* on October 31:

> The call for separation between Israel and the territories will remain an empty slogan until Israel manages to give specific answers to three main ques-tions: there can be no real separation as long as Israel holds on to all the set-tlements, and if Israel wishes to keep only part of them, are we talking about separation between Israel—including main blocs of settlements—and the PA? . . . Does Israel intend to separate Jerusalem and the territories? . . . Does separation mean stopping masses of workers from the territories from enter-ing Israel, including the severe implications of such a step, especially for the Palestinians?

Whenever Barak tried to put some content into his "plan," he pre-sented the media with a new, impressive turn of phrase: On October 22, for example, the public was introduced to the concept of "the breathing bor-der." A member of Barak's planning team told *Ha'aretz* that "the breathing border is a unique concept, a border between countries that is not a tightly closed border, and not an alligator moat, but an open border zone, where all the economic and civic interaction between Israel and the PA will take place." On October 25 the prime minister's office issued a "clarification," now mentioning a "separation space." It was announced that "interface areas," facilitating the movement of people and goods, would be created "along the line"—which had not been set yet. These, to be sure, are empty words, clarifying nothing. Separation between Israel and the Palestinians is impossible as long as the settlements are not evacuated; it is impossible to create a tight defensive border between Israel and the Palestinians without starving the Palestinian people; and it is impossible to "restore personal safety" while planning an "open border space." All this is quite obvious, yet the newspapers swallowed the PM's "clarifications" whole, and did nothing to nip this manipulation in the bud. *Ha'aretz*—reputedly an independent, critical newspaper—devoted yet another main headline to the separation plan on October 18. It announced: BARAK STEPPING UP PREPARATIONS FOR UNILATERAL SEPARATION FROM PALESTINIANS.

Arafat's "Green Light": Evaluations, Reports, and Headlines

On Wednesday, October 11, one day after readers were told that the ultimatum had expired, the three newspapers handed them a new message: Arafat had decided to change his war tactics. *Ma'ariv's* banner states:

> "ARAFAT ORDERS CEASE-FIRE AND CONTINUED STONE THROWING
> —AND GIVES TERROR A GREEN LIGHT"

Yediot Ahronot's banner:

> ISRAEL: ARAFAT ORDERS HIS MEN TO PUT DOWN ARMS, BUT
> ALLOWS HAMAS TO PERFORM TERROR ATTACKS

And *Ha'aretz's* main headline:

> ARAFAT ORDERS TANZIM TO HOLD FIRE
> IN TERRITORIES AT THIS STAGE

Note the similarity in these headlines' phrasing. They have a common source: "senior officials" in the Israeli defense establishment. These officials told journalists that Arafat had released dozens of "high-profile" Hamas militants from prison on Monday, and thus "allowed the Islamic Jihad and Hamas to commit acts of terror within Israel"; they also said that the heads of the Palestinian security apparatuses received an "explicit order" to hold fire. They estimated that "Arafat gave the order to cease fire because of the UN Secretary General's visit to the region," and made it clear that as far as they were concerned, "the relative calm reigning in the territories yesterday proves that Arafat is able to fully control events." Let us, then, take a closer look at both sides of this equation.

First, Arafat's order to cease fire: Intelligence assessments of this type are obviously legitimate news material, but anyone going through the list of assessments released to the media throughout the week would arrive at the conclusion that they are of limited value. One day earlier, when Arafat's forces still had no "explicit order" to stop fire, official sources told the newspapers that Arafat controlled the field—his forces were still shooting, after all—and that he was determined to continue fighting. *Ma'ariv*, for example, told its readers that according to "military intelligence," Arafat was doing nothing to stop the violence "and has no intention of doing anything in the foreseeable future." *Yediot Ahronot*'s Ron Ben-Ishai provided an amazingly detailed analysis of Arafat's goals and intentions. "Arafat's models are Kosovo, Bosnia, and Timor," he wrote, "and he wants to emulate them in the territories." The escalation in violence, according to Ben-Ishai, "serves this purpose." The next day, updated intelligence had it that Arafat was *again* in control of the field—his forces did, after all, reduce the level of violence—and that he was now worried about the UN secretary-general's visit. The next day, on Thursday, shooting was resumed. Defense sources now presented the journalists with a refurbished evaluation: Arafat was in control—his forces, after all, had resumed shooting—and he was interested in maintaining a high level of violence in the territories. According to Amir Oren, on *Ha'aretz*'s first page, this was because he "prefers to try to drive Israel out of the territories by force, and is now speaking Arabic, not English." Other intelligence sources, quoted by Amos Harel on page two of the same paper, have a different version. According to them, Arafat's control of the field is not complete, "and it is doubtful whether he wants it to be," since "there will always be someone who will use the right pretext to open fire." In other words, even Arafat's lack of control somehow serves his goals.

This shifting line of argument continues throughout the entire period: As the situation gets more and more complicated and unclear, the defense sources' evaluations become clearer and simpler, and they are updated—and changed—on a daily basis. It is possible, of course, that Arafat maneuvered between different positions and occasionally changed his tactics. But it is hard to believe that he changed his overall perspective every twenty-four hours, following each diplomatic development, and it is hard to understand how every one of these dramatic changes proved—unequivocally—that he was in full control of every development. Certainly, obtaining information regarding Arafat's intentions is a difficult and complex undertaking, but a minimal degree of critical analysis, and an independent working relationship with *Palestinian* sources, would certainly have taught the press a thing or two about the shortcomings of its intelligence sources. The fact of the matter is that the newspapers reported intelligence evaluations in a totally factual way. They did not confront intelligence officials with their own previous evaluations, only one or two days old, and they did not check these evaluations against Palestinian reports. Even *Ha'aretz*, which continuously published Amira Hass's reports from the territories, never tried to use her material to challenge the reports sent in by the military correspondents. During the entire period, the front page lead stories—those forming the basis for the main headlines—were written by the military correspondents, reflecting the defense establishment's point of view. Hass's stories, dealing with the very same topics, were published separately, on internal pages: They were framed as an attempt to bring in "the other side's perspective"—which they did—but were never actively used by *Ha'aretz* to examine the overall factual perspective, which it accepted wholesale from IDF and government officials.

The second part of the equation—Arafat's license for terror—captured the main headlines on October 11 and 12. *Ma'ariv*'s main headline on the 12th is:

BARAK: TERROR ATTACKS ARE THE WRITING ON THE WALL

The headline on pages 2–3 of the same paper reads:

"HAMAS AND JIHAD PLAN NOTHING LESS THAN MEGA-ATTACKS"

On Friday, when the newspapers dedicated their main headlines to the Ramallah Lynch, *Yediot Ahronot*'s sub-headline states: PALESTINIANS RELEASE TERROR MASTERMIND MUHAMMAD DEF; SECURITY FORCES ON TOP ALERT. The head-line on page 8 reports, in huge letters: NUMBER I ON MOST-WANTED LIST FREE TO ACT. One of *Ma'ariv*'s front page headlines reads: ARCH-TERROR-ISTS SET FREE: ARAFAT RELEASES HAMAS LEADERS MUHAMMAD DEF AND ABU-HUNOD. TERROR ATTACKS FEARED. The huge headline sprawl-ing across page 9 reads: ARCH-TERRORISTS RELEASED. In its front page MAIN FACTS box, *Ha'aretz* reports: PA RELEASES DOZENS OF HAMAS PRISONERS, AP-PARENTLY INCLUDING MUHAMMAD DEF AND ABU-HUNOD. The headline on page 6 reads: HAMAS: ALL OUR BROTHERS ARE FREE; ISRAEL WILL PAY DEARLY. Next to the headlines appear the pictures of the Hamas leaders, including Def and Abu-Hunod.

How much of this was based on hard facts? Not a lot. One fact was clear: Arafat had indeed ordered the release of a few dozen Hamas and Is-lamic Jihad activists from the PA prisons. However, it was not at all certain *who* was released, and what Arafat intended to achieve with this step. Let us start, then, with the first question: All three newspapers, as we have seen, mention the names of Muhammad Def and Mahmud Abu-Hunod, two of the major, most infamous leaders of the Hamas military branch, on their front pages. For Israeli readers these are terrifying names, and their release came as a shocking piece of news. According to the headlines, they were indeed released. According to the news reports, however, the release was a matter of *conjecture*. First, consider the material presented by Ma'ariv's reporters on October 1, on page 9:

> The first name in the list of released prisoners is Muhammad Def—head of Hamas's military branch in the Gaza Strip and for many years the number one terrorist on the IDF's most-wanted list, the man responsible for the terror campaign in February–March '96. A senior defense source claimed yesterday that Def was released on Yasser Arafat's personal order, following Hamas pressure. It is not yet clear whether Abu-Hunod, a West Bank Hamas leader, was released too.

According to this story, then, it was not at all clear whether Abu-Hunod was released. We find no traces of this lack of clarity on the front page: There, Abu-Hunod's release is presented as solid fact. The parallel story in Ha'aretz offers the critical reader an additional surprise:

> There has been contradictory information regarding the release of Hamas leaders Muhammad Def and Mahmud Abu-Hunod. A senior defense source said that "at this point in time we are dealing with rumors, but in this case we believe them. I am sure we shall verify them very soon."

According to the report in Ha'aretz, then, Def's release was questionable too. Ha'aretz reflected some of this uncertainty in its MAIN FACTS box, but apparently Ma'ariv and Yediot Ahronot were not troubled by these epistemic nuances: They simply turned rumor into fact.

Were Def and Abu-Hunod actually released? According to later reports by Amira Hass, they were not. They may have been transferred from jail when the PA evacuated its buildings and facilities, following Israel's warning that it would start bombing them in reprisal for the Ramallah Lynch, and held in custody somewhere else. According to later reports published in other newspapers, they were released—and sent back to prison only a week later. Either way, during the week we are dealing with, their release was never unequivocally confirmed by the IDF. For intelligence officials, it remained a "rumor"; for readers, it became a fact.

Let us return, then, to our central question: Why did Arafat give the order to release Hamas activists from prison? According to the headlines, this order marked a strategic change in Arafat's policy—he had decided to give terror a "green light." What was the actual basis for this startling piece of news? Consider the following report, published on October 11, on page 2 of *Ma'ariv*:

> In the past days the PA has released about ninety Hamas and Islamic Jihad militants from prisons in the territories. "These are people deeply involved in terrorism, and whose return to the field certainly raises the concern about terror attacks," said a senior Israeli officer. Another defense source said that the release was accompanied by "a wink," which suggested to the terror organizations that they "should set to work." According to this source, the meaning of their release is that Arafat has, in practice, given terror a "green light."

According to this paragraph, then, we are no longer dealing with a "green light" for terror attacks, but rather with a *wink*—which, according to an IDF source, meant that Arafat had, *in practice*, given terror a "green light." Yet again, an intelligence evaluation has become hard fact. But there is more. The next paragraph adds some further details:

> However, other sources in the defense establishment believe that Arafat is not interested in terror attacks at the present time, especially on the eve of a possible summit with President Clinton, and before the Arab summit. "Such attacks would not serve his interests at the moment, because they would only detract from the international support for the Palestinians and improve Israel's image as the victim," said a senior IDF officer. However, he also made it clear that "when so many dangerous people captured after tremendous efforts are released, the danger of terror attacks obviously increases."

It now appears, then, that the troubling intelligence evaluation we read earlier—the one that had turned into front page fact—was merely the evaluation of *certain* sources in the defense establishment. Other sources actually thought Arafat was "not interested in terror attacks." And there is more. On October 12 *Ma'ariv*'s commentator Oded Granot explains the reasoning behind the pessimistic intelligence evaluation:

> At this moment in time, there is no conclusive proof that Arafat authorized Hamas terror attacks within Israel. But there is no proof to the contrary— that he released the prisoners on the condition that they should do no such thing. The main question, it turns out, is how the Hamas leadership will interpret the release of its militants: as a mere wish of Arafat's to threaten Israel, or as a "green light" for killing.

And to complete the picture, Granot also reminds us: "Needless to say, the Hamas military branch can carry out an attack without waiting for more militants to be released from Palestinian prisons."

Let us, then, take stock: Arafat had released a few dozen activists, and certain sources in the security establishment *assumed* this release was accompanied by a "wink"; there was no "conclusive proof" for this assumption, but there was no "proof to the contrary," even though other sources in the security establishment assumed that Arafat was not interested in attacks: Either way, the very fact that militants were released increased the danger of attacks. The defense establishment sounded a warning; it is its duty to do so. Defense sources also had contradictory opinions about Arafat's intentions: Some hypothesized that he wished to give Hamas a sign that he was interested in attacks; others hypothesized that Arafat was actually trying to threaten Israel, a threat of the same kind as Barak's flaunted invitation for Ariel Sharon to join his government. Prime Minister Barak quickly endorsed the more pessimistic evaluation—as we saw, his contention that "terror attacks are the writing on the wall" captured *Ma'ariv*'s headline on the 12th—and the newspapers hurried to present Arafat's "green light" as a newsworthy fact. This, to be sure, is one of the most alarming examples of the gaps we find throughout the month between reality, its interpretation by Israeli officials, and its representation in the media.

The Lynch:
Emotional Expression and News Coverage

By the time the October 13 newspapers were published, the question of Arafat's intentions was swept aside by a stream of horrifying pictures from Ramallah. These pictures, already shown on television throughout the previous day, told an unbearably painful story: One of them showed a Palestinian youth standing at the police station window, waving his hands—covered with the soldiers' blood—at the cheering crowd outside; another picture showed one of the corpses being thrown out of the window to the masses. If any additional proof were needed for the decisive role played by the television cameras in this Intifada—if such proof were still required after the televised death of Mohammed al-Durra—the pictures of the Lynch, the close-ups of the murderers' expressions, their bloodstained hands, the circle of rioters kicking one of the bodies apart, provide us with ample evidence. "This is the most televised battle in the history of mankind," wrote commentator Chemi Shalev in *Ma'ariv*'s October 13 issue; "it is literally a ratings bomb. A small, densely populated country, surrounded by VCRs . . . both sides trading in horror pictures against each other. The television images inflame emotions in Gaza and Jerusalem, in Seattle and Dubai."

The Lynch itself, as well as its visual images, were branded on the Israeli collective consciousness as the most appalling, most traumatic event of the first months of the Intifada. It is precisely because of these feelings of horror and disgust, because of the emotional scar left by the Lynch, that we should critically examine the way the newspapers covered the event. Using Shalev's words, we should ask whether the papers had joined those trading in horror pictures and inflaming emotions or offered their readers a reasonable coverage of the event. The notion of *reasonable coverage* does not mean that the papers were somehow expected to suppress their feelings of rage and shock at such an event. On the contrary: Newspapers are entitled—even required—to express and reflect the sentiments of their readers. This is one of their main roles in the modern state. The point is that newspapers are also required to give their readers credible reports, and the real question is that of a reasonable *balance* between these two roles: Where is the middle point between emotional expression and news coverage? To what extent do the papers abandon their role as providers of information at such traumatic moments, and uncritically—even intentionally—focus on amplifying the painful emotional experience?

Ha'aretz manages the task impressively, though as we shall see, it prefers not to stress the critical questions hovering over the Lynch story—questions we shall return to later. The newspaper's headline reads:

TONIGHT: IDF ATTACKS ADDITIONAL TARGETS IN PA;
WEST BANK CITIES BLOCKADED

The banner above this headline says:

TWO SOLDIERS MURDERED BY PALESTINIAN MOB IN
RAMALLAH; ISRAEL RESPONDS WITH ATTACK
AGAINST TARGETS IN PA TERRITORIES

The newspaper's main headline, then, focuses on more recent events, while the Lynch is mentioned as a reminder, above the headline. Below it we find a picture of one of the corpses being thrown out of the window of police headquarters in Ramallah, and next to it a photograph of one of the victims, Vadim Norzich, as well as a picture of the police station after it was hit by IDF air force missiles. The headlines on pages 2–3 are:

DOZENS OF PALESTINIANS BEAT SOLDIERS
TO DEATH, THEN MUTILATE THEIR CORPSES

ISRAEL: WE SHALL SETTLE SCORE WITH MURDERERS

PA: AN UNFORTUNATE EVENT RESULTING FROM ISRAEL'S POLICY

PALESTINIANS: THE LYNCH—AN EXCUSE FOR IDF ATTACK

ISRAELI AIR FORCE CHOPPERS ATTACK IN RAMALLAH AND GAZA

IDF MAY ENTER PA TERRITORIES

The two other newspapers produce very different representations of the event. Most of Ma'ariv's front page—a weekend, double-sized page— is covered with a picture of one of the victims being thrown out the window. This is not the same photograph that appears in Ha'aretz: it is very fuzzy, most of it showing the police station wall in brown and yellow shades with the window at the center. The corpse, tossed out head first, appears as a featureless black shape, like a shadow on the wall. The overall effect is not that of a news photograph, but of a dramatic, poster-like processed television image. Above the picture, in huge red letters, the headline says:

LYNCH IN RAMALLAH

On the left side of the picture are photographs of the two victims and beneath them a sub-headline, as well as an additional picture of the police station window after it was hit by the air force. The sub-headline reads:

THE HORROR: "I JUST KILLED YOUR HUSBAND"—SAID THE ARAB YOUTH TO THE WIFE OF RESERVE SOLDIER YOSSEF AVRAHAMI WHEN SHE CALLED HIS CAR CELL PHONE. AVRAHAMI AND VADIM NORZICH, IN THE SAME MILITARY UNIT, LOST THEIR WAY, ARRIVED IN RAMALLAH, AND WERE ARRESTED BY THE PALESTINIAN POLICE. AN ANGRY MOB ATTACKED THE POLICE STATION, THEN MURDERED THE SOLDIERS WITH FISTS AND KNIVES. THE CORPSES WERE LATER THROWN TO THE SQUARE, WHERE THEY WERE MUTILATED. BARAK: "AN ABOMINABLE, BRUTAL MURDER." IDF: WE ARE CHECKING THE POSSIBILITY THAT THERE WAS ANOTHER SOLDIER IN THE CAR

On the lower part of the page, below the fold, appears an additional headline: BARAK MAKES EFFORT TO SET UP EMERGENCY CABINET.

The air force's raids on the PA territories are only mentioned in the sub-headline—a point we shall return to later. Next to the headline are two commentaries: one by Ron Miberg, quoted at the beginning of this chapter, titled WE WON'T FORGET—WE WON'T FORGIVE; the second, by Hemi Shalev, also mentioned before and to be discussed further on, under the headline BROADCAST LIVE FROM HELL.

The Lynch pictures reappear on page 3, under the huge headline:

"I JUST KILLED YOUR HUSBAND"

Other headlines in the news pages read:

BLOOD FEUD

PALESTINIANS SET FIRE TO ANCIENT JERICHO SYNAGOGUE

PALESTINIANS TRIED TO PREVENT
BROADCASTING OF HORROR IMAGES

SISTER OF VICTIM LYNCHED SIX YEARS AGO:
"THESE PICTURES MAKE ME TREMBLE ALL OVER"

"HUMAN BEASTS"

Yediot Ahronot spreads two huge pictures on the center of its front page. The first shows one of the murderers waving his bloody hands; the other shows the corpse thrown out the window. Above the pictures we find the headline:

IDF SOLDIERS LYNCHED

Under the pictures, below the fold, another headline reads:

MISSILES FIRED AT RAMALLAH, GAZA, AND JERICHO

Unlike *Ma'ariv*, then, *Yediot Ahronot* gives the Israeli attack its own separate headline. Beneath it appear two pictures: one showing Vadim Norzich on his wedding day, a week before he was murdered; the other showing his wife after hearing the news. Next to the pictures there are two commentaries: one by Nachum Barnea, titled A NO-CHOICE WAR (the opening paragraph of which is quoted at the head of this chapter), and the other by Ron Ben-Ishai, titled THE END OF RESTRAINT.

Page 3 is entirely dedicated to the horror pictures, printed around the central headline THE LYNCH. Each picture has its own headline: BLOOD; HORROR; FRENZY; CELEBRATION. Page 2 tells the story of the Lynch, hour by hour, under the gigantic headline:

INHUMAN

Other headlines read:

NIGHTMARE

NEWS OF LYNCH LEAKED BEFORE FAMILIES WERE NOTIFIED

"THIS IS NOT YOUR HUSBAND SPEAKING; I'VE MURDERED HIM"

"A SHOCKING, NASTY, UNFORGIVABLE CRIME"

"THESE PALESTINIANS ARE ANIMALS, NOT HUMAN BEINGS"

PALESTINIANS GAIN CONTROL OF CNN

IDF STILL CHECKING: WAS A THIRD SOLDIER LYNCHED?

LYNCH ON LIVE TV

FROM HAPPINESS TO GRIEF IN ONE WEEK

Note the following fact, then: In both tabloids, the headlines as well as the huge pictures spread on their first pages do not provide readers with any *news*. All the readers already knew that two soldiers had been murdered in Ramallah, and they had all repeatedly seen the appalling television images. Many of the headlines include the word itself—*Lynch*—which appears again in some of the banners and many of the captions, and is repeated over and over again in the texts themselves, as if the newspapers were trying to extract all the horror encapsulated in this term. The other headlines, those not using the word itself, exhaust the Hebrew language's lexicon of shock and outrage: BRUTAL AND ABOMINABLE MURDER; WE WON'T FORGET—WE WON'T FORGIVE; BLOOD FEUD; FEAR AND TREMBLING; HUMAN BEASTS; BLOOD; HORROR; FRENZY; INHUMAN; NIGHTMARE; SHOCKING, NASTY, AND UNFORGIVABLE CRIME. Some of these expressions appear as headlines of op-ed articles, with writers expressing their rage and disgust, but most of them appear in the *news* section. In this case, the newspapers have simply renounced their reporting function and dedicated the headlines of their news pages to a blunt, raw, unprocessed venting of rage and aversion.

This emotional surge leaves no room for a more sober examination of the event even though the reporters once again brought in extremely newsworthy materials. First, the papers do not dedicate a single headline to the decisive fact that the soldiers' tragic voyage to the Palestinian roadblock in Ramallah, just like the kidnapping of the soldiers on the northern border almost a week earlier, revealed a series of scandalous IDF blunders. According to *Yediot Ahronot*'s Roni Shaked, for example, the soldiers' reserve unit sent them to the Beit-El military base, near Ramallah, in one of their cars. "For some reason," writes Shaked, "no one in this reserve unit paused to think whether they should be sent on their own to such a 'hot' area." It later turned out that army regulations explicitly forbade such a practice. The soldiers lost their way and somehow arrived at the Palestinian police roadblock. They may have passed an IDF roadblock on their way, but the soldiers there let them through, apparently thinking they were on their way to a nearby base. Thus, two reserve soldiers, civilians unfamiliar with the field, were sent by the army in a private car to an unknown zone, practically a war zone—and the newspapers never even mention this fact in a *sub*-headline. *Yediot Ahronot's* story is punctuated with little headlines reporting the stages of the event, hour by hour. The first of these headlines, accompanied by an illustrated watch showing the time 9:30, says: **ON THE WAY TO RESERVE DUTY.** The next, at ten past ten: **GETTING LOST.** The third, at twenty past ten: **THE SOLDIERS ARE KIDNAPPED.** The army failure simply isn't mentioned.

This failure was so profound that when the news of the kidnapping reached the IDF, sources there believed—according to Roni Shaked—that the soldiers were "undercover agents disguised as Palestinians." In Ramallah, of course, people thought along similar lines. The funeral of a Palestinian civilian, Halil Zahran, who was killed in clashes with the IDF two days earlier, had just ended. Thousands of mourners approached the police station, eager to vent their rage upon the two "undercover agents." The mob arrived at the police station and tried to break in. What did the police do in this situation? Here is Shaked's report, based on the eyewitness testimonies of two journalists who were there at the time of the Lynch (note Shaked's rhetorical questions at the beginning of the paragraph):

> We do not know for certain what happens at the police station at this stage: do the Palestinian police beat up the soldiers? Stab them? Shoot them? The Italian reporter says that "the angry mob broke into the police station and demanded that the soldiers be given over, but the police tried to push them back. The policemen were able to hold out only 7–8 minutes, but then were forced to give in. I am convinced that they feared for their lives. Had they continued to resist, the mob would have trampled them underfoot." Palestinian police officers did indeed claim later that they tried to stop the mob but were not able to. Etti Wieseltir, a producer for one of the foreign television channels, was one of the few journalists at the scene. She also had the impression that the police tried to stop the Lynch, but not forcefully. "They only yelled. They had clubs, there were many of them, but they did nothing. I think they tried to stop the crowd, but with shouts—not force."

Let us try to understand this: Two journalists *who were at the scene* testify that the policemen at the station tried to prevent the Lynch. Possibly they did not use enough force, possibly they feared for their lives, but they clearly did not join the riot. *Ha'aretz's* Amira Hass reports that about thirteen Palestinian policemen were wounded while trying to stop the Lynch, and a similar claim appears in Ma'ariv's report. None of the newspapers thought these testimonies worthy of highlighting.

Moreover, the two witnesses only saw what happened *outside* the building, which is what the Italian television cameras captured—but in this paragraph Shaked uses a series of *rhetorical questions* to suggest that perhaps the policemen beat/tortured/shot the soldiers inside the station before the mob broke in. There is no evidence to back up this statement—there can be no such evidence—except for the fact that some uniformed people were photographed among the Lynch perpetrators. But note the fact that the Ramallah station police wear black uniforms, while the policemen seen participating in the Lynch wore combat fatigues. This fact, mentioned only by Amira Hass, the one Israeli reporter who spends all her time in the territories, indicates that the policemen who participated in the Lynch may have come to the station with the funeral crowd. Some pictures may be worth a thousand words, but their interpretation sometimes requires *verbal* investigation.

Three days later, on Monday, October 16, reporter Gideon Levi tried to conduct such an investigation. He interviewed the Ramallah station commander, Colonel Camal A-Sheikh. The interview was published, quite appropriately, on Ha'aretz's front page. The police commander defined the Lynch as "the PA's greatest failure" and as "an insult to the Ramallah station and to me personally." According to A-Sheikh, there were twenty-one policemen at the station when the mob broke in—some of them administrators and cooks. Most policemen were scattered throughout the city because of the demonstrators' funerals that were taking place at the time. He said that the few policemen at the station were unable to stop the raging crowd, and he claimed that when the mob tried to break into the station he moved the Israeli soldiers to the safest room in the building and even offered one of them a cigarette before the mob broke into the room. He then tried to protect the soldiers but was shoved away.

Do we have to believe Colonel A-Sheikh's story? Of course not. He may have told Levi a pack of blatant lies. This is always possible. But once again the crucial point is that a reasonable presentation of the other side's version should not depend on its factual truth. The colonel may have lied to Levi, but he may have also been telling the truth, and he may have been telling a partial truth—at the very least, his story tallies with the testimonies of both witnesses and is not refuted by the pictures. This possibility is simply too important to be ruled out *a priori*: the sheer horror of the Lynch is beyond dispute, but there is still a tremendous difference between murder by a frenzied mob, on its way back from yet another funeral, and an organized murder orchestrated by the Palestinian police in Ramallah. This difference bears directly on the central question of this chapter—the one having to do with the "true nature" of the Palestinians. It may have been hard to remember, on such a day, that murderous acts committed by mobs do not attest to the "true nature" of an entire people, or the "true intentions" of their regime, but the newspapers were nevertheless obliged, as news providers, to present their readers with more than a passive reflection of their own rage, and to remind them of this distinction.

Obviously, those components of reality suppressed by the newspapers (the IDF failure, the rumors about undercover agents, the atmosphere created by constant Palestinian funerals, the consistent claims about the Ramallah police's attempts to prevent the Lynch) would not have lessened the outrage provoked by the event; but they would definitely have given the story a more credible, more balanced, more complex dimension. They would have gone some way toward divesting it of its apocalyptic significance, and toward incorporating it in the appropriate context. After all, the Palestinians remained Israel's "negotiating partners" even after the Lynch: A summit was convened in Sharm el-Sheikh in Sinai only four days later. And the Lynch was not the only terrible act of violence committed during those days. It was part of a total reality—a violent, tragic, complex, and thoroughly paradoxical reality. The tabloids, however, turned it into an event of mythical significance, disconnected in time and in space, that revealed once and for all the "murderous nature" of each and every Palestinian. And it was as such that the Lynch was engraved in the Israeli collective memory throughout the Intifada.

Within this context, the papers' coverage of the Israeli retaliation bombings exudes satisfaction with the "natural response," pride about the "precise" hits, and a slight dissatisfaction with the "overly restrained" nature of the response. Ma'ariv dedicates two pages to the bombings. The headline on page 5 says:

"MISSILES ON RAMALLAH AND GAZA ARE JUST A WARNING"

The headline on page 6 stresses yet again:

ISRAEL WARNED SENIOR PA OFFICIALS
BEFORE CHOPPERS STRUCK

Yediot Ahronot also dedicates two pages to the bombings. The headline, spread over both pages, reads:

DOZENS OF MISSILES DEEP INSIDE TERRITORIES

Seven pictures proudly parade around this headline, each with its own identical headline—THE TARGET: the transmitters of "Voice of Palestine"; the Palestinian naval bases in the Gaza Port; the Ramallah police station, and so on. Alex Fishman's commentary is titled THIS IS ONLY THE BEGINNING:

> October 12 might go down in the annals of history as a critical turning point in the relationship between Israel and the Palestinians. Since yesterday, both sides are ready for all-out war. We are no longer talking of Palestinian security officers taking the initiative, or scattered shooting by Tanzim men. There is talk in the PA about a declaration of war. By this they mean that uniformed Palestinians will act against Israel in an established and organized way—in the territories but also within the Green Line—together with the Islamic Jihad and Hamas. The IDF is indeed preparing for war. The alert was raised yet another notch: complete closure of all the territories, and blockades on all large Palestinian cities in the West Bank, with no one allowed in or out. The tanks have already been deployed. . . . Yesterday the air force choppers attacked very specific and select targets in the Palestinian towns. This was only a hint. Israel made it clear to the Palestinians exactly how it intends to act in case of war. Next time there will be no two-hour warning to enable people to flee in time.

The headlines and Fishman's article repeatedly emphasize the careful choice of targets, the warnings given to the PA before missiles were launched, and the "specific and selective" nature of the operation. As far as the Palestinians were concerned, however, there was nothing "restrained," "selective," or "specific" about the IDF bombings. From the Palestinian point of view, these bombings marked a dramatic escalation in Israeli violence, now directly and collectively turned against them, making use of the most advanced technological warfare. In a tiny item on Ma'ariv's page 6, Eli Buhadna reports that "yesterday, convoys of Palestinian vehicles were seen leaving the city of Gaza to the southern part of the strip. The Palestinians hope that the IDF won't strike in that area." For those residents fleeing from Palestinian towns, the bombings were possibly the most traumatic, constitutive event of the first weeks of the Intifada. And as these bombings were accompanied by complete, suffocating closure of Palestinian towns— with "no one allowed in or out"—the Israeli operation was naturally perceived as a "declaration of war." This is what the PA's senior spokesmen were referring to in the international media throughout October 12. They were not talking about preparations for war on *their* side. This basic insight is voiced only by Ma'ariv's commentator Chemi Shalev:

Certainly, many Palestinians were upset by the horrible Lynch in Ramallah. But even they will probably remember this day by another picture—that of Israeli combat choppers bombing defenseless Palestinian targets. This will be the image engraved in their memories, symbolizing predatory American technology crushing their very being. They have taken us back to a primitive stone age; we have given them a glimpse into a cruel future.

From the point of view of those Palestinians who fled from their homes, the bombings were also an incredibly *arbitrary* act: Israel had defined the bombings as an act of retaliation for the Ramallah Lynch, but even the harshest analysts did not claim that that atrocity was carried out under orders of Arafat or any of his senior staff. From the Palestinian point of view, the bombings were only loosely related to the Lynch and were interpreted as yet another crackdown message to the PA, a direct sequel to the declaration that the ultimatum had expired and to the "escalated response" at the beginning of that week. Could there be some truth to this? Definitely so, according to an analysis by *Ha'aretz*'s Ze'ev Schiff, published on page 2 on October 13:

It was clear that Barak authorized the operation with one eye directed to Israeli public opinion, which was appalled by the Ramallah Lynch, and another eye directed toward Egypt and the Arab world, which were preparing for the summit. All this was done while bearing in mind that there is still a chance to resume negotiations with the Palestinians and avoid an all-out military conflict. Actually, this was not a punitive operation in retaliation for the Lynch of two reserve soldiers who had lost their way, but a hint to the PA, a "signaling operation."

All this is of crucial importance, but the three newspapers—including *Ha'aretz,* which published Schiff's analysis—endorsed the definition of the bombings as a direct "response" to the Ramallah Lynch, and thus gave Barak, who had his "one eye directed to Israeli public opinion," the support he needed in the internal political arena. And as we saw in chapter 4, the very fact that Barak used considerable military force in order to appease public opinion played a crucial role in the unfolding of events throughout the Intifada. The newspapers not only failed to point out this pattern, and warn against it, but actually played a central part in its perpetuation.

In the years after the Oslo agreement, the Israeli public suffered severe blows, as hard as the Ramallah Lynch: Dozens of Israelis were killed in terror attacks on buses in Tel Aviv, Ramat-Gan, and Afula. But the prime ministers at the time, Itzhak Rabin and Shimon Peres, emphatically distinguished between the perpetrators and their commanders on the one hand, and the Palestinian people and their leadership on the other. Ehud

Barak actually adopted Benjamin Netanyahu's position on this issue: The Palestinian people and the Palestinian Authority were considered a monolithic entity, and any violent action of the Palestinians was perceived as absolute and immediate proof of Arafat's evil intentions. The IDF bombing of Palestinian towns following the Lynch expressed this view more eloquently than a thousand speeches—and made it easier for the newspapers to provide their readership with an inflamed coverage that convicted the entire Palestinian people of each and every violent action.

This, then, is the second vicious circle characterizing the relationship between Barak, the press, and public opinion throughout the Intifada: Barak systematically de-legitimized Arafat and his regime; the newspapers reflected this strategy in a completely uncritical way; public opinion predictably responded with a clamor for severe action against Arafat; Barak "escalated" his responses; the Palestinian response inflamed public opinion even further. At the end of the day, this strategy accomplished much more than it set out to achieve: It persuaded the overwhelming majority of Israelis, even those who had traditionally supported the peace process, that Arafat was simply not interested in peace; it helped put an end to the diplomatic process; and it determined Barak's own political fate.

7

"We Have Turned Every Stone"

The Palestinians do not want peace? Too bad, but never mind.
Let them create their state, and Israel will cling to its holdings
and see where they are headed. Should the Likud agree, a
long-term unity government, with Ariel Sharon, Benjamin Netanyahu, and others, may be an option.

—Dan Margalit, *Ha'aretz,* October 12

On Monday, October 16, only four days after the Palestinians were "exposed in all their murderous ugliness," Ehud Barak and Yasser Arafat met
again, at the Sharm el-Sheikh summit in Sinai. The newspapers reporting
the planned summit, on Sunday the 15th, expressed considerable pessi-
mism: with all due respect to President Clinton's feverish efforts, what could
possibly be expected of this summit, when Arafat showed no signs of changing his violent ways? *Yediot Ahronot*'s main headline says:

SUMMIT—UNDER SHADOW OF TERROR ATTACK THREAT

The banner and the sub-headline elaborate:

> BARAK, CLINTON AND ARAFAT DUE TO MEET TOMORROW IN
> SHARM EL-SHEIKH TO NEGOTIATE CEASE-FIRE. SHARON:
> WE WILL NOT JOIN THE GOVERNMENT TILL RESULTS OF TALKS
> ARE PUBLISHED
>
> CONCERN IN THE U.S.: TALKS MAY FAIL. LIKUD BACKS PM: SUPPORTS DELIBERATIONS
> FOR A CESSATION OF VIOLENCE. SECURITY ESTABLISHMENT ALERTS: HAMAS AND
> JIHAD WILL TRY TO BRING ABOUT A CANCELLATION OF THE SUMMIT. FORMER HEAD
> OF SHIN-BETH AMI AYALON: ARAFAT HAS LOST CONTROL

Ma'ariv's main headline also attempts to lower readers' expectations:

> PESSIMISM ON WAY TO SUMMIT; BARAK AND SHARON PLANNING
> "EMERGENCY GOVERNMENT" AFTERWARDS

The banner reports the latest security assessment:

FEARED TERROR ATTACK INTENDED TO
UNDERMINE SHARM SUMMIT TOMORROW

The sub-headline elaborates:

CONCERN: ARAFAT WILL RESUME "PARIS TACTICS" AT THE SUMMIT. BARAK AND
SHARON ARE CLOSE TO AN AGREEMENT ON A SHARED DIPLOMATIC PLAN,
INCLUDING CONTINUED STATUS QUO IN JERUSALEM. RISING OPPOSITION
TO EMERGENCY GOVERNMENT IN LIKUD AND THE LEFT.

Ha'aretz's main headline reports:

SUMMIT IN SHARM TOMORROW, ATTEMPT TO ACHIEVE
CEASE-FIRE; RENEWAL OF NEGOTIATIONS IS NOT EXPECTED

The sub-headline adds:

PARTICIPANTS: CLINTON, BARAK, ARAFAT, MUBARAK, AND KING ABDALLAH; DEFENSE
ESTABLISHMENT IS SKEPTICAL ABOUT CHANCES FOR A COOL-DOWN

Two days later, on Tuesday, October 18, a few hours after the summit
ended with a bilateral cease-fire agreement, it "turned out" again that the
pessimistic assessments were right on the mark: Arafat had been put to the
test—and had failed yet again. He had indeed signed the agreement in
Sharm, but at the very same time had ordered his people to resume shooting on Gilo—the contradiction already discussed in the opening chapter of
this book. Two days later a group of settlers who had taken their children
on a day trip to Mount Eival in the Nablus area were shot at by Palestinians. One of the settlers, Benjamin Herling from Kdumim, was killed. Four
were wounded. Once again, the prime minister had "no choice." On the
next day, Friday, October 20, one day before the Arab leaders' summit in
Cairo, Barak announced that Israel was taking "a time-out" from the
diplomatic process. On Saturday night, after the Cairo summit ended with
a moderate condemnation of Israel, the prime minister's office released the
following statement:

Given that the Palestinians did not comply with the Sharm el-Sheikh understandings, and as a result of the Arab countries' summit in Cairo, this
time-out is necessary. Our purpose is to reassess the state of the diplomatic
process in light of the past weeks' events. The prime minister reiterates that
Israel will continue striving for peace and searching for a way to attain it.
Only someone who is blind on the diplomatic as well as the defense level can
think it possible to continue negotiations, as if nothing had happened. This
time-out is a self-evident necessity, dictated by common sense.

And senior sources in Barak's office added:

> Those who try to represent the time-out as an Israeli-initiated interruption of
> the diplomatic process are wrong. They weaken our position in the entire
> world, and mislead others in a way that furthers the arguments raised against
> us by the Palestinians and the Arab world.

With Barak's decision to "reassess" the diplomatic process, we approach the
end of this book. The present chapter will focus on the Sharm el-Sheikh
summit and Barak's "time-out," and will continue with a more compre-
hensive investigation of the newspapers' coverage of the diplomatic front:
Barak's diplomatic style; his "generous offers" to Arafat; Arafat's "rejection"
of these offers. These issues, to be sure, lie at the very heart of the acute
sense of betrayal shared by most Israelis throughout October 2000 and ever
since: the belief that Barak did everything possible to achieve a final settlement with the Palestinians, only to discover—in Dan Margalit's words,
quoted in the beginning of this chapter—that they simply "do not want
peace." The diplomatic events of the third week of the Intifada will thus
provide us with a fascinating example of the way the newspapers systematically suppressed Barak's decisive contribution to the collapse of the diplomatic process.

The Sharm el-Sheikh Summit: Low Expectations and Hidden Interests

Let us return, then, to the Sharm el-Sheikh summit and follow the story as
told by the headlines. The members of the Israeli delegation were already
in Sharm el-Sheikh on Sunday, October 15. On Monday the 16th the newspapers reported the preparations for the summit, the atmosphere at the
hotel, and the low expectations shared by Barak and his people regarding
the coming talks.[1] The headline on *Yediot Ahronot*'s front page says:

LOW EXPECTATIONS AT SUMMIT

The sub-headline informs readers that

**ARAFAT THREATENED TO TORPEDO THE SUMMIT TILL THE VERY LAST MINUTE.
STRICT SECURITY MEASURES AND A CHILLY RECEPTION FOR ISRAELI DELEGATION
MEMBERS IN SHARM EL-SHEIKH**

The same injured tone—the one we encountered in the coverage of the
Paris summit—is reflected in the inner page headlines. The main headline
on pages 10–11 reads: **AT LAST MOMENT ARAFAT THREATENS TO TOR-**

PEDO SUMMIT. Next to this headline, beside the logo HOSTILE ATTITUDE we find the headline "DO YOU REMEMBER THE PALESTINIAN CHILD?" The sub-headline explains: ISRAELI "VANGUARD" IN SHARM EL-SHEIKH RECEIVES A CHILLY RECEPTION FROM EGYPTIANS. On page 10 we find two headlines:

IN SPITE OF TENSION BARAK INTENDS TO SHAKE ARAFAT'S HAND

CROWDED DELEGATION: PM TAKES ALONG TEN SPOKESMEN

The headline on page 14 deals with the IDF's assessments before the summit. It leaves little room for doubt:

"ARAFAT NOT INTERESTED IN SUCCESSFUL
SUMMIT—TERROR ATTACKS TO COME"

Ma'ariv's headlines tell a similar story. The main one reads:

TO SHARM SUMMIT—WITH HEAVY HEART

The sub-headline tells the readers:

ISRAEL WILL SETTLE FOR A CEASE-FIRE AGREEMENT. NEGOTIATIONS FOR
"EMERGENCY GOVERNMENT" TO CONTINUE AFTER SUMMIT

And the banner removes all doubt regarding the chances for a summit breakthrough:

BARAK: PRESENT PALESTINIAN LEADERSHIP UNRIPE FOR PEACE

The inner page headlines are:

CHANCES FOR AGREEMENTS AT SHARM—"SLIM"

CHIEF OF STAFF: "QUIET IN TERRITORIES WILL NOT LAST"

AN "ARMY" OF ISRAELI SPOKESMEN WILL
"CONQUER" SHARM EL-SHEIKH

AMERICAN GOAL: KEEP THINGS QUIET TILL
PRESIDENTIAL ELECTION

PALESTINIANS: "ARAFAT IS PUTTING TO WASTE
ALL OUR SACRIFICE"

THREATS: TOP-GRADE TERROR ALERT CONTINUES

INCITEMENT: "OH BROTHERS IN FAITH, SLAUGHTER THE JEWS"

The last headline, it turns out, is also related to Barak's spokesmen's effort before the summit. The call to slaughter Jews was part of a sermon by a Palestinian preacher, Ahmed Abu-Halbiah, broadcast on Palestinian television. Barak brought the videotape to Sharm in order to present it to the international press.

And finally, *Ha'aretz*'s main headline reads:

SHARM SUMMIT TODAY; BARAK: AGREEMENT TO END
VIOLENCE IS POSSIBLE

The sub-headline elaborates:

AT THE SUMMIT CLINTON WILL TRY TO SET A TIMETABLE FOR RENEWAL OF
NEGOTIATIONS; IDF PESSIMISTIC ABOUT SUMMIT'S CHANCES OF SUCCESS

The headlines on page 2 are:

ISRAEL PREPARING FOR "INFORMATION OFFENSIVE"

CLINTON: EXHAUSTED, FRUSTRATED, DISILLUSIONED

ON WAY TO SHARM: FAREWELL PARTY FOR PEACE TEAM

"SLIM CHANCES OF SUCCESS," SAY SOURCES IN PA

IDF: TANZIM SHOULD BE MADE TO DISARM

This, then, is the situation on the eve of the summit, according to the newspapers: Arafat is threatening to torpedo the summit; he is not interested in its success; terror attacks are on the way; the IDF is very pessimistic; the Israeli delegation has already received a chilly reception in Egypt; and Barak, who does not believe that the present Palestinian leadership is ripe for peace, nevertheless takes along an army of spokesmen and departs for Sharm, and he even intends to shake Arafat's hand.

The next day, Tuesday the 17th, the newspapers report the nerve-wracking drama of the first day of talks. *Yediot Ahronot*'s main headline reads:

NIGHT OF CRISES

The banner and the sub-headline explain yet again, just as they did on the previous day, that it is hard to expect any real results:

SEVERE CLASHES IN TERRITORIES YESTERDAY. DEFENSE
ESTABLISHMENT: ESCALATION ENCOURAGED BY ARAFAT

FOREIGN MINISTER BEN-AMI'S ASSESSMENT YESTERDAY: SUMMIT WILL END WITH
AN AMERICAN CALL FOR A CEASE-FIRE. ISRAELI SOURCES ASSESSED: VIOLENCE
WILL NOT STOP

Under the sub-headline appear the pictures of Clinton, Barak, and Arafat.
Each picture has a small, one-word headline above it: Barak, according to
Yediot Ahronot, is PESSIMISTIC; Clinton is EXHAUSTED; and Arafat is sim-
ply COMPLACENT. Three words is all it takes for the paper to sum up the
Sharm situation: Clinton is putting in a tremendous effort to salvage peace;
Barak, all too familiar with the situation, is not optimistic; and Arafat just
isn't interested.

And there is more. The headline of pages 2–3 tells readers:

BARAK: I'M FED UP WITH ARAFAT

And the sub-headline describes the atmosphere during the talks:

TENSE ATMOSPHERE DURING SUMMIT TALKS YESTERDAY. BARAK IS ANGRY WITH
THE PALESTINIANS AND OFFENDED BY THE EGYPTIANS. THE PALESTINIANS ARE
CROSS WITH THE AMERICANS; BEN-AMI "GOT HIS" FROM SAEB ERIQAT—AND
ANSWERED BACK IN KIND. AFTER MIDNIGHT YESTERDAY, ISRAELI DELEGATION
SOURCES ASSESSED A CEASE-FIRE AGREEMENT AS POSSIBLE. BUT SENIOR ISRAELI
SOURCE REMAINS PESSIMISTIC: EVEN IN CASE OF AN AGREEMENT, CEASE-FIRE
WILL NOT LAST

Additional headlines are:

CLINTON'S SPEECH: "IN SPITE OF EVERYTHING, DO NOT
GIVE UP ON PEACE"

MUBARAK'S SPEECH: "ANARCHY MIGHT SPREAD"

WHAT A MEETING—CLINTON AND BARAK CLOSETED
IN RESTROOMS FOR FIFTEEN MINUTES

FRUSTRATED ADVISOR: "ARIK [SHARON] CAN STAY CALM,
THERE'S NOTHING GOING ON HERE"

EMBARRASSING INCIDENT—BARAK TO EGYPTIANS: "RETURN MY
MOBILE PHONE IMMEDIATELY!"

INFORMATION OFFENSIVE—ISRAELIS DISTRIBUTE VIDEOTAPE OF
RAMALLAH LYNCH

PREACHER WHO CALLED FOR MURDER OF JEWS ARRESTED

"SHARON HAS RIGHT TO VISIT TEMPLE MOUNT"

Ma'ariv's perspective is very similar, yet somewhat more balanced. The main headline says:

DIFFICULTIES AT SUMMIT

The banner and sub-headline elaborate:

SHARM EL-SHEIKH: ALL PARTIES YELL AT EACH OTHER. BARAK, YESTERDAY: SITUATION IS COMPLICATED

CLINTON STRIVING FOR A "PRESIDENTIAL ANNOUNCEMENT" CALLING FOR CESSATION OF VIOLENCE; SHOOTING IN THE TERRITORIES: IDF ON ALERT IN CASE THE SUMMIT FAILS. POLITICAL ESTABLISHMENT GETTING READY FOR POSSIBLE EMERGENCY GOVERNMENT

Under the sub-headline are the three pictures already encountered in *Yediot Ahronot*—without the "explanations." The caption reads: LEADERS' FACES RE-VEAL TENSION. *Ma'ariv*, unlike *Yediot Ahronot*, at least concedes that Arafat is not just strolling through the hotel grounds, enjoying his vacation.

The headline on pages 2–3 reads SHOUTING SUMMIT. The sub-head-line elaborates:

BARAK AND ARAFAT DID NOT MEET OR TALK. DELEGATES EXCHANGED ACCUSA-TIONS AND SHOUTS. CLINTON AND MUBARAK PRESSURED FOR SOME AGREEMENT. BARAK REFUSED TO DISCUSS A RENEWAL OF THE DIPLOMATIC PROCESS. BOTH SIDES REJECTED A COMPROMISE PROPOSAL BY MEDIATOR TERJE LARSEN. NEVER-THELESS, SECURITY TALKS WERE HELD, AND THE SUMMIT WILL CONTINUE TODAY

Additional headlines are:

THEY ALL SHOUT AT EACH OTHER

IN SPITE OF DISPUTES, THERE'S STILL A CHANCE
FOR AN AGREEMENT

MEDIA BLACKOUT; JOURNALISTS WATCH CEREMONY
ON CHANNEL 2

"RARE ITEM": ISRAELI FLAG

CLINTON'S SPEECH: "GET THE PEACE PROCESS GOING"

MUBARAK'S SPEECH: "AVOID SETTING FIRE TO REGION"

ISRAELI SPOKESMEN DISTRIBUTED LYNCH VIDEOTAPES

ANGRY DEMONSTRATIONS IN ARAB COUNTRIES: "START JIHAD
AGAINST ISRAEL"

IDF WARNING: DETERIORATION IN TERRITORIES
SHOULD SUMMIT FAIL.

And finally, *Ha'aretz*'s main headline adds an element that never appeared in *Yediot Ahronot*'s headlines, and is only mentioned in *Ma'ariv*'s sub-headline on pages 2–3:

SHARM SUMMIT: BARAK ASKS CLINTON TO POSTPONE RENEWAL OF NEGOTIATIONS

The sub-headline adds:

DELIBERATIONS CONTINUE TONIGHT TO PREVENT SUMMIT FAILURE

The lead story on *Ha'aretz*'s front page "explains" Barak's request:

> Prime Minister Ehud Barak asked President Bill Clinton to postpone the renewal of the Palestinian-Israeli diplomatic process for a period of "weeks or months," said a senior source in the Israeli delegation in Sharm el-Sheikh yesterday. Barak had two conversations with Clinton yesterday, and there was disagreement regarding the timetable and format for renewal of the process. According to the Israeli source, "the correct way to resume negotiations—if indeed they should be resumed—is to make sure the situation in the field is calm, and then examine where we stand in our relations with the Palestinians. This may take a long time." Barak suggested the U.S. should be the one to examine whether conditions are ripe for renewal of the permanent status talks, in what way they should be resumed and on what basis.

Additional headlines on *Ha'aretz* pages 2–3 are:

TENSE ATMOSPHERE DURING TALKS; BEN-AMI TO ERIQAT:
"RELAX, THIS IS NOT A CNN SHOW"

WORDS EXCHANGED AT FOREIGN MINISTERS' MEETING

JORDAN: LACK OF PROGRESS WILL LEAD REGION TO DISASTER

SUMMIT PROCEEDINGS—PARTIES TAKE PRIDE IN VERBAL BLOWS

CLINTON POSTPONES DEPARTURE IN ORDER TO MEET ARAFAT
FOR THIRD TIME

BARAK'S SPOKESMEN SWOOP DOWN ON INTERNATIONAL PRESS

The next day, as we have already seen, the newspapers informed their readers that the summit did indeed end with some sort of agreement, but Arafat was quick to break it. In a commentary published on *Yediot Ahronot*'s front page, Ron Ben-Ishai sums up the situation quite simply and clearly:

The understandings reached by the Israeli-Palestinian-American security team were good and satisfactory, as such. Should they be implemented, the field will indeed calm down, and the danger of terror attacks will decrease significantly. But there is more than considerable concern that implementation on the Palestinian side will be incomplete and will not be enough to bring about a real cease-fire. At this time, Arafat has no real interest in a complete cessation of violence in the field. He returns from Sharm with no real achievement and is about to leave for the Islamic summit—where he wants to arrive with the field still on fire.

As usual, however, a careful reading of the stories published during those days, as well as on that weekend, reveals a somewhat different picture. First of all, it turns out that the members of the Palestinian delegation did not spend all their time complacently strolling through the hotel grounds, and were not exclusively busy with CNN appearances. The Palestinians had also prepared for the summit, thus suggesting, on the face of it at least, that they too were interested in leaving Sharm el-Sheikh with some sort of achievement—for example, an end to the closure of the territories. Consider, for instance, the story by *Yediot Ahronot*'s three senior reporters, Nachum Barnea, Shimon Shiffer, and Smadar Perry, published on the summit's first day. The report appears on page 2 of the October 17 issue, opening with Israeli assessments about the possible results of the summit (including an evaluation by a "senior source" who says that even if a cease-fire agreement were formulated, Arafat would not respect it). The story then goes on to describe the talks, the tense relations between the parties, and the chilly Egyptian reception; then, in a clearly apologetic tone, we find the following paragraph:

> Nevertheless, Arafat did do one thing that seemed to indicate that he was interested in reaching some joint agreement. After it turned out that the Palestinian delegation did not bring a single security expert, Arafat urgently called in Gibril Rajub, head of the West Bank preventive security apparatus. Under the sponsorship of CIA head George Tenet, Rajub and Shin-Beth head Avi Dichter held detailed talks and went into minute details of the security situation.

Why "nevertheless"? Because this step by Arafat's contradicted Barak's "pessimistic assessment." Other members of the delegation, it turns out, had a different perspective:

> Within the Israeli delegation there were different perspectives. Barak was pessimistic. Ben-Ami emphasized difficulties. [Amnon] Shahak was a little more optimistic. He believed that the pressure on Arafat, by the U.S. and espe-

cially by Egypt, might result in a joint statement. In his opinion, Arafat came to Sharm el-Sheikh in order to reach an agreement, not to torpedo the talks.

From Shahak's point of view, then, calling in Rajub was not a step that "nevertheless . . . seemed to indicate" that Arafat had some intention of reaching an agreement. That sentence owes its apologetic structure to the fact that it was formulated within the frame constructed by Barak's views. Note, moreover, that the reporters do not at any point turn to senior PA officials and ask *them* what they think about Arafat's intentions. To be sure, this was the first real opportunity they had since the Paris summit to do just that, but no such attempts were reported at all.

On the other hand, a close look at *Ha'aretz*'s lead story on October 17 reveals that, from the point of view of at least one Israeli source, "the information team encountered some difficulties in explaining the Israeli refusal to renew negotiations immediately." The Israeli refusal itself is reported in the newspaper's headline, as well as in a *Ma'ariv* sub-headline. But what about those difficulties? Was this yet another case of a hostile international press? Was there another aspect to this refusal—beyond the "obvious" need to wait for the cessation of violence—that created such difficulties for the team? According to the headlines, not at all. But the report by Nachum Barnea and Shimon Shiffer, published in *Yediot Ahronot*'s political supplement on October 20, tells a very different story:

> The confrontation between Clinton and Barak was related to . . . the renewal of the diplomatic process. There, Barak was torn between his dependence on Clinton and his dependence on Sharon. At this stage of his term he had no choice but to prefer Sharon; but he found it very hard to say no to Clinton. On Tuesday at 10:30 AM Barak was called in by Clinton. This was after Clinton got Arafat to agree to his statement, in Mubarak's presence. Clinton presented Barak with the document. "I cannot accept this," said Barak. The last paragraph stated that negotiations would be resumed within two weeks, based on UN Security Council resolutions 242 and 338, and "on the work done since." Such a formulation would scratch any chances of creating an emergency government: The Likud vetoes any renewal of the peace process and considers the understandings reached at Camp David a national calamity. Clinton was angry; he saw this dependence on Sharon burying his main foreign policy effort during eight years of presidency. Each word was fought over. The two weeks remained, but their meaning was glossed over. The allusion to Camp David was erased. When Barak left Clinton he asked to be put on the phone with Sharon: "We've done it, Arik. A cease-fire, and that's it."

What does this mean? What precisely was it that Barak and Sharon set out to accomplish? Is it indeed possible that Clinton saw Barak's "dependence on Sharon" bury his main foreign policy effort? Definitely so. According to the newspapers, Barak had already agreed with Sharon on the main terms for a unity government *before* the summit, and the summit's success would in fact have undermined the possibility of such a government. Here is Nachum Barnea, in an analysis published in *Yediot Ahronot* on October 17:

> The Palestinians are not Barak's only problem. He is fighting on two contradictory fronts—the Clinton front, and the Sharon front. Clinton demands his acceptance of the American proposal announcing the renewal of the peace process. According to this proposal, renewal of talks will be contingent on the fulfillment of all terms of the Oslo agreement—in letter and in spirit. Barak, in fact, agreed to accept the proposal. He could not embarrass Clinton. It is easy to say that the "Palestinian leadership is unripe," but harder to face the results. The problem is that any willingness to renew the process raises great difficulties for the creation of an emergency government. Barak will need Houdini's tricks in order to extricate himself from this impasse. Here is an example: among the Israeli demands presented yesterday was one calling on Arafat to extradite the perpetrators of the Ramallah Lynch. Israel raised this demand knowing that no such extradition will ever occur. In the past, moves of this kind were typical of Likud governments.

The "impasse" Barnea mentions is of course the acceptance of the American proposal and the renewal of the peace process, while the "Houdini tricks" are steps meant to create the feeling that the diplomatic process was buried because of *Palestinian* non-compliance. The purpose of such tricks is to pave the way for a government with Sharon. It takes no great expertise in political sciences, and no anti-Israeli orientation, to understand that Barak came to the summit with an inherent interest in its failure. All the newspapers' commentators wrote about this in the most straightforward manner—always in the back pages. Consider *Ma'ariv*'s Chemi Shalev on October 15; *Ha'aretz*'s Aluf Ben on October 17; and *Yediot Ahronot*'s Sima Kadmon on October 18, following in that order:

> Barak is counting on Arafat to do the dirty work; he doesn't want to be the one to tell everyone present that they are wasting their time. He therefore sounds "determined"—this time, the purpose is to get Ariel Sharon into his government. Barak, perhaps, does not fully appreciate to what extent Sharon's inclusion in the government "at the present time" will be considered a clear provocation, in the region and in the entire world—no less so, and perhaps more so, than Sharon's visit to the Temple Mount.

> The summit's real hero did not come to Sharm. He remained at his ranch, surrounded by his supporters and the TV cameras, receiving live cell phone briefings from Barak's delegation every fifteen minutes. On his way back to

government, Ariel Sharon has once again managed to shape the region's diplomatic and political agenda, and Barak was forced to justify to President Mubarak his controversial visit to the Temple Mount.

Barak's feet were in Sharm el-Sheikh, but his mind was at the Likud convention. He knows that the more impressive his achievements at the summit, the shorter his [political] course; that his diplomatic success is his political downfall; that any victory will be a Pyrrhic victory as far as he is concerned: implementation of the Sharm understandings may be the end of his administration, and disregarding them may be his only chance for survival.

Note the alarming gap between all this and the perspective represented by the newspapers' headlines: How can one start out with all these crucial pieces of information—the collusion between Barak and Sharon; Barak's refusal to sign Clinton's statement; the "minute details" worked out by the security committee; Barak's inveterate interest in the summit's failure—and end up with a "pessimistic" Barak saying that the situation is "complicated"; a "complacent" Arafat wishing to "torpedo" the summit; and "a frustrated advisor," as *Yediot Ahronot* put it, saying that "Arik can stay calm, there's nothing going on here"? How could the newspapers just ignore reality, and join Ehud Barak wherever he was standing at any particular moment? In an article published in *Ha'aretz* on October 17, next to the lead story on page 2, Aluf Ben explains:

The journalists who came to Sharm yesterday remembering the secrecy and high walls of the Camp David summit found it hard to keep up with the stream of briefings, interviews, and leaks from the Israeli delegation. In times of crisis, the press has an easy life: each side must show the public back home that it has been adamant in defending its positions. The large number of spokesmen and aides surrounding Ehud Barak and Shlomo Ben-Ami created a veritable flood. Messages were not always coherent. Danny Yatom spoke of lack of progress, and expectations that the summit will collapse. Gilad Sher assessed that everything would be fine. Shlomo Ben-Ami, only recently thrilled with the depth of his understanding with the Palestinians, sent his spokesmen to tell how he defeated Eriqat with his wit. The members of the Israeli delegation were proud of their firm stand in face of the Egyptian-Palestinian front, and sounded like Israeli diplomats in the years preceding the peace process. "The whole world is against us," one of them proudly said.

This is what it comes down to, then: Danny Yatom talks of "expectations that the summit will collapse," and the newspapers report "expectations that the summit will collapse." Shlomo Ben-Ami sends "his spokesmen to tell how he defeated Eriqat with his wit" and the newspapers report how Ben-Ami paid Eriqat back "in kind." The entire delegation is proud of its "firm stand in face of the Egyptian-Palestinian front," and the newspapers report that "the whole world is against us." It is true indeed: "In times of crisis, the press has an easy life."

Throughout the week the newspapers enthusiastically reported Israel's new "information offensive." *Ma'ariv*, as we have seen, reported on October 16 that

AN "ARMY" OF ISRAELI SPOKESMEN WILL
"CONQUER" SHARM EL-SHEIKH

The sub-headline elaborates:

ENGLISH? ARABIC? ITALIAN? FRENCH? THE PRIME MINISTER HAS EQUIPPED
HIMSELF WITH SPOKESMEN FLUENT IN EVERY LANGUAGE. THE GOAL: TO CREATE
A MEDIA HEADQUARTERS THAT WILL ACT AND RESPOND IN REAL TIME, ON ALL
TELEVISION AND RADIO NETWORKS WORLDWIDE, CLARIFYING THE ISRAELI
POSITION

But throughout the period we are examining, the newspapers proceeded as if they did not understand, or did not wish to understand, that all those spokesmen also spoke Hebrew, and that the joke, so to speak, was mostly on them. It seems that they did not understand, or did not wish to understand, that they themselves were Barak's main propaganda tool, and that Barak's propaganda was meant primarily for the Hebrew-speaking audience—their readers—and not for television viewers in Rome or Paris. This unawareness is seen most clearly whenever the newspapers deal with the distinction between the Palestinian "propaganda machine" and the Israeli "information offensive." On October 15, for example, *Yediot Ahronot's* daily supplement has a long story about the Palestinian side of the equation. On the supplement's cover we find the following headline, in large white letters against a red background:

REPORTING HATE

Under the headline is a picture of Arafat visiting a Gaza hospital. The caption reads: "Arafat visits a wounded Palestinian at the hospital after the air force attack on Gaza. Some of the patients with whom he was photographed were not even wounded in the Israeli attack." In this story, reporters Roni Shaked and Itamar Eichner describe the Palestinian propaganda system's methods of operation: They indicate, for example, that the Palestinians added a citizen killed in a car accident to the list of Intifada casualties, and that they tried to portray the victims of the Ramallah Lynch as members of the army's undercover unit. "Every day," Eichner and Shaked write, "the Palestinian television broadcasts pictures of children throwing stones and IDF soldiers shooting at them, as well as close-ups of the dead, the funerals, and proud militant youths carrying the Palestinian flag." According to Shaked and Eichner, "the radio and television speak 'Palestinian,' not Arabic. The term 'Zionists' is always derogatory. The word 'settlers' is always attached to the word meaning extremists, or, in Palestinian code, lunatics. The 'Tel Aviv government' is the Israeli government, and the IDF is the enemy's army, the army of occupation."

Much could be made of these assertions—for example, the implication that the meaning of "Zionists" in Arabic, as opposed to "Palestinian," is positive; the claim that broadcasting pictures of confrontations between stone throwers and IDF soldiers, as well as pictures of the dead and the funerals, is inherently different from the Israeli television coverage of these same confrontations, including Israeli casualties and funerals; the implied claim that the IDF is not really an occupation army—but all these are minor points. The truly important issue lies elsewhere: In the very same newspaper, on pages 16–17, two stories deal with what is termed the Israeli "information offensive." The stories tell of ten video cameras distributed to soldiers in the territories—"in order to aid Israel's information effort, which is increasingly emerging as the main front in the present battle." According to the report, "the IDF will decide which pictures to distribute in order to show what IDF soldiers are facing." In another story, Eitan Amit reports that the Knesset's chairman, Avraham Burg, has come to New York to boost the Israeli information effort there, mainly because of his fluent command of English. According to Amit, "Burg briefed the spokesmen of Jewish communities and emphatically instructed them to refrain from any type of apology to the Palestinians." The newspaper's front page refers readers to these stories. One of the signposts reads:

THE WORKINGS OF THE PALESTINIAN PROPAGANDA MACHINE

The other, however, reads:

THE INFORMATION FRONT: IDF WILL EQUIP
SOLDIERS WITH CAMERAS

This, then, is the entire story from the newspaper's point of view: *They* (the Palestinians and their media) are dealing in *propaganda; we* (the Israeli government) are giving out *information;* and the Israeli press simply reports. But, of course, as we have seen throughout this book, the Israeli newspapers were not sitting back and observing events from an impartial viewpoint—

they were chin-deep in the "information offensive." Even the story dealing with the Palestinian "propaganda machine" was an integral part of the information battle: The reporters interviewed Captain-Major Yarden Vatikai, head of the foreign press section at the army spokesman's unit; Nahman Shay, "who because of the emergency situation was enlisted to head the Israeli information offensive"; and another source in the Foreign Office, "who closely monitors the Palestinian propaganda broadcasts." None of these three sources was a neutral observer; they all had a clear interest in disseminating the view shared by Barak and the security establishment, a view that included, as we have seen, a systematic de-legitimization of the Palestinians, especially Arafat.

The Arafat File:
De-legitimization and Psychological Explanations

The Arafat de-legitimization campaign reached its peak on October 20, the day Barak announced he was taking his diplomatic "time-out." On this day *Yediot Ahronot*'s weekend magazine published a five-page story dealing exclusively with Arafat's "personality." The cover shows the picture of the PA chairman, and over it, diagonally, we find the headline, framed in a red square, not unlike an office stamp:

THE ARAFAT FILE

The sub-headline reads:

THE PARANOIA. THE MOTIVES. THE MOODS. THE WHIMS. THE PERSONALITY CULT. THE INHIBITIONS. THE BRAINWAVES. THE ANXIETIES—THE PSYCHOLOGICAL PROFILE OF YASSER ARAFAT, THE MAN WHO SET FIRE TO THE MIDDLE EAST.

The magazine's table of contents, on page 5, offers the readers a pun: One altered letter in the Hebrew word for "file" changes the headline into **THE ARAFAT TIC.** Under this headline, the story is introduced with the following lines:

IS THERE A PARTNER? OR PERHAPS NOT? IS ARAFAT NORMAL? HAS HE LOST HIS MARBLES? IS HE IN CONTROL? OR PERHAPS NOT? WAS THIS PREDICTABLE? OR PERHAPS NOT? ALL THE RIGHT QUESTIONS

The entire story is organized so as to show that there is no partner, and Arafat is not normal; that he has indeed lost his marbles, and that he is absolutely in control, and that all this was definitely predictable—from the point of view of the Israeli defense establishment, of course. The story is based on "research conducted by the defense establishment in the months prior to the riots" dealing with "Arafat's complex patterns of behavior." According to the report, the Arab division of the Shin-Beth employs a "team of psychologists and researchers" who analyze Arafat for "psychological traits related to the negotiations with Israel." This team has discovered "formulas for almost every one of Arafat's typical behavioral patterns." According to a senior researcher, the work was not particularly hard:

> This is no precise science, but we are definitely dealing with fixed patterns, and after all, we have known this man for over forty years. We have all put in tens of thousands of "Arafat hours." Just between us, if people could be compared to computer programs, Arafat is a relatively simple and outdated BASIC program, not a super-computer or C++. Not something too complicated or complex to understand.

What, then, are the "psychological aspects" of this BASIC program called Yasser Arafat? Here are a few quotes from the researchers' contributions:

> Whenever Arafat compromises, he has an urge to give militant statements in order to feel that he has paid Israel back in kind, that he has humiliated it. If he makes a concession at night, he will hurry the next morning in search of some memorial service for a well-known terrorist, and grab the microphone.

> He finds it difficult to cross the divide separating the leader of a terror organization and the leader of a state. Note, for example, that he is unable to sit still for one moment. He moves between houses every day, between Gaza and Ramallah, between Jericho and Bethlehem. He has to be on the move all the time, as he used to be in the past.

> Arafat is not big on ideology. He is not a socialist or a capitalist. He is simply a national leader, pragmatic and even flexible to a certain extent, who does everything possible to create a state for his people and turn it into a member of the western community of nations. But on the way to statehood he upholds two principles: first, his top concern is the unity of the Palestinian camp. . . . The second principle is maintaining the independence of the Palestinian struggle.

> Regarding Israel, he suffers from a persecution complex. After many years as a wanted terrorist, with opponents within and without frequently trying to liquidate him, a man becomes obsessively suspicious. This suspiciousness turns him into an almost intolerable partner for negotiations. He is always certain that we are trying to trap him. How can one try to persuade him that we have no intention of harassing him and certainly none of liquidating him?

Are these the "discoveries" that the researchers working on the "Arafat File" managed to accumulate in all their tens of thousands of working hours? He "grabs the microphone" at memorial services? He "moves between Gaza and Ramallah, between Jericho and Bethlehem"? He is "always certain that we are trying to trap him"? This does not sound very impressive. Where are the whims? The moods? The marbles? What about the tics? They are simply not there. And if Yasser Arafat was a partner for peace in Rabin's time, and in Peres's time, and even in Netanyahu's time—though it might be assumed that then, too, he was "unable to sit still for one moment"—how is it possible that he has suddenly become a BASIC program with paranoid tendencies? And where were all these researchers during the past years? How is it that the "Arafat File" suddenly emerges from the offices of the defense establishment and is published in *Yediot Ahronot*'s weekend magazine on the very day that Barak discredits the chairman for all time? The writers, Roni Shaked and Ron Leshem, "explain":

> The Arafat puzzle has caused frustration and anger at the prime minister's office over the past weeks. Barak's people could not quite understand how it could be that the Palestinian state is practically on its way to independence, but Yasser Arafat chooses to endanger everything. Right now—when he has a flag, an anthem, license plates, stamps, a national Palestinian passport, a stock market, a consumer's price index, and even a state comptroller. . . . So why on earth did Arafat shuffle the decks now, when Ehud Barak even agreed to discuss Jerusalem? What does he want? Does he want to find himself on a plane on his way out, does he want to undo everything and resume his expatriate's life in the villas of Tunisia? At this rate, he will lose what opportunity he had. He is setting fire to the entire region, and this fire will consume him too. Only the Arab studies specialists in the defense establishment could console themselves over the last weeks, with a bitter "we told you so."

This, then, is the key issue: Barak and his people were simply unable to understand how it could be that the prime minister agreed to "discuss Jerusalem" and Arafat for his part "chose to endanger it all." Given this situation, only one possible conclusion remained: Arafat is insane. This "Arafat riddle"—the fact that he refused to accept Barak's peace proposal—lies at the heart of the conceptual confusion that took hold of the Israeli consciousness throughout the entire Intifada. We shall deal with this riddle in detail later on in this chapter. At this stage, however, it should be noted that Arafat was not the only Arab leader who suffered from the newspapers' fondness for psychological explanations. The newspapers are used to "explain" the conduct of all Arab leaders in terms of personality whenever they do not conform to the goals of the Israeli establishment. Thus, for example, after the Syrian president, Bashar Assad, gave some "extremist" speeches, the newspapers promptly told their readers that the man was simply insane. On October 31, for instance, *Ma'ariv* dedicated the cover of its daily supplement to a psychological diagnosis of Assad. The headline reads:

MANIPULABLE, TENSE, IRRITABLE

The sub-headline says:

MORE SIGNS THAT BASHAR ASSAD, THE YOUNG SYRIAN PRESIDENT, IS LED ALONG BY EXTREMIST ADVISORS. THIS WOULDN'T HAVE HAPPENED TO DAD

And when the king of Morocco, Mohammed VI, decided to sever relations with Israel a few days after the diplomatic "time-out" was announced, both tabloids were quick to characterize the young king's action in the same terms. The sub-headline of the *Ma'ariv*'s story on October 24 reads:

SOURCES IN RABAT: "THE DECISION MADE BY THE YOUNG KING, MOHAMMED VI, CONTRADICTS HIS FATHER'S LEGACY"

Yediot Ahronot's headline on page 9 the next day adds:

MOROCCAN KING CAUSES ANGER: "THIS WOULDN'T HAVE HAPPENED IN HIS FATHER'S TIME"

This consistent perspective, explaining every Arab step that Israel does not approve of in terms of the Arab leaders' defective personality (paranoid, young, irritable) clearly has no foundation in reality: Assad the elder was not quite the ardent Zionist; the king of Morocco was not necessarily betraying his father's legacy. Note, moreover, that while the disruption of relations and the extremist speeches merit main headlines in all three newspapers, the efforts of Egyptian president Mubarak and the Jordanian king Abdallah, who throughout the entire period tried to bring about a renewal of the diplomatic process, are only minimally reported. During the Cairo summit, for example, Mubarak and Abdallah led a policy clearly committed to diplomacy, and they prevented the adoption of more militant resolutions as demanded by Bashar Assad and the representatives of Iraq, Sudan, and Yemen. On October 22, for example, *Ma'ariv*'s analyst, Oded Granot, wrote that the summit ended with the "relative triumph" of the moderate line, and that "none of the leaders, including the representatives of the militant bloc, suggested starting or joining a war against Israel." And yet *Ma'ariv*'s front page carries four pictures under the headline WAR ON FOUR FRONTS. The fronts are GAZA (the picture shows an injured Palestinian); RAMALLAH (demonstrators carrying a missile); NORTH (soldiers who prevented a terrorist infiltration); and, of course, CAIRO (Arafat talking to Arab leaders at the summit).

The Israeli Copernicus and the Arafat Riddle

Let us return, then, to the "Arafat riddle": After long years of floundering between interim agreements, with occasional territorial concessions, periodic crises, and sporadic terror attacks, one Israeli prime minister decided to examine once and for all, *scientifically*, whether indeed it was possible to finalize the process with a real peace agreement. This prime minister— Ehud Barak—cut through procedures, put an end to the pattern of interim agreements, and offered Arafat a permanent status agreement on unimaginable, unprecedented, "generous" terms. How did Arafat respond to this proposal? By igniting the flames of the Intifada. Why did he do that? Why did he not seize the opportunity Barak presented him to end the historical conflict between Israelis and Palestinians once and for all, and sign a peace agreement? The answer to the riddle is clear and simple: Arafat was not interested in peace. Why? Two options present themselves: either he decided to "conquer Palestine by blood" instead of gaining independence "in diplomatic ways," or else—he was mentally unstable. Since he was only too well aware that conquering Palestine would be impossible (for Israel would win the war), the only remaining conclusion was that the leader of the Palestinian people was truly and simply insane; and so, the reasoning goes, Israel had to wait patiently for a change in the Palestinian leadership. This answer to the riddle is unpleasant, disappointing, frustrating—but this is reality. One simply has to get used to it.

This perspective was most eloquently expressed in an extensive and very influential article published by Ari Shavit in *Ha'aretz*'s weekend magazine on October 27. The signpost on the magazine's cover says:

KNOW THINE ENEMY: BARAK'S CONCEPTUAL REVOLUTION

The magazine's table of contents elaborates:

THANKS TO EHUD BARAK, THE PEACE PROCESS FAILED THE REALITY TEST—
A FAILURE THAT IS ALL HISTORICAL BLESSING

The article itself, under the title BARAK'S COPERNICAN REVOLUTION, begins with a lengthy historical review of the defeat of the geocentric perspective lying at the heart of ancient astronomy: This perspective, which had the sun as well as the stars revolving around the earth, gave the world "stability, order and optimism, and a deep sense of rational meaning." But then, at a certain historical moment, a *Copernican* moment, it turned out that this perspective was no more than "a figment of our imagination; a wish; a false dream; a cock-and-bull story." "The present historical moment," writes Ari Shavit, is a Copernican moment—and Ehud Barak is no other than the

Israeli Copernicus, since he has proven that the "autocentric" perspective of Israeli culture was no more than "a figment of our imagination; a wish; a false dream; a cock-and-bull story":

> Two complementary assumptions were the basis of this autocentric perspective: the assumption that the Israeli occupation since 1967 lies at the heart of the conflict; and the assumption that since Israeli occupation lies at the heart of the conflict, the solution is at hand, for it depends primarily on Israel and its willingness to put an end to this occupation. . . . Thus, the real historical importance of the events of October 2000 is the fact that they undermined this autocentric perspective along with its two assumptions. For the Palestinian national movement's decision to land a violent attack on Israel was made just after Israel offered that same movement to put an end to occupation, recognize a Palestinian state, retreat from 95% of the territories, and even divide Jerusalem. Moreover, the religious-nationalist and at times atavistic nature of this sudden attack proves that the Palestinian national movement represented by Arafat is interested not in reconciliation with Israel (like Sadat) but in defeating Israel (like the Hizballah). . . . In the months preceding this outburst of violence Ehud Barak actually subjected the old peace hypothesis to a critical experiment. He took the autocentric perspective's assumptions, stretched them to their limit, and subjected them to a decisive empirical test. . . . This is the real meaning of Barak's term in government so far. This is Barak's real revolution. . . . Now the masquerade is over. The makeup has been removed, the costumes have been shed. And now we can all see the actors' true images. Now we all look this cruel reality— revealed by Barak and personified by Arafat—in the eye.

Throughout October, and much later as well, it was hard to find an Israeli who would not readily accept Ari Shavit's words. This was true not only of the political Right, who celebrated quite a victory during those days, but also of the moderate Left, which at the time was going through intense conceptual stock-taking, after years of being trapped, as it were, by the pre-Copernican "false dream," the dream of ending the Palestinian-Israeli conflict by peaceful means. The simple fact, however, is that Ari Shavit's perspective, the perspective formed by Ehud Barak's propaganda, is completely unfounded—for two fundamental and complementary reasons. These reasons were well known throughout October; they were freely discussed by reporters and analysts, but the newspapers completely avoided any attempt to explicitly deal with them, thus helping to perpetuate Barak's perspective in the Israel consciousness to an extent that now seems almost irrevocable.

The first point has to do with the very notion of the *experiment*: Ehud Barak, deeply familiar with scientific thought, was probably well aware that whoever conducts an experiment cannot participate in it—this is a completely basic scientific insight. Yet Barak obviously participated in his own experiment, and quite actively at that. He participated in it not only after the outburst of the Intifada, and not only in the ways already dealt with throughout the book—the supposedly restrained military activity in the territories, the systematic de-legitimization of Arafat—but also, and primarily, in the way he handled negotiations with the PA: He totally ignored the need for confidence-building measures; he put an end to Israel's staged withdrawal from the territories, as envisioned in the Oslo process; he did not hand over *any* territory to the Palestinians throughout his term; he severed the deep relationships between Israeli and Palestinian peace-process veterans; he authorized more building in the settlements than his rightwing predecessor Benjamin Netanyahu; he humiliated Arafat and his staff from his first day in office; he never entered a process of *negotiation* with the Palestinians, but rather asked them to sign finalized dictates for agreements; he raised the sensitive issues of the division of Jerusalem and control of Mount Temple without previous diplomatic groundwork; and mainly, he let it be felt all along that he thought of what he was doing as an experiment—with Arafat as his guinea pig.

Every one of these facts was reported in the newspapers during the month of October, but they always appeared in the weekend magazines and in section B of *Ha'aretz*—and they were never once mentioned in the newspapers' news pages. Here are three examples, out of many. In *Yediot Ahronot's* political supplement on October 13, Sima Kadmon reports a special cabinet meeting convened after Yom Kippur:

> The atmosphere was tense. People came with very heavy hearts. . . . The question hovered in the air, but no one dared ask it: how did we come to this pass? Everyone knew the answer. It had to do with the personality of the person in charge of negotiations, namely, the prime minister. With Barak, it was all or nothing. Black or white—retreat from Lebanon within a year; reach a peace agreement with the Palestinians within fifteen months; a comprehensive agreement—or no agreement at all; the end of the conflict, or nothing. And without an agreement, there is indeed nothing. And nothing means violence. Terror. The unilateral declaration of Palestinian statehood. This is true this week, and it has been true all along. Talented people like Rabin, Peres, Beilin have put into this process years of work. They understood that this road must be traveled in stages. Haim Ramon warned Barak: don't try to do it all. Settle for less. Barak thought he knew better. He gambled. He sacrificed everything, including his administration, on a wager that now seems mistaken.

That same day, Chemi Shalev published a similar article in *Ma'ariv's* political supplement. Shalev reports the opposition to Barak within his cabinet and says that "more than a few cabinet members are critical of the tactics he adopted, the steps he initiated, and the efforts he aborted. But these are days of national rallying, of consensual defensiveness, and when the guns roar, the critics are silent." Shalev then goes on to say:

Barak does not admit to any mistake, of course, and rightly so, as far as he is concerned. If indeed his steering was misguided, then perhaps we didn't really have to come to this, perhaps someone else could have gotten different results with the same starting point, and then it would be impossible to say that we had no choice. Nevertheless, here is a very partial list of things that could have been done differently:

[a] Channeling the conflict into a situation of black and white dichotomy—agreement or conflict, with no middle ground, no shades of gray. Barak invented the "end of the conflict" as the Archimedean point for the entire process, and this implied the need to finalize everything, here and now—including Jerusalem, the Temple Mount, and the right of return. Barak went for the all-or-nothing approach. Not only did he fail to leave himself escape exits, he was quick to block those that others tried to open.

[b] Unleashing the religious demons as a direct result of the need to discuss the holiest of holies on the way to the "end of the conflict." Raising the issue of the Temple Mount, and the failure to prevent Ariel Sharon's visit to the place, unleashed primordial, apocalyptic, Jihadic spectres. According to this approach, the Temple Mount should have been discussed by two independent states who had already learned how to live with each other, and not by Israelis and Palestinians who do not trust each other one bit.

[c] Ignoring the personal dimension of the conflict; the lack of respect and the deprecation he often showed Yasser Arafat; the analytic, rational thought that does not recognize the importance of the psyche and emotions. The ambivalence regarding the peace process and the Palestinians, keenly felt in Ramallah and in Nablus. The lack of communication skills, which finds its expression in the widespread sense of estrangement from Barak, both in the internal political arena and in public opinion.

[d] The attempt to dictate from the outset all the rules of the game, from A to Z, including non-viable framework agreements, meaningless deadlines, and the procrastinating, patronizing attitude toward the Palestinians. First he asked for two months' time for thought, then he turned up with the synergetic and simultaneous peace vision, and later he nevertheless ordered the Palestinians to sit back and wait till he finished his flirt with Assad. Finally he brought them back on stage, and still complained that they were not in as much of a rush as he was.

[e] Publicly and blatantly cornering Arafat in the international arena, starting with Clinton's one-sided speech at the end of July, after the Camp David summit (which earned the praise of local nearsighted analysts) and ending with quite an impressive success in changing the European position. As September 13 approached and Arafat heard an international "no" to his intent of declaring independence, cries of joy were heard in Jerusalem. But

this achievement sowed the seeds of disaster: Arafat felt the need to turn the tables and was willing to pay a high price. Such battles, said a cabinet minister this week, should never be won.

And finally, here is a paragraph from an article by Akiva Eldar, published on October 26, on page 3 of *Ha'aretz*'s section B.

According to Central Bureau of Statistics data, Sharon does not need to join the government. Barak is doing his work better than Sharon did, and even better than Benjamin Netanyahu. In the second quarter of this year there was a 51 percent rise in new building in the territories (740 units, as opposed to 490 in the second quarter of 1999). While it is true that the most impressive rise (from 130 to 290—123 percent) is in the private sector, public building has also registered an impressive 25 percent rise (from 360 to 450). All in all, during the first half of 2000, Barak's government has outdone the rate of the Netanyahu administration during the same term last year by 44 percent (from 1,240 to 1,790).

These are not political claims raised by radicals in the opposition but facts of crucial news value: One reporter writes that the atmosphere in a cabinet meeting was tense, and everyone knew that the answer resided "in the personality of the person in charge of negotiations"; another reporter says that "more than a few" people in government made a long and detailed list of basic failings in Barak's political conduct, including "efforts he aborted"; another one presents data from the central bureau of statistics indicating an increment in building in the settlements—and none of the newspapers take notice, and none of these facts ever appear in a single headline in the news pages.[2]

This, then, is the first point: Barak ran his diplomatic affairs in a way that contradicted, by definition, the image of an objective experimenter testing the possibility of achieving peace. It is not necessary to adopt the radical perspective about Barak's behavior—according to which he *set up* his experiment so as to reach the outcome obtained—in order to analyze his policy in an independent and critical way. It is certainly possible that Barak sincerely thought he was "turning every stone" on the way to peace; it is certainly possible that he thought he could put an end to the conflict with the Palestinians within fifteen months. But Barak's private perspective was not supposed to win automatic acceptance from the newspapers—they should have examined the possibility that Barak actively contributed to the collapse of the peace process. This simply never happened.

The second point has to do with the experiment's basic assumption—the assertion that the Intifada broke out, as Ari Shavit put it, "just after Israel offered that same movement to put an end to occupation, recognize a Palestinian state, retreat from 95 percent of the territories, and even divide Jerusalem." What was the origin of this assertion? Did anyone *know* for a fact that Israel had indeed offered to put an end to the occupation, withdraw from 95 percent of the territories, and divide Jerusalem? It is indeed true that this was what Ehud Barak told the journalists (or let them understand, or failed to deny) from time to time, but the fact is that throughout the month, and later as well, the newspapers never once tried to find out what *exactly* it was that Barak offered the Palestinians—not what Barak *said* he had offered, but what he had *actually* offered. Where exactly was the border supposed to lie? Which settlements were supposed to remain, and which were supposed to be evacuated? Did he, for instance, offer to dismantle the settlement in Kiryat Arba, a constant locus of friction with Palestinians in Hebron? And if not, in what sense did he offer to "put an end to occupation"? How many Palestinians were supposed to remain under Israeli sovereignty? How many separate territories was the PA supposed to be divided into as part of this agreement? And how were the Palestinians supposed to move between these areas? How was Jerusalem to be divided? What was the exact nature of his solution for the refugee problem? What about the Temple Mount? What about water, and economic relations? Such an examination could and should have also included real research into the Palestinian positions, publication of the maps Barak used when presenting his offer (if indeed there were any), etc. Yet no such research was conducted, and the discussion about Arafat's political intransigence was exclusively based on Barak's suggestions. Consider, for instance, the following lines by Akiva Eldar, on November 16, and Uzi Benziman, on November 19, both published in section B of *Ha'aretz*:

> Almost everyone in the political establishment now understands that peace, as well as this government, will stand or fall on the "Camp David understandings" of July 2000. Almost no one knows what these understandings were. No one saw the document summing up these understandings, since there is no such document. Experienced diplomats cannot recall diplomatic talks of this kind whose content was not written down.

> Ehud Barak's version about turning every stone on the way to a peace agreement with the Palestinians was engraved in the public consciousness to such an extent that no one demands that he prove what he says. God is in the details, and one who strives for internal national unity in this emergency situation cannot get himself off the hook with a general claim that he did everything possible to reach an agreement with Yasser Arafat. Detailed evidence is called for. No one knows, for instance, to which borders Barak agreed to withdraw: did he demand that 18 percent of the territory be left in

Israeli hands, or 12 percent, or only 5 percent? The maps presenting Barak's vision of the borders of the permanent status agreement were never revealed—not to the Palestinians, not to the Israeli public, not to cabinet members. Acquaintance with such a withdrawal map is necessary in order to appreciate correctly the viability of a Palestinian state, and in order to be convinced that the present crisis is all Arafat's handiwork. . . . The same applies to the proposals for settling the dispute over Jerusalem. Various leaks informed the public about far-reaching concessions made by Barak at Camp David regarding this issue, but they remain vague. . . . And what are Barak's ideas for finding a settlement for the Temple Mount? Barak's position regarding the Palestinian demand to implement the right of return remains unclear as well. . . . Until now, he has evoked tactical needs in order to explain his refusal to present his precise position during negotiations: ambiguity improves his bargaining ability. . . . No more. When the impasse in negotiations leads to fresh graves, the prime minister must stand up and present his proposal in full detail, so as to convince us that this is indeed a necessary war.

Of course, there was no reason to assume, at any stage of the process, that Barak would volunteer to "present his proposal in full detail, so as to convince [Israelis] that this is indeed a necessary war." First, Barak indeed needed the vagueness in order to "improve his bargaining ability"; second, such exposure of his plan might have proven that this was no necessary war at all. The task of exposing his proposals fell of course to the media—the so-called watchdogs of democracy—but the papers preferred to keep their distance, and were content with stating that Barak did indeed "turn every stone" on his way to peace, and that Arafat had lost his sanity and was dragging the entire region to another war.

8

Conclusion

> If the Likud were in office, all hell would break loose. The Left
> would accuse the government, the media would sound the
> alarm. . . . If the Likud were in office, the leaders of the Left, in-
> cluding Ehud Barak, would vehemently attack the prime min-
> ister and accuse him of leading us all to our destruction. Who
> are you, they would mockingly defy him, to decide that Arafat
> is no longer a partner?
> —Chemi Shalev, *Ma'ariv,* October 20

During the first month of the Intifada, the Jewish public in Israel went
through a radical transformation in its perception of the Israeli-Palestinian
conflict. In social-psychological terms, this change can be characterized on
the basis of the distinction between *tractable* and *intractable* conflicts (Kriesberg 1993; Bar-Tal 1998, 2000, 2001): In the Oslo period, from 1993 till the
outbreak of the Intifada, a significant proportion of the Jewish public gradually came to view the conflict as a tractable one, in which "the parties in
dispute attempt to resolve [the conflict] through negotiations, . . . avoid violence, recognize mutual interests, and accept each other's identity and
rights" (Bar-Tal 1998, p. 23). In October 2000, however, the Jewish public
quickly retreated into a consensual perception of the conflict as totally *intractable*. Intractable conflicts "are prolonged, involve great animosity and
vicious cycles of violence"; they are "exhausting, demanding, stressful,
painful, and costly"; they seem to be "irreconcilable and self-perpetuating"
(Bar-Tal 1998, p. 23).

As Bar-Tal shows, societies immersed in intractable conflicts form particular sets of *societal beliefs*, which "strengthen the society to help it cope
with the conflict as such," but which also "constitute a certain psychological investment in the conflict and thus perpetuate its continuation" (Bar-
Tal 1998, p. 23). The following list comprises eight themes common to
different societies in intractable conflicts—from the Protestant and Cath-

olic communities in Northern Ireland to the Turks and Kurds in Turkey. The list impressively reflects the essence of the newspapers' coverage throughout October 2000, as analyzed throughout this book:

[a] Societal beliefs about the justness of one's own goals: These beliefs not only "outline the goals and establish their justice" but also "provide the rationale for the eruption of the conflict"; they "rest on the assumption of the supreme and vital importance of those goals: failure to achieve them threatens the existence of the society" (p. 26).

[b] Societal beliefs about security: "the issue of security becomes the main preoccupation of such society's members and a central and determinative societal value" (p. 27).

[c] Societal beliefs that de-legitimize the opponent: These explain, so to speak, "why the opponent has 'far-reaching', 'irrational,' 'malevolent' goals that negate the honorable and worthy goals of one's own society, and why the adversary is intransigent and unwilling to reconcile." They also help "explain" the "violence, viciousness, and atrocities of the opponent," and "serve as justifications for one's own violence and destructiveness" (p. 28).

[d] Societal beliefs that create a positive self-image: "attributes that are often used for this purpose are humaneness, morality, fairness, and trustworthiness, on the one hand, and courage, heroism, and endurance, on the other" (p. 28).

[e] Societal beliefs about victimization: "The focus on the injustice, harm, evil, and atrocities of the adversary, in combination with the society's self-perception as just, moral and human, leads society to assume that it is a victim" (p. 28).

[f] Societal beliefs about patriotism: "patriotism increases the cohesiveness of the society. . . . In the name of patriotism, members of the society can be asked to forget their personal convenience, wishes, or even needs" (p. 29).

[g] Societal beliefs about unity: These "focus on the importance of setting aside any internal conflicts, controversies, and disagreements and unite the group's forces in face of the external threat" (p. 29).

[h] Societal beliefs about peace: These "present the society members, both to themselves and to the world, as peace loving and peace seeking. This peace, however, is usually conceived of in utopian terms as a vague dream or wish" (p. 29).

A crucial question arises in connection with such beliefs: What comes first? Do societies develop these sets of societal beliefs in order to cope with an already *existing* intractable conflict, or do they form such beliefs in the process of *making* the conflict intractable? In other words, do these beliefs actually contribute to the intractability of the conflict? In the case of Israeli society in October 2000—at least as far as the press is concerned—this seems to be beyond doubt. As we have seen again and again throughout this book, the reality that the newspapers' reporters described was that of a tractable conflict in crisis: Violence erupted, people were killed, there was a sense of danger in the air, but at the same time representatives of both sides were constantly negotiating. Barak and Arafat met in Paris (chapter 3) and in Sharm el-Sheikh (chapter 7); senior Israeli and Palestinian officials negotiated security arrangements on the Temple Mount (chapter 3) and tried to work together to reach a cease-fire (chapter 6). The papers, however, had already told their readers a story of an intractable conflict during the very first week of the Intifada—and then kept repeating this story: They stated as fact that Arafat had planned and initiated the Intifada, even though a great majority of their sources insisted that it was a spontaneous outburst (chapter 2); they immediately characterized Arafat himself, and the entire Palestinian people, as irrational and malevolent (chapter 6); they obsessively portrayed the Israeli side as the victim of Palestinian violence and flatly suppressed reports about the dire results of Israeli violence (chapter 4); they framed the demonstrations within the Green Line, in which thirteen Arab citizens were killed, as an attempt to activate a fifth column inside Israel (chapter 5); they uncritically echoed Barak's contention that Israel did everything it could to achieve peace with the Palestinians (chapter 7); they sent their readers an anxious message about an all-out war just around the corner (chapter 3); and they projected the sense of patriotism and togetherness so typical of societies in intractable conflicts. Thus, it seems, there can be little doubt that the press actually framed the conflict as intractable *before* it reached that stage in reality: After all, as we have seen, the two sides kept negotiating toward a final settlement until the very last days of Barak's term.

The very fact that the Israeli press presented its readership with a one-sided, simplified, apocalyptic, and emotional representation of reality should come as no surprise to anyone acquainted with the literature on media and conflict, media and racism, and media and elite ideology. This book, however, has attempted to show more than just that: It has set out to reveal the dramatic contrast between the newspapers' overall representation of reality and *the factual reports sent in by the newspapers' own reporters.* It has attempted to show, in other words, that the slanted patterns of representation were first and foremost the result of *editorial policy:* the reports sent in by the reporters by and large told a much more reasonable story of a tractable conflict in crisis, a crisis in which the Israeli side played as much of a destructive role as the Palestinian side. The editors, however, turned this into a completely different story.

This state of affairs raises a fundamental question: Why should there be such a dramatic gap between the story told by the reporters and the story eventually told by the edited papers? Was there a conscious editorial decision to provide readers with a slanted representation of reality? Did editors simply reflect their own ideology, which was somehow different from that of the reporters, in their decision making process? Surprisingly, the existing literature does not seem to be very helpful. As Schudson (1997) notes, "there has been much more attention to reporter-official relations than to reporter-editor relations. . . . Most research focuses on the gathering of news rather than on its writing, rewriting, and 'play' in the press" (p. 272). This is particularly unfortunate, Schudson claims, because

> research suggests that it is in the *play* of a story that real influence comes. Hallin (1986), Herman and Chomsky (1988) and Lipstadt (1986) all argue that in the press of a liberal society like the United States lots of news, including dissenting or adversarial information and opinion, gets into the newspaper. The question is where that information appears and how it is inflected. Hallin interestingly suggests there is a "reverse inverted pyramid" of news in much Vietnam reporting. The nearer the information was to the truth, the farther down in the story it appeared.

To be sure, much of the work done within the framework of *Critical Discourse Analysis* (cf. Fairclough 1989, 1995; van Dijk 1983, 1985, 1988a,b, 1991), and much of the work done on *framing* (cf. Gamson 1992; Iyengar 1991; Pan and Kosicki 1993), is *implicitly* exactly about this: A lot of the research, for example, concentrates on the influence of headlines on the interpretation of news stories. But this type of research deals only with the frames and formulations themselves, not with the editorial decisions that brought them about. Much of the work on *gatekeeping* (cf. Shoemaker 1991) is *explicitly* about editorial decision making, but only with respect to the question of what gets in the paper and what does not. It seems that the impact of editorial work on the ideological slanting of the news that does get published has not been given the attention it deserves.

In the next section I will suggest an explanatory account of the editing patterns we have seen throughout this book.

Toward an Explanation (1):
On Editors as Epistemic Agents

Between September 2001 and July 2002 I conducted eighteen background interviews with senior editors, reporters, and commentators from the three newspapers. All of them were already familiar with the research results presented in this book.[1] Interestingly, I received very similar reactions from my interviewees: They all seemed to agree that the discrepancy between the reporters' original reports and the final product was the result of a paradoxical combination of professional, ideological, and sociological realities.

To begin with, all my interviewees viewed as unrealistic the assumption that editorial work is always done *on the basis* of the reporters' information. One senior reporter called it "naïve." This is especially true with respect to the formulation of headlines. This is what another reporter said:

> In most cases, the editors have their own agendas. First they formulate their headline, on the basis of whatever information they have, mostly from the news on television, and then they look for a report they can use for their headline. Sometimes the reporters are asked to bring in material that does not really fit what is going on in the real world.

A senior editor in one of the papers described the following scenario as commonplace:

> On many occasions, the head of the news department would read a report or two from the agencies, watch the television news, listen to the radio, talk to people in the building, and then formulate the main headline. Sometimes, having seen the headline, I would tell myself: let's go look at the reports we've received from the reporters to see if we have something similar there. All this has to do with the professional mechanism: the editors are in many ways autonomous from the reporters.

All this deeply echoes the general view my interviewees had of the essence of editorial work: Far from being engaged in a technical task, editors are supposed to be able to look at the "big picture," beyond the specific perspectives of the reporters, and provide their readers with generalized answers to the "big questions" of the day. In theoretical terms, reporters are supposed to produce the news; editors are supposed to produce the *frame*. One commentator simply said that "editors are the ones responsible for the spin." A senior editor said:

> I would say that editors tend to see themselves as having a wider perspective. You are supposed to answer those questions which the public, rightly or not,

expects you to answer: What is the meaning of all this? What is going to happen? Is this good or bad? Is it getting better or worse? To do this, you need to simplify things, make them simple, even simplistic.

This perception, however, is highly paradoxical, for two complementary reasons: First, both the reporters and the editors I spoke to agreed that in complex and volatile periods—such as the first crucial weeks of the Intifada —most editors by and large know *less* about the intricacies of the general picture than the senior reporters do. Here is how a senior reporter puts it:

> These people spend all their time in the headquarters in Tel Aviv. They are ignorant. Who among the senior editors of the papers has been on a single visit to the territories since the outbreak of this Intifada? Who among them knows what a settlement or a Palestinian village looks like? Who among them saw a demonstration with his or her own eyes? They have no way of making judgments about what is happening there.

Second, both editors and reporters agreed that editors regularly establish their views on (what they think is) the general picture on the basis of what they learn from the other *media*. Specifically, newspaper editors often prefer to rely on the TV news broadcasts rather than on the information brought by their own reporters. Says a senior editor:

> Editors are influenced by other media more than they are influenced by reporters. There is a feedback mechanism here, which in the end creates a unified message. It's a twenty-four-hour cycle: I watch the news on television; the morning shows' editors read the paper I edited; the evening news' editors watch television all day long; and so on. From time to time a reporter would call me and say: Did you see that report they just had on TV? My sources tell me it is not true. I must say I do not always trust the reporter in such a situation.

One reporter felt that television news had another negative effect in this complex situation:

> Editors watch a televised report of a certain event, and they feel they know exactly what happened there. Assume there was a small demonstration at Netzarim junction. The cameramen shoot it from a certain angle, to make it look big. The editors see it on TV. It looks huge. Now try and persuade them that there were no more than fifty people there, that it was relatively quiet.

This, then, is the paradox: Editors are supposed to make certain types of epistemic judgments—what is the significance of a given story, what should be its proper headline, where should it be placed, and most importantly, which version of the story is closer to the truth. But generally speaking, they are not in the position to make these judgments. What do they do, then? The consensus among my interviewees was that in this type of situation editors work according to the following strategy: They adopt the political and military establishment's judgments as the basis for their editorial decisions, and try to present the "big picture" in a way that would minimize friction with the establishment *and* the public. On the basis of this strategy, editors inevitably highlight those reports based on formal Israeli sources, suppress reports based on Palestinian sources or otherwise contradict the hegemonic story, and formulate headlines that tend to simplify the story and amplify its emotional significance.

In a real sense, then, this editorial strategy leads to slanted representation almost by default. Working against it would amount to an explicit assertion that the paper prefers the other side's version. Here is another senior editor's view:

> Sometimes I would get two reports from my reporters on the number of Palestinian casualties. One report would indicate, say, that according to Israeli sources six Palestinians were killed, whereas the other report would say that according to Palestinian sources eight people were killed. Both the reporters and I know that the Palestinians are probably right. They have the more accurate numbers when it comes to their own dead. But I have no choice: I formulate a headline, or a sub-headline, saying that six Palestinians were killed, and leave their own count in the text. This is almost routine procedure. Otherwise, I could get into trouble. We cannot explicitly show that we believe the Palestinian sources more than we believe our own.

Note—and this is crucial—that the reporters in this case do *not* face the same quandary. They simply report what their sources told them. The factual judgment in this case has to be made by the editor—and it is made in a way that grants the official sources on the Israeli side "certain positive rights" (Schlesinger 1989, p. 287) as far as decisions about truth are concerned. From the readers' point of view, as we have seen in chapter 1, all this remains obscure. They read the news from the first page onward, from the headlines down to the texts—and they receive a message that in a real sense reflects the editors' emotional and cognitive perspective much more than the data collected by the reporters.

Toward an Explanation (2): Taking Barak at His Word

All this has relatively little to do with the specific context of the outbreak of the Intifada. This context, however, seems to have aggravated the general tendency outlined above in more than one way. First, some of my interviewees thought that the editors, detached as they were from the reality in the territories, were in a way much more susceptible to the surge of anxiety, confusion, and anger that flooded the Jewish public in Israel in those days. Thus the emotionally laden editorial patterns they produced actually reflected to a certain extent their own sincere feelings. One commentator thought that the crucial element here was the events that took place within the Green Line:

> The October events within the Green Line were critical here. I think it gave everybody in Tel Aviv a sense that we really were surrounded, that this was not just a second round of the Intifada. It must have made a difference.

Second, and much more important, the almost routine tendency to accept the establishment's perspective as the basis for editorial decisions was strengthened to a large extent by the editors' shared general feeling that Barak could be fully trusted at his word. Many of my interviewees thought that the significant distinction was that between Barak and his predecessor, Benjamin Netanyahu. A senior editor remarked:

> There was so much negative emotion toward Netanyahu in the media, his personality strengthened the general suspicion toward the Right. When Barak was elected, there was a real sense of relief. It probably gave Barak some very valuable points.

Paradoxically, then, it seems that the fact that many of the senior editors traditionally subscribe to the moderate Left actually contributed to their inclination to slant the news in this particular way. Some of them actually said that they were quite captivated by Barak's rhetoric: the determination he showed, the rigid timetables he set up, the tremendous energy he brought into office, his vision of himself as Rabin's political heir, the speeches he gave about the "heart-wrenching decisions" that he, and only he, was able to make—and first of all the fact that he did indeed break the taboo regarding the division of Jerusalem. This last fact, of course, is definitely significant. But his short administration also provided the best proof of the tremendous, inconceivable gap between the rhetoric political leaders can adopt and the realities they create. A free press, at least in principle, is supposed to try to expose this gap. In this case, exposure did not happen. Here is what a senior editor said:

> If you take into account the type of offers he brought up, the fact that he broke the taboo regarding Jerusalem, for example, you have to understand

that all this seemed very close to the Left's rosiest dreams. What could we criticize? And if he said there's no partner, you felt you should probably take his word for it.

This editor's words echo another insight shared by some of my interviewees. They observed the events through the prism of internal Israeli politics: Barak, after all, was the prime minister of the Left. By definition, then, he was the type of prime minister who yearns for peace, acts with restraint, is willing to make generous concessions, and understands the Arab perspective. By definition, again, it was inconceivable that he himself should put obstacles on the way to peace. If *he* said there was no partner, then there probably was no partner for peace. In October 2000, this basic insight was expressed only once, in a commentary by Chemi Shalev, published in *Ma'ariv* on October 20, quoted in part in the epigraph to this chapter:

If the Likud were in office, all hell would break loose. The Left would accuse the government, the media would sound the alarm. Peace Now would demonstrate at road junctions. Shimon Peres and Yossi Beilin would try to work something out with Arafat, in spite of everything, and behind everyone's backs. If the Likud were in office, the leaders of the Left, including Ehud Barak, would vehemently attack the prime minister and accuse him of leading us all to our destruction. Who are you, they would mockingly defy him, to decide that Arafat is no longer a partner? . . . If the Likud were in office, difficult questions would be raised regarding the force we are using, the citizens killed by the police, the excessive success, so it seems, of the IDF's sharpshooters' courses. If the Likud were in office, many would stand in the breach, they would call on the public to stay calm, and the public, including the media, would not get carried away. Not to this extent. Peace-oriented commentators would advise restraint, not crackdowns. Television interviewers would not become self-appointed preachers and inquisitors, grilling every Arab who comes their way. The horrifying Ramallah Lynch would be broadcast frequently, but not hundreds of times, by some sort of compulsion bordering on incitement. If the Likud were in office, someone on the Left besides Yossi Beilin would take the trouble to remind the public that there are other Palestinians as well. From the moment Barak adopted the right-wing terminology, all barriers collapsed. Uniformity of thought took hold of us all, the Left collapsed and the Right began to celebrate its historical triumph. Barak and his information experts carelessly adopted the harmful propaganda methods of the eighties, and distributed horror tapes in the style of [right-wing advisors] David Bar-Ilan and Yigal Carmon, doing [right-wing radio] channel 7's work for it, as the heads of the station themselves noted with satisfaction. Our information experts took no prisoners, they gave not a single thought to the day after, when the government will be called to explain why, after all, it is concluding a peace agreement with the Devil himself. It was once said that only the Likud can bring peace. This point is still debatable. But for going out to war, there is nothing like the Left. The tragic results are identical, but the Left makes despair so much more comfortable, and we all feel so absolutely justified.

This insight proved only too true when Ariel Sharon became prime minister in March 2001. On March 12, only four days into Sharon's term, the IDF's closure policy suddenly became front page material. *Yediot Ahronot's* main headline on that day reads:

CRACKDOWN IN TERRITORIES; IDF SURROUNDING TOWNS

The banner says:

CRITICISM WITHIN THE GOVERNMENT: PERES, VILNAI, AND SNEH OPPOSE NEW POLICY

The sub-headline takes the trouble to elaborate:

THE STEPS WERE AUTHORIZED BY SHARON. IDF SOURCES: WE MOVED FROM "BREATHING CLOSURE" TO "SUFFOCATING CLOSURE." PALESTINIANS: UN SECURITY COUNCIL SHOULD BE URGENTLY CONVENED

The page's central picture, under the headline **NO THROUGHWAY**, shows a soldier stopping a Palestinian driver at the A-Ram junction between Jerusalem and Ramallah. The headline on pages 2–3 reads: **SHARON AUTHORIZES "SUFFOCATING CLOSURE" ON WEST BANK TOWNS.** The opening paragraph states:

The IDF has begun to implement a tighter closure policy in the territories. The goal is to move from what the IDF terms "breathing closure" to a "suffocating closure." This means that towns and villages will be completely isolated by means of trenches and roadblocks. The step was authorized by Prime Minister Ariel Sharon and Defense Minister Binyamin Ben Eliezer. Voices opposing this measure are already heard within the new government.

And the opening sentence of Alex Fishman's commentary, which stands by itself as the lead paragraph, explains yet again:

It was Sharon who gave this plan the green light.

Ma'ariv also dedicates its main headline to this topic:

CLOSURE ON RAMALLAH BECOMES TIGHTER; PALESTINIANS: WE WILL FORCE OUR WAY THROUGH

Under the headline appears a picture of an IDF armored personnel carrier with a soldier seated on it who is looking at the line of Palestinian cars trying to exit Ramallah. Next to the picture, we find the following head-line:

PERES: THE CLOSURE POLICY IN RAMALLAH NEEDS RETHINKING

And the headline on pages 2–3 says:

RAMALLAH—CITY UNDER SIEGE

The sub-headline, quoting Palestinians, says: "THE ISRAELIS ARE TRYING TO LOCK US UP IN HUGE PRISONS." On page 3 appears a large picture of a Palestinian family, a mother and three children, passing the IDF roadblock with sad faces.

This theme continues the next day, March 13. *Ma'ariv*'s daily supple-ment headline reads PRESSURE COOKER. The headline on pages 2–3 quotes a Palestinian again: "ANYONE WHO THINKS THIS SIEGE WILL CALM THINGS DOWN IS INSANE."

Yediot Ahronot's page 3 shows a huge picture of Hannan Ashrawi, mem-ber of the Palestinian legislative council, participating in an attempt to top-ple an IDF dirt roadblock at one of the entrances to Ramallah. The headline reads:

BEHIND THE ROADBLOCKS: "IT FEELS LIKE JAIL"

The story starts with a quote from a Ramallah resident, Um-Tarek: "I live in the prison that is Ramallah—afraid, worried. Why are you doing this to us? Aren't we human beings?" And on page 2, we find two boxes: CLOSURE—THE PROS; CLOSURE—THE CONS. In the second of these boxes, commentator Roni Shaked explains:

> The continuous suffering created by the closure only increases Palestinian vindictiveness and hatred toward Israel. Collective punishment emphasizes the Palestinians' weakness and suffering and the immorality of occupation. The results are international pressure and anger in all Arab countries. The suffering caused by the closure only serves Arafat's purposes. He is now call-ing for international protection and aspires to "internationalize" the conflict. From the security point of view as well, the closure cannot seal off territorial units completely, especially against a terrorist making his way by foot.

All this is extremely significant, because as we have seen throughout this book, the closure and the siege, the dirt roadblocks and the trenches, the "continuous suffering" and the "vindictiveness and hatred" were there all along—since the outbreak of the Intifada (and in many ways since the beginning of the occupation in 1967). The closure of Ramallah may have tightened somewhat in these first days of Sharon's administration, but there was no significant change of policy. Here is what *Ha'aretz* reporter Amos Harel wrote on March 13:

> Day before yesterday, at noon, the IDF still found it hard to understand the sudden (and at that time, also limited) interest the media took in the strict closure of Ramallah. After all, the closure measures had gradually tightened over the past two weeks in an attempt to restrict the movement of Palestinian armed squads, which had turned the area's roads into a nightmare for Israeli drivers. . . . Reports about the closure consistently appeared on the newspapers' back pages during the last days of these past weeks. But it took a Channel 2 televised report from the Ramallah area, the day before yesterday—a report that became the evening's opening story due to a scarcity in news items—to turn this into a main headline story.

Can the sudden interest in the closure really be explained as a result of a "scarcity in news items"? This is hard to believe. Consider Harel's closing paragraph:

> The Labor ministers, led by Shimon Peres, were quick to attack the decision to enforce closure, even before the unity government met for its first session. Thus it is not at all certain that the unity government will provide a wider umbrella for harsh measures in the territories, as the IDF hoped. . . . It is all a question of politics. This also holds for the Peace Now activists, who have resumed their demonstrations against the occupation in front of the Defense Ministry—something they did not often do during the five months of Intifada under Barak's government.

And in the last paragraph of another story, on the same page, we find the following sentence:

> Ben Eliezer noted that the policy of closure and blockades is not new, and was already implemented by the previous government.

A few days later, the press's interest in the closure and blockades lessened. The conduct of the press during Sharon's tenure, however, has indeed changed in significant and specific ways, which seems to support the notion that Barak's political affiliation did play a crucial role in this complex story. First, as I show in Dor (2003b), both *Ha'aretz* and *Yediot Ahronot* have since maintained a significant level of critical coverage of Sharon's policies, whereas *Ma'ariv* took its nationalistic perspective to new extremes. Second, and much more important, all three newspapers have consistently framed their coverage in terms of Barak's original narrative: Arafat bears full responsibility for the collapse of the diplomatic process and the continuation of the armed struggle, leaving Israel no choice but to defend itself with the means at its disposal. Within this framework, *Ha'aretz* and *Yediot Ahronot* have regularly criticized Sharon for "not having a serious plan," for "using excessive force," or for refusing, for a long time, to build a fence along certain parts of the Green Line, a fence that experts claimed could reduce the number of terror attacks in Israeli cities. They have not, however, criticized Sharon for refusing to try to get back to diplomatic negotiations, or for declaring that he would not be willing to evacuate settlements. Such criticism would, at least by implication, indicate that they assume there might be a partner for peace on the other side. In a real sense, then, Barak's perspective remained at the very foundation of the Israeli perception of the Intifada long after Barak himself lost the elections and left the political arena.

Final Remarks on Democracy, the Press, and Theoretical Complexity

All too often, the literature on the cluster of topics discussed in this book suffers from a tendency to look for clear-cut, one-dimensional theoretical bottom lines (*head*lines, actually): What is the final conclusion? Did the Israeli press engage in an all-out propaganda campaign in direct subservience to the establishment? Or did it unwittingly reflect social power relations and cultural undercurrents? Was the slanted coverage simply a deterministic derivative of the production process and the social roles played by reporters and editors? Are we talking about *hard* hegemony or *soft* hegemony?

As I have tried to show in this book, things are probably never as simple as that. In the period examined, the Israeli press worked under a complex array of influences, and its specific conduct can only be explained on the basis of the convergence of all these influences: the surge of fear and anger, the undercurrents of racist stances, the deep-seated ignorance concerning the realities of occupation, the massive propaganda campaign led by the government and the military establishment. These influences, moreover, targeted different echelons in the newspapers in different ways and, together with the specific patterns of professional conduct, determined the type of coverage eventually produced. It is not *either* propaganda *or* culture, *either* emotion *or* professional determinism—but propaganda, *and* culture, *and* emotion, *and* professional determinism.

This complexity makes a narrative form of analysis and presentation an absolute necessity. Going through the events, day by day—deconstructing the representations constructed by the papers, and then reconstructing them as they were reported by the reporters—makes it possible to identify fine-grained patterns in this web of complexity. Thus, for example, we can detect how pseudo-factual, propagandist contentions of the establishment become part of the cultural background. The assertion of yesterday is today's presupposition. The notion that Arafat is no partner for peace is of course the ultimate example. We can see how short-term fluctuations in the establishment's view reconfirm or weaken deep-seated cultural assumptions. Think, for example, about the newspapers' reactions to Barak's decision to create a committee of inquiry for the events within the Green Line. And we can detect patterns of emotional and ideological development in the coverage itself. The best example is probably the Lynch in Ramallah.

This mode of patient analysis also allows for critical judgments that escape the danger of oversimplification. Think about *Ha'aretz*, for example. Unlike the two tabloids, it consistently provided its readers with considerable amounts of information about the Palestinian perspective. But it also consistently published this information on back pages, making it clear—in main headlines and editorials—that this is indeed no more than the Palestinian *perspective*, and that it accepts the reports from the Israeli side as factually accurate. This duality makes it impossible to provide a clear-cut evaluation of *Ha'aretz's* conduct in terms of the traditional, liberal conception of the role of the press in democratic societies. It does, however, tell a much more revealing story about what Israeli society, and especially the moderate left, went through during the critical period of the outbreak of the Intifada.

All of which should raise skeptical sentiments about this very notion of the *role* of the press in democratic societies. Liberal wishful thinking notwithstanding, it seems quite clear that the moment when democratic societies need their free press most is the very moment when the press actually fails most miserably in doing what it is supposed to do. The literature, of course, tells us quite clearly that it was never really supposed to do that, that the press in liberal democracies has always aligned itself with the establishment and popular sentiment—in most cases against the very interests of the people it is supposed to serve. The only problem remaining, then, is that the public has not been given appropriate notice of this fact. Citizens of non-democracies are well aware that their press does not tell the truth, the whole truth, and nothing but the truth. They know how to read between the lines. The press in democratic societies, of course, does not get its orders directly from the *politburo*, and as far as domestic politics are concerned, it has internalized some reasonable rules of proper conduct. But in times of crisis, especially military crisis, it plays a role not totally dissimilar to that of the press in non-democracies—and this is something that the public does not really understand. It may indeed be the case that the press cannot do otherwise, that this is what its very existence within the fabric of liberal democracies dictates. But if this is the case, we should help the public develop a more acute sense of skepticism: If newspapers cannot be expected to act differently, then we have to re-learn how to read them.

Notes

1. Introduction

1. According to the Peace Index, a project of the Tel Aviv University's Tami Steinmetz Center for Peace Research, 44 percent of the Israeli Jewish respondents thought in July that Barak's positions at Camp David were too conciliatory, and only 35 percent felt they were appropriate. (For the full results, see the Steinmetz Center web page, at <www.tau.ac.il/peace/Peace_Index/p_index.html>.)

2. According to the Peace Index, by July, 65 percent held the Palestinians mainly, or wholly, responsible for the failure of the talks. In August, 76 percent shared the view that "even if Israel were to agree to a Palestinian state with East Jerusalem as its capital, attaining a peace agreement would remain uncertain, since the Palestinians would then present additional demands." Significantly, this view was shared by a clear majority of Barak voters (62%). In October, 73 percent of the respondents estimated that "at this time the Palestinian Authority has no vested interest in peace with Israel." For the sake of comparison, it should be noted that only four months before, in June 2000, the Jewish public was "evenly divided between those who believed the PA to be interested in peace and those who felt that this was not the case." An even steeper drop was evident in Arafat's personal image. In October, 71 percent felt that his behavior was "that of a terrorist." Two years before, this view was shared by 41 percent. According to the Gallup poll published in *Ma'ariv* on October 13, 62 percent said Israel does not have "a partner for peace" on the Palestinian side.

3. According to the November 2000 Peace Index, 80 percent of the Jewish public blamed the Palestinians for the outbreak of the Intifada. In the Gallup poll published in *Ma'ariv* on November 10, 77 percent shared this view.

4. According to the November Peace Index, 78 percent of the Jewish public believed that "the Palestinians have little regard for human lives and therefore persist in using violence, despite the high number of their own casualties." Eighty-six percent claim that the Palestinians realize "how strongly Israel values human lives" and therefore "persist in their violence, in order to erode Israel's power to resist."

5. According to the October Peace Index, only 29 percent believed that political negotiations with the Palestinians should be called off altogether, while 45 percent believed that the talks should merely be suspended until the violence stopped.

6. According to the latest available figures, published in 1995 by the Israel Advertisers Association, 68.7 percent of Israeli readers are exposed to *Yediot Ahronot* on weekends, and 54.4 percent are exposed to it on weekdays. Note that *exposure* figures are better indicators of popularity than *circulation* figures.

7. According to the Israel Advertisers Association figures, 26.7 percent of Israeli readers are exposed to *Ma'ariv* on weekends and 23.9 percent are exposed to it on weekdays.

8. This notion of relevance is developed in Sperber and Wilson (1986, 1995) and is arguably the most important theoretical notion used in contemporary pragmatics.

2. "Under Arafat's Baton"

1. Historically, the term "Land of Israel" refers to the entire area between the Mediterranean and the Jordan River—the state of Israel and the occupied territories. In present-day Hebrew, its usage is usually associated with right-wing ideology. Guri's formulation thus reflects the notion, prevalent at the time, that the riots signify the end of the distinction between the Land and the State.

2. As part of the Oslo agreement, IDF soldiers and Palestinian policemen joined forces patrolling certain sensitive areas. This ended, of course, as soon as the riots broke out.

3. Settlements on high topographical ground, mostly within the Green Line, especially in the Galilee area. Literally, "lookouts."

4. Chief of Palestinian Security.

5. Armed wing of the Fatah.

3. "Make No Mistake, Yasser"

1. This is the traditional term used to refer to the days between Rosh Hashana, the Jewish New Year, and Yom Kippur, the Day of Atonement.

2. The newspapers' coverage of the background negotiations between Barak and Sharon makes it clear that the papers viewed the possible formation of an emergency government as a necessary step. A picture on page 2 of *Yediot Ahronot* on October 5, for example, shows Barak and Sharon shaking hands during the parachute brigade's yearly memorial service. The caption's first words are: "A moment of unity." None of the newspapers warn their readers about the negotiations' possibly disastrous results in terms of the peace process. One paradoxical exception stands out: On *Yediot Ahronot*'s first page, one person, "a private citizen," publishes a long article calling Israelis to "return to their senses" and to rally "around the firm principles of national agreement," thus countering "the Arab belief that the Jewish State is a passing phenomenon"—without ever mentioning the concrete idea of a unity government. The writer was none other than former prime minister Benjamin Netanyahu.

3. It should be noted that *Ha'aretz*'s front page on Friday morning also included a report from Gaza by Amira Hass titled CHILDREN IN GAZA SUFFER NIGHTMARES FOLLOWING MOHAMMED AL-DURRA'S DEATH. The real difference between *Ha'aretz* and the two tabloids is to be found not in the editorial line but rather in the very fact that *Ha'aretz* employs reporters Amira Hass and Gideon Levi—the only two reporters in the Israeli press who regularly bring in factual reports from the territories. As we have seen and will show in further detail in the coming chapters, these reports in no way shape or even affect the overall picture of reality which *Ha'aretz* constructs for its readers. Yet the very fact that their stories are published regularly is obviously significant.

4. Until the very last days before its evacuation, the head of the yeshiva attached to the Tomb was none other than Rabbi Itzhak Ginsburg. Ginsburg is known for the eulogy he wrote for Baruch Goldstein, who in February 1994 broke into the Tomb of the Patriarchs in Hebron and massacred twenty-nine Palestinians.

4. "The Limits of Restraint"

1. The other papers state that the child was actually 9 years old.

7. "We Have Turned Every Stone"

1. These reports are slightly overshadowed by the dramatic story of Colonel (Ret.) Elhanan Tenenbaum's kidnapping by the Hizballah, but the preparations for the summit do occupy a prominent place on the front pages.

2. Only once during October, after the diplomatic "time-out" was announced, did the newspapers emphasize cabinet criticism of Barak in their front page headlines. Ma'ariv's banner on October 22 reads: ANGER ON LEFT: BARAK ZIGZAGGING TO RIGHT. AMONG THE CRITICS: PERES, BEN-AMI, AND BEILIN. That day, the newspaper's editor, Yaakov Erez, publishes a front page article under the headline THE PEACE PROCESS SHOULD NOT BE PUT ON HOLD. The newspaper dedicates pages 2–3 to this topic, under the headline INNER OPPOSITION TO TIME-OUT, and quotes a senior source in the Labor party, saying: "The goal of this process is to save Barak's seat at any cost." The same day, Yediot Ahronot's front page headline reports: BARAK'S "TIME-OUT" ANNOUNCEMENT HARSHLY CRITICIZED IN THE U.S. AND WITHIN THE CABINET. Ha'aretz's main headline reads: BARAK ANNOUNCES A "TIME-OUT IN NEGOTIA-TIONS" IN ORDER TO PREVENT ANOTHER SUMMIT. The next day, October 23, the criticism appears again on Ma'ariv's front page; the banner of one of the page's headlines reads MINISTERIAL ATTACK ON BARAK'S "TIME-OUT"—and more implicitly in Yediot Ahronot, with one of its front page headlines reporting that BARAK WANTS AGREEMENT ON EMERGENCY GOVERNMENT BY WEEKEND. These two days, then, represent the only occasion throughout the month on which the newspapers dedicate headlines to the deep inner conflict within the government and the severe criticism of Barak's conduct voiced by senior ministers.

8. Conclusion

1. The Hebrew version of this book, titled Newspapers under the Influence, was published by Babel Publications in September 2001.

Bibliography

Bar-Tal, Daniel. 1998. "Societal Beliefs in Times of Intractable Conflict: The Israeli Case." *International Journal of Conflict Management* 9: 22–50.

———. 2000. *Shared Beliefs in a Society*. Thousand Oaks, Calif.: Sage.

———. 2001. "Why Does Fear Override Hope in Societies Engulfed by Intractable Conflicts, as It Does in the Israeli Society?" *Political Psychology* 22: 601–627.

Bell, Allan. 1984. "Good Copy, Bad News: The Syntax and Semantics of News Editing." In P. Trudgil, ed., *Applied Sociolinguistics*. London: Academic Press.

———. 1991. *Language of News Media*. Oxford: Blackwell.

Bleske, Glen L. 1995. "Schematic Frames and Reader Learning: The Effect of Headlines." Paper presented at the Annual Meeting of the Association for Education in Journalism and Mass Communication, Washington, D.C.

Caspi, Dan, and Yehiel Limor. 1999. *The In/Outsiders: The Media in Israel*. Cresskill, N.J.: Hampton Press.

de Cillia, Rudolf, Martin Reisigl, and Ruth Wodak. 1999. "The Discursive Construction of National Identities." *Discourse & Society* 10, no. 2: 149–173.

Cohen, Akiba, and Gadi Wolfsfeld. 1993. *Framing the Intifada: People and Media*. Norwood, N.J.: Ablex Publications.

Cottle, Simon. 1997. "Reporting the Troubles in Northern Ireland: Paradigms and Media Propaganda." *Critical Studies in Mass Communication* 14, no. 3: 282–296.

Dor, Daniel. 2003a. "On Newspaper Headlines as Relevance Optimizers." *Journal of Pragmatics* 35: 695–721.

———. 2003b. *Behind Defensive Shield* (in Hebrew). Tel Aviv: Babel Publications.

Erjavec, Karmen. 2001. "Media Representation of the Discrimination against the Roma in Eastern Europe: The Case of Slovenia." *Discourse & Society* 12, no. 6: 699–727.

Fairclough, Norman. 1989. *Language and Power*. London: Longman.

———. 1995. *Critical Discourse Analysis*. London: Longman.

Fang, Yew-Jin. 2001. "Reporting the Same Events? A Critical Analysis of Chinese Print News Media Texts." *Discourse & Society* 12, no. 5: 585–613.

Gamson, W. A. 1992. *Talking Politics*. Cambridge: Cambridge University Press.

Gamson, W. A., and A. Modigliani. 1989. "Media Discourse and Public Opinion on Nuclear Power." *American Journal of Sociology* 95, no. 1: 1–37.

Geer, J. G., and K. F. Kahn. 1993. "Grabbing Attention: An Experimental Investigation of Headlines during Campaigns." *Political Communication* 10, no. 2: 175–191.

Gibson, Rhonda, and Dolf Zillmann. 2000. "Reading between the Photographs: The Influence of Incidental Pictorial Information on Issue Perception." *Journalism & Mass Communication Quarterly* 77, no. 2: 355–366.

Gramsci, Antonio. 1971. *Selections from Prison Notebooks*. Cambridge: Cambridge University Press.

Hallin, Daniel C. 1986. *The "Uncensored War": The Media and Vietnam*. New York and Oxford: Oxford University Press.

Harrison, Martin. 1985. *Television News: Whose Bias?* Berkshire: Hermitage.

Henley, N. M., M. Miller, and J. A. Beazley. 1995. "Syntax, Semantics, and Sexual Violence: Agency and the Passive Voice." *Journal of Language and Social Psychology* 14, no. 1–2: 60–84.

Herman, Edward, and Noam Chomsky. 1988. *Manufacturing Consent: The Political Economy of the Mass Media.* New York: Pantheon.

Ilie, Cornelia. 1998. "The Ideological Remapping of Semantic Roles in Totalitarian Discourse; or, How to Paint White Roses Red." *Discourse & Society* 9, no. 1: 57–80.

Iyengar, S. 1991. *Is Anyone Responsible? How Television Frames Political Issues.* Chicago: University of Chicago Press.

Jenkins, F. 1990. "Train Sex Man Fined: Headlines and Cataphoric Ellipsis." In M.A.K. Halliday, J. Gibbons, and H. Nicholas, eds., *Learning, Keeping, and Using Language: Selected Papers from the 8th World Congress of Applied Linguistics, Sydney, 16–21.* Amsterdam: Benjamins.

de-Knop, Sabine. 1985. "Linguistic and Extralinguistic Aids for Reconstruction and Interpretation of Metaphors in Headlines." In W. Paprotte and R. Dirven, eds., *The Ubiquity of Metaphor: Metaphor in Language and Thought.* Amsterdam: Benjamins.

Kriesberg, Louis. 1993. "Intractable Conflict." *Peace Review* 5: 417–421.

Leon, J. A. 1997. "The Effects of Headlines and Summaries on News Comprehension and Recall." *Reading and Writing* 9, no. 2: 85–106.

Liebes, Tamar. 1997. *Reporting the Arab-Israeli Conflict: How Hegemony Works.* New York: Routledge.

Limor, Yehiel, and Rafi Mann. 1997. *Journalism* (in Hebrew). Tel Aviv: The Open University.

Lindemann, B. 1989. "What Knowledge Does It Take to Read a Newspaper?" *Journal of Literary Semantics* XVIII, no. 1: 50–65.

———. 1990. "Cheap Thrills We Live By: Some Notes on the Poetics of Tabloid Headlines." *Journal of Literary Semantics* 19, no. 1 (April): 46–59.

Lipstadt, Deborah, E. 1986. *Beyond Belief: The American Press and the Coming of the Holocaust 1933–1945.* New York: Free Press.

McCombs, M., D. Shaw, and D. Weaver. 1997. *Communication and Democracy: Exploring the Intellectual Frontiers in Agenda-Setting Theory.* Hillsdale, N.J.: Lawrence Erlbaum.

Nir, Raphael. 1993. "A Discourse Analysis of News Headlines" (in Hebrew). *Hebrew Linguistics* 37: 23–31. (Hebrew.)

Pan, Z., and G. M. Kosicki. 1993. "Framing Analysis: An Approach to News Discourse." *Political Communication* 10, no. 1: 55–75.

Perfetti, C. A., et al. 1987. "Comprehending Newspaper Headlines." *Journal of Memory and Language* 26, no. 6: 692–713.

Phillips, Louise. 1996. "Rhetoric and the Spread of the Discourse of Thatcherism." *Discourse & Society* 7, no. 2: 209–241.

Price, Vincent, David Tewksbury, and Elizabeth Powers. 1997. "Switching Trains of Thoughts: The Impact of News Frames on Readers' Cognitive Responses." *Communication Research* 24, no. 5: 481–506.

Rhee, June Woong. 1997. "Strategy and Issue Frames in Election Campaign Coverage: A Social Cognitive Account of Framing Effects." *Journal of Communication* 47, no. 3: 26–48.

Roeh, Itzhak, and Raphael Nir. 1993. "Reporting the Intifada in the Israeli Press: How Mainstream Ideology Overrides 'Quality' and 'Melodrama.'" In Akiba Cohen and Gadi Wolfsfeld, eds., *Framing the Intifada: People and Media*, 176–191. Norwood, N.J.: Ablex Publications.

Schlesinger, Philip. 1989. "From Production to Propaganda?" *Media, Culture, and Society* 11, no. 3: 283–306.

Schudson, Michael. 1978. *Discovering the News: A Social History of American Newspapers*. New York: Basic Books.

———. 1997. "The Sociology of News Production." In D. Berkowitz, ed., *Social Meanings of News*. Thousand Oaks, Calif.: Sage.

Semino, Elena, and Michela Masci. 1996. "Politics Is Football: Metaphor in the Discourse of Silvio Berlusconi in Italy." *Discourse & Society* 7, no. 2: 243–269.

Shinar, Dov, and Gina Stoiciu. 1992. "Media Representations of Socio-political Conflict: The Romanian Revolution and the Gulf War." *Gazette* 50: 243–257.

Shoemaker, Pamela. 1991. *Gatekeeping*. Thousand Oaks, Calif.: Sage.

Sperber, Dan, and Dierdre Wilson. 1986, 1995. *Relevance: Communication and Cognition*. Oxford: Blackwell.

Stevenson, Nick. 1995. *Understanding Media Cultures: Social Theory and Mass Communication*. Thousand Oaks, Calif.: Sage.

Teo, Peter. 2000. "Racism in the News: A Critical Discourse Analysis of News Reporting in Two Austrian Newspapers." *Discourse & Society* 11, no. 1: 7–49.

Tuchman, Gaye. 1973. "Making News by Doing Work: Routinizing the Unexpected." *American Journal of Sociology* 79: 110–131.

Valkenburg, Patti M., Holli A. Semetko, and Claes H. De Vreese. 1999. "The Effects of News Frames on Readers' Thoughts and Recall." *Communication Research* 26, no. 5: 550–569.

van Dijk, Teun A. 1983. "Discourse Analysis: Its Development and Application to the Structure of News." *Journal of Communication* 33: 20–43.

———. 1985. *Communicating Racism*. London: Sage.

———. 1988a. "How 'They' Hit the Headlines: Ethnic Minorities in the Press." In G. Smitherman-Donaldson and T. A. van Dijk, eds., *Discourse and Discrimination*, 221–262. Detroit: Wayne State University Press.

———. 1988b. *News as Discourse*. Hillsdale, N.J.: Erlbaum.

———. 1991. *Racism and the Press*. London: Routledge.

Williams, Raymond. 1977. *Marxism and Literature*. New York: Oxford University Press.

Wolfsfeld, Gadi. 1997. *Media and Political Conflict: News from the Middle East*. New York: Cambridge University Press.

Index

Dr. Daniel Dor teaches at the Department of Communication, Tel Aviv University. He is a graduate of Stanford University. His research interests include, among other topics, the role of the mass media in the construction of political hegemony, the linguistic consequences of globalization, and the cultural-biological evolution of language. He has worked as a senior news editor in two of Israel's leading newspapers.